SUICIDE IN MIND

SUICIDE IN MIND

Arthur Lawrence

Book Guild Publishing
Sussex, England

First published in Great Britain in 2009 by
The Book Guild Ltd
Pavilion View
19 New Road
BN1 1UF

Typesetting in Times by
Keyboard Services, Luton, Bedfordshire

Printed and bound in Great Britain by
CPI Antony Rowe

A catalogue record for this book is available from
The British Library

ISBN 978 1 84624 302 8

Contents

Introduction

Writers are more likely to contemplate suicide than any other profession.

That conclusion was drawn by Professor Arnold Ludwig, Professor of Psychiatry at the University of Kentucky Medical Centre, following his research over a ten-year period covering over 1,000 eminent professional and artistic people.

In a further study, Professor Ludwig surveyed 60 writers attending a Women Writers' Conference, at the University of Kentucky in 1993. He compared the results with an identical survey of 60 women occupied in non-creative professions, and he found that the results supported the conclusions of his long-term studies.

Many other modern surveys and studies of the psychology of writers have been published in the UK and the USA. Most notable are *Creativity and Mental Illness: Prevalent Rates in Writers* (Andreasen 1987), *Relationship Between Creativity and Psycho-pathology* (Richards 1981), *Mood Disorders and Patterns of Creativity in British Writers and Artists* (Jamison 1989) and *Strong Imagination: Madness, Creativity and Human Nature* (Nettle 2003). These contemporary studies do establish the belief that fictional writers more than any other profession are subject to mental disorders and strong suicidal tendencies.

We can go back and find comments from the nineteenth-century writer Edgar Allen Poe: 'The question is not yet settled, whether madness is or is not the loftiest intelligence; whether all writing that is profound does not spring from disease of thought.' Even further back, we find Socrates saying, 'The sane compositions of writers never reach perfection, but are utterly eclipsed by the inspired madman.' He should know, being himself a writer who committed suicide.

All of these studies and social commentaries concern themselves with the fact that writers are far more prone to suicidal thoughts than any other profession. They substantiate the view that there is a clear link between mental instability and creative writing. Yet this is an opinion that has long been held by writers themselves. What this book looks at is the fact that, for writers, these tendencies often become realities. The truth is more writers do commit suicide than in all other non-creative professions added together. That is a tremendous preponderance.

What causes writers with suicide in mind to take the deadly step of committing the act? That is the question for the reader.

Early on in my research, I was able to identify a long list of well-known writers who have committed suicide. At random, I have selected for the reader's consideration eight internationally-known writers. The only restriction I placed upon my choice was to confine it to nineteenth- and twentieth-century writers. Sarah Kane, Ernest Hemingway, Sylvia Plath, Thomas L. Beddoes, Cesare Pavese, Virginia Woolf, Hunter S. Thompson and Anne Sexton. The eight essays, which are in essence short life stories, contained in this book, will invite the reader to find common threads running through these writers' lives and leading to their death by suicide. The usual suspects: drink, drugs and depression, will suggest themselves. They play their part, but they are only upon the surface. The reader will need to crawl below and into the psyche of these writers to discover why they have suicide in mind.

Acknowledgements

The author and publishers are grateful to the following for permission to reproduce material in this book:

Peter Owen Ltd, London for Cesare Pavese's *Festival Night* (translator A.E. Murch), *Selected Letters* (editor and translator A.E. Murch), *Among Women Only* (translator D.D. Paige), *This Business of Living, Beautiful Summer* (translator W.J. Strachan) and *The Moon and the Bonfire* (translated by Louise Sinclair); Anne Sexton's works reprinted by permission of SLL/Sterling Lord Literistic, Inc. Copyright © by Anne Sexton. Extracts from *The Diary of Virginia Woolf* edited by Anne Olivier Bell and from *The Letters of Virginia Woolf* edited by Nigel Nicolson and Joanne Trautman, published by Hogarth Press. Reprinted by permission of The Random House Group Ltd.

Every effort has been made to trace copyright holders of material included in this book. The publishers would be pleased to hear from any we have been unable to contact.

Sarah Kane

A Prophet Not Honoured

Once in a while a new star erupts into the firmament, shines brightly for a short time, then explodes and is gone for ever.

One such was Sarah Kane, who burst upon the world's theatrical stage at the age of 23 when her first play *Blasted* was performed at the Royal Court Theatre in Sloane Square, London. That she was shattered and gone, destroyed by her own hand, at the tender age of 28, is now considered by most reviewers to be one of theatre's greatest tragedies. Yet, as we read her brief life story, we shall discover what a crucial role those same theatrical reviewers played in her death.

Photo: akg-images/ullstein bild

1

Sarah Kane was born on 3 February 1971 at Kelvedon near Brentwood, Essex; but a stereotype 'Essex Girl' she most certainly was not. Both her parents were journalists and devout evangelists. As a young girl Sarah was a fervent born-again Christian; the rest of her world was dominated by the written word in all its forms and by drama. Her mother was also a teacher but gave up her work to care for Sarah, and it seems that she devoted more time to Sarah than to her older brother, Simon. The result was that Sarah developed into an intelligent child who enjoyed learning.

The paradox was that she was later to frequently state: 'I hated school until the sixth form.' Yet she also acknowledges: 'My English and Drama teachers were excellent – I was encouraged to read, write and act, which were things I wanted to do.' If there was anything she hated during those early teenage years it was the superior attitude of her neighbours: 'They thought that certain things could not happen here. Yet there is the same amount of abuse and corruption in Essex as anywhere else, and that's what I want to blow open.'

While at Shenfield Comprehensive School she became involved in acting and directing with local drama groups. She directed *Macbeth* and *Oh! What a Lovely War* at the school; later she was in trouble for playing truant to work as assistant director in a production of Chekov's *The Bear* at Soho Polytechnic.

As a teenager she was known as a tomboy. Typical of this was her interest in football. She was a keen Manchester United supporter. When I met her in 1996, one of the things I asked her was where and how she had gathered the astonishing vocabulary of four-letter words that she spewed forth in *Blasted*. She told me: 'I think I picked most of it up watching Man U from the terraces at London clubs.'

The first turning point in her life came in her 18th year. It was in this year that she lost her Christian faith, rejected God and became an agnostic.

I believed in God but not in the lifestyle that Christianity demanded. I knew a lot of Christians who I thought were fundamentally bad people and a lot of non-Christians who I thought were utterly beautiful, and I couldn't understand that, so I made a conscious decision to reject God. According to the Bible I am now utterly damned. The point ... is that if you're not sure God exists you can cover your arse living your life carefully, just in case ... or you can live your life as you want to live it. If there is a God who can't accept the honesty of that then, well, tough.

She was later to say that she gave up on God '...to get a life'. She viewed it as her '...first relationship break-up'. There were to be several more in her short life.

This was also the year of her A level exams; she passed with good grades, which enabled her to obtain a much sought-after place on a BA course in Drama at Bristol University. Kane said, 'I chose to do Drama at Bristol because it was the only course I could find any genuine enthusiasm for. Until I got there, when suddenly I found far more interesting things to do.'

Indeed she did. She immediately fell in with the theatrical crowd and soon became very popular. She enjoyed the company of her peers to the full, joining them in leading a riotous social life. They were frequently to be found in Bristol's late night clubs, where Sarah was noted for her chain-smoking and ability to drink vast quantities of beer. She also had several lesbian affairs during her three years at the university.

Her original intention was to become an actor and director. In her first 18 months at Bristol she demonstrated her acting talents in a number of plays, the most noteworthy being the part of Bradshaw in Howard Barker's Jacobean drama *Victory*. Outstanding amongst productions she directed were *Top Girls* and *Macbeth*. But at some point during the spring of 1991 she became disillusioned with acting and for the first time she began writing seriously. The first production piece was *Sick*, a collection of three monologues, entitled *Starved*, *Comic Monologue* and *What She Said*, relating to sexual identity, rape and bulimia. *Comic Monologue* was part of a production entitled *Dreams and Screams* where she combined with Vincent O'Connell (Sore Throats Theatre Company). It was performed at the Edinburgh Fringe Festival in August 1991, where it was considered by critics to be disturbing and coarse. *Starved* and *What She Said* were performed in August 1992 at the Edinburgh Festival, again with Vincent O'Connell.

The Drama course at Bristol was an academic one and Sarah was not an academic. Her attitude towards her tutors became increasingly confrontational. One often quoted example concerns an occasion during the autumn seminar of 1991 when she was required to produce a piece of work for a tutorial. The tutor criticised her harshly for what he described as a pornographic essay. Kane's response was to purchase a number of explicitly pornographic magazines, which at the next tutorial she threw at him, saying: '...that's pornographic. Perhaps that will help you to understand the difference between pornography and experiential writing.' That, of course, got her into trouble with the university's authorities, as she was to be on several occasions. At one point it was suggested that she leave the university and it took lengthy efforts to enable her to stay.

But stay she did, graduating in the summer of 1992 with a First-Class Honours Degree. That she was able to achieve that, despite a great deal of irresponsible behaviour, speaks for her natural ability to understand drama. Whilst at Bristol, she had studied Edward Bond's play *Saved* (notable for the stoning of a baby); she had been moved and shocked by it. 'But, I thought there isn't anything you can't represent on stage.' For the first time she began to think seriously about writing plays. That summer she went to see *Mad* by Jeremy Weller at the Edinburgh Festival. This play was performed by professional and amateur actors, all of whom had first-hand experience of mental illness. It was to have a profound effect on her life and death. In Kane's own words, '...the night I saw it I made a decision about the kind of theatre I wanted to make – experiential. It remains the only piece of theatre to have changed my life. As an audience member I was taken to a place of extreme mental discomfort and distress – and then popped out the other end.' Kane said it took her to hell and made her ill for days afterwards, but she believed that experience prevented her from having more serious mental breakdowns when she later confronted the violence and extremes of her own writings.

Sarah came away from this experience wanting to write a play incorporating more than one character.

By the time she graduated from Bristol, Sarah was clear how she wanted her career to develop. She wanted to become a playwright. First, she needed to see whether she could write a full-length play with more than one character in it. One problem was that she was unemployed and without funds. Almost immediately she located an MA course in Playwriting at Birmingham University, where the tutor, and founder of the course, was dramatist David Edgar. She was able to obtain a financial grant from the Education Authority and joined the course in September 1992. Sarah told me, in 1996, that she only joined the course to please her mother and to get the grant. At Birmingham she encountered the same problems that got her into difficulties at Bristol. The MA was an academic course; but according to Sarah:

> I didn't want to be an academic. Inevitably, what you're studying is what's already been discovered. As a writer, I wanted to do things that hadn't been done, to invent new forms, find new modes of representation. So sitting in seminars discussing the three-act structure switched me off completely.

Certainly it did; she did not go to most of the lectures, but spent much of her time drinking, experimenting with drugs and feeling miserable, living in a city that she hated. However, living in Birmingham was to give her that first desire to write plays set in a large, unpleasant, industrial city; and from this wish *Blasted* was born.

Another problem for Kane was that the writers she was interested in talking to – Edward Bond, Howard Barker, Harold Pinter – were not lecturing at the course. In the end it was all too academic and anecdotal for Sarah; she did not complete the course.

What she did complete was the first two scenes of *Blasted*. These are acted out by the two principal characters, Ian (a middle-aged hack journalist) and Cate (a naïve, epileptic, young woman) in an expensive hotel room in Leeds; they could stand alone as a short play lasting about 45 minutes. The advantage of being at the university was that *Blasted* was given a student workshop production in the summer of 1993 at the Allardyce Nicoll Studio in Birmingham. At the end of the performance there was complete silence. This was followed by several students in the audience complaining loudly about the play's racist remarks, foul language and the rape of a retarded girl. Kane then got up and defended the play with great passion and fire.

Present at that performance was Melanie Kenyon (the literary manager), who was to become Sarah's agent and an intimate friend. In a conversation with Graham Saunders (author of *Love Me or Kill Me: Sarah Kane and the Theatre of Extremes*), Kenyon said, '...the writing was exquisite, passionate, raw, truthful. I thought,

God she's talented, but she's going to be a handful.' Mel Kenyon soon wrote to Sarah asking to see the completed play.

Kane's only interest now was in completing *Blasted* and it was obvious that the MA course would not allow her sufficient free time to draft and re-draft a major play. Shortly after the Birmingham production she left the university. The problems now were to find somewhere to live and an income to replace her student grant. She soon found a small studio flat in South London at Brixton. Perhaps not the ideal area for Sarah. She was already smoking cannabis and had experimented with cocaine. In Brixton in the 1990s every kind of drug was readily available on most street corners.

Upon arriving in Brixton, Kane signed on the dole. However, within a short time she had found part-time work as a literary assistant with the Bush Theatre in West London at Shepherds Bush. This, moreover, gave her sufficient scope to concentrate her energies on *Blasted*. She now began a pattern of writing throughout the night, which was to continue for the rest of her life. To keep her going through the late hours she would stimulate herself with tea, coffee, Prozac, cannabis and occasionally cocaine. The side-effect of these stimulants was invariably headaches, sometimes severe. On those irregular times when she had the opportunity to sleep, she relied upon Temazepam.

Sarah was dedicated to completing *Blasted* and could visualise the development of the two main characters, but was unable to see her way forward into the second act. By sheer chance events during the war in Bosnia were to open the door and shed an illuminating light upon her problem. During a break from her night-time writing, she switched on the TV news. Horrifying events in Srebrenica unfolded before her. At once she felt a need to do something about it, to write about it. Yet she was still dominated by her story of Ian and Cate in the Leeds hotel room. Suddenly she saw the connection. It is in the actions of peace time civilisation that the origins of war can be found. Now Sarah began to write feverishly, extending the first act of *Blasted* into further scenes, which introduce a soldier and turn the hotel room into a vision of a Bosnian battlefield. Kane completed the play within a few weeks. But she was determined to hone the dialogue to spare dramatic lines; it took 15 re-drafts before she was satisfied. She dedicated the piece to Vincent O'Connell, with whom she had written and co-produced at the Edinburgh Festival. Now she sent the completed work to Mel Kenyon and to other agents.

Kenyon was keen and soon arranged a meeting with Sarah. Shortly afterwards Sarah agreed to Kenyon becoming her agent. Mel Kenyon advised Sarah that, in her view, the only London theatre that might be persuaded to produce the play was the Royal Court. At that time the Royal Court had been given a grant of public money, through the Jerwood Foundation, for the purpose of choosing six new young playwrights and producing their work. By coincidence, Mel Kenyon also knew the work of one of the Royal Court associate directors, James Macdonald; and she believed he was probably the only one capable of producing the play.

Kenyon now approached him with *Blasted*; he was interested and the Royal Court did a reading in January 1994, which Macdonald directed. He was impressed by Kane's economic use of language, her control of pauses through punctuation and her format of telling the story through images rather than text. The Royal Court had already given grants to three new playwrights in Judy Upton (*Ashes and Sand*), Nick Grosso (*Peaches*) and Joe Penhall (*Pale Horse*). However, they offered Sarah a grant, to be used either to complete *Blasted* or to write another play. As we now know, Sarah had for all practical purposes completed *Blasted*. She did accept the grant but carried out only one minor re-draft on *Blasted* before delivering it up to the Royal Court.

Now followed a period of frustration and distress for Sarah. The Royal Court scheduled *Peaches* and *Ashes and Sand* and committed to *Pale Horse*, but would not programme *Blasted*. Sarah conferred with Melanie Kenyon and they concurred that *Blasted* was moving backwards in the queue for production; they speculated that there was disagreement amongst the Royal Court executive about the play. Sarah's depression was exacerbated by her work at the Bush Theatre coming to a close, causing her again to rely upon the dole for her income. Suddenly, in the autumn of 1994, the Royal Court did a reading of the completed play; Sam Kelly taking the lead part of Ian. James Macdonald was very keen and the play was programmed for January 1995.

In summary, the play's plot, if one can dignify it by saying that it had one, is this: it takes place in the bedroom of a five-star hotel anywhere (the Royal Court production chose Leeds). Ian, a middle-aged, second-rate journalist, also a third-rate undercover agent, appears with his ex-lover, Cate, a young, naïve, epileptic girl. It is soon clear that Ian is dying of lung cancer. He is

7

homophobic, sexist and grossly racist. He wishes to have sex with Cate, but she refuses. Whilst Cate has fainted, Ian rapes her. When Cate recovers she takes revenge by performing oral sex on Ian, but biting his penis very hard just as he is about to climax. Cate escapes through the bathroom. There are sounds of soldiers outside. Someone knocks loudly on the door. Ian foolishly opens it. An armed soldier bursts in. He sees Cate's knickers and goes looking for her, hoping to rape her. When he realises she has gone, he urinates on the bed (we are not told why). Suddenly there is a huge explosion; the hotel has been blasted by a mortar bomb. As they sit amongst the ruins, the soldier describes to Ian horrors he has committed during war, particularly sexual degradation and rape, which he has inflicted on men and women. Ian tells him this is a story no one wants to hear. The soldier then rapes Ian, sucks out his eyes, eats them and shoots himself. Cate returns, holding a baby. The baby dies. Cate buries it under the floorboards and then leaves to search for food. Blind and helpless, Ian defecates, masturbates and eats the baby. Ian is now beneath the floorboards with only his head poking out (shades of Samuel Beckett). Ian dies; rain falls upon his head. Cate returns with food; end of play.

Describing the events that take place within the play does not examine the work. The play is about language and the use of imagery, rather than text to tell the story. Importantly, it tears apart the strict three-act structure that had dominated British theatre since the days of Shakespeare.

The play's opening night at the Royal Court was 17 January 1995. Not a good choice. The Royal Court executive were still unsure about the play, so it was given very little build-up publicity, and deliberately programmed immediately after Christmas, in the hope that it would draw limited attention. The press were invited for the first two nights, as was usual. But most of them were free only on 18 January; thus it was that the audience in the 60-seat Theatre Upstairs on the 18th was mainly theatre critics. The play did not get off to a proper opening. Kane had incorporated an element of black humour into the work. This was to be established in the opening scene, which is set in a luxurious bedroom in an expensive hotel; enter Ian who says, 'I've shat in better places than this.' Unfortunately, the Royal Court produced a set more akin to a cheap bedsitter; the opening humour was lost and the scene was never set for this feature of the play. Played without an interval, it lasted almost two hours and for most of the audience it felt punishing.

Thus it was that, from the next day onwards for the length of the run, the newspaper critics furiously attacked the play. It seemed that on 18 January they had agreed together as one man (and they were almost all middle-aged men) that the play was disgusting and without dramatic merit and they would castigate it. Leading the charge was Jack Tinker of the *Daily Mail*, who phoned his newspaper that night to ensure he was first with the headlines! 'This Disgusting Feast of Filth' was his banner and he went on to say, '... I was utterly and entirely disgusted by a play which appears to know no bounds of decency, yet has no message to convey by way of excuse.' In a later review he wrote: '... *Blasted* was a bucket of bilge dumped over the audience at the Royal Court'. However, Tinker's colleague at the *Mail on Sunday*, Louise Doughty, said, '... Kane has an acute grasp of sexual politics and her dialogue is both sparse and stunning.'

Irving Wardle, for the *Independent on Sunday*, wrote, '... I cannot recall having seen an uglier play. The trouble with the piece is not its atrocities, but failure to relate them to any believable context. It ... lacks even the logic of a dream.'

In the *Guardian*, Michael Billington ridiculed it, saying:

> ... the play contains scenes of masturbation, fellatio, frottage, micturition, defecation – ah those old familiar faeces! – homosexual rape, eye-gouging and cannibalism. I was simply left wondering how such naïve tosh managed to scrape past the Court's normally judicious play selection committee.

This review provoked a letter from David Greig (the playwright) in which he says '... *Blasted* will last. It's a very good play indeed and after the hysteria dies down it remains to be read and performed for years to come.'

In fairness to Michael Billington, we should note that he was later to state, on BBC Radio 3 in June 2000, '... I deplored the tone with which I reviewed it, which was one of lofty derision. I can see now that it was a serious play driven by moral ferocity.' Certainly David Greig proved to be an accurate prophet and indeed his reaction was typical of other playwrights. Edward Bond said, '... It has a strange, almost hallucinatory quality, it is revolutionary.'

9

Later he wrote to the *Guardian*: '... It is the only contemporary play I wish I'd written.' Harold Pinter (*Daily Telegraph*, 16 March 1995) drew a distinction between the violence portrayed in *Blasted* and what he called the gratuitous violence of films (Quentin Tarantino was of course quoted). Pinter said, '... *Blasted* faces something actual and true and ugly and painful – and therefore received the headlines saying this play should be banned.' Probably these were reactions by other playwrights in support of one of their own.

The newspaper critics did not agree and their barrage of adverse criticism continued. *The Spectator* said it was '... a truly terrible little play'. Charlie Spencer for the *Daily Telegraph* called it '... this vile play' and said, '... hardened theatre critics looked in danger of parting with their suppers'. In the *Evening Standard*, Nick Curtis described the final scenes as '... a systematic trawl though the deepest pits of human degradation'.

The criticism was itself sensational. Public interest was now aroused. Stephen Daldry (Artistic Director for the Royal Court) was called back from a fundraising tour in the USA to appear on *Newsnight* and *The World at One* in defence of the production. He compared it to Osborne's *Look Back in Anger* and Bond's *Saved* and said that the symbolic landscape had either not been understood or had been obscured by media-created controversy and he echoed David Greig in saying it would later be hailed a classic. The play's director, James Macdonald, was also forced to defend it. Writing in the *Observer*, he called it, 'a moral and compassionate piece of work'.

All this violently adverse public criticism had a devastating effect on Sarah Kane. It might be seen as the beginning of the end of her life. She was emotionally and physically exhausted and became clinically depressed. In principle she went into hiding from the press. She was not at her flat, no one knew where she was, her agent Mel Kenyon would give no details of her whereabouts and would not even discuss the play or the writer. The press could get no interviews with her. This infuriated the journalists. Writing for the *Daily Express*, Polly Graham led with the sensational headline, 'Rape play girl in hiding'; she quoted a source at the Royal Court who said: 'She's gone into hiding, which is a bit rich. If she has so much to say in her plays, surely she should have the backbone to explain why she did what she did.' In practice, if the news hounds had gone back to the Court's Theatre Upstairs, they would have found Sarah tucked away at the back of the theatre, where she attended every performance of the play. Polly Graham was also the first journalist to reveal that the Royal Court had already commissioned the 23-year-old to write another play. This was to be *Cleansed*. She had already started writing it and had discussed it with James Macdonald, but it would be three years before it was produced and, in the meantime, many dramatic events were to take place in Sarah Kane's young life.

In the immediate aftermath of *Blasted*, Kane's only income was dole money plus some small revenue from *Blasted*. She kept herself busy, accepting invitations to attend readings of *Blasted* in New York, Berlin and Bucharest. She began to draft *Cleansed*, taking as her theme the survival of love in the most extreme situations for even the most objectionable of characters. The protagonist was to be drawn as a sadist, and with a touch of irony, Sarah named him Tinker, after her main adversary of the same name from the *Daily Mail*.

That summer, of 1995, she was approached by TV producer Mark Barker (best known for *Superstars*), who tried to interest her in writing a piece for TV or film production. She told him she was not interested because there was too much censorship of the writing and no audience reaction for the writer to analyse. But the thought stuck with her and within weeks she had written *Skin*, a short film of about ten minutes playing time. It was an explicit portrait of a skinhead racist thug, who falls in love with a black woman. It was screened at the London Film Festival in late 1995. Although it was filmed again in Edinburgh in September 1996 by Tapson Steel Films for Channel 4 Films, it was not broadcast by Channel 4 TV until June 1997. Originally scheduled for screening at 9.30 p.m., it was put back until 11.30 p.m. due to concerns about the scenes of violence and body-carving. Sarah got her own way with the choice of director; it was her long-time friend Vincent O'Connell. The producer was David Love, who was to renew his acquaintance with Sarah Kane only a few months later when they were both on the same ward at Maudsley Hospital in south east London, where they were both being treated for severe depression following drug overdoses. *Skin* was certainly successful; it has been repeated several times since and currently can still be seen occasionally on cable TV.

In May 1995, Sarah was commissioned by the Gate Theatre at

Notting Hill to write and direct a play based on a European classic. Her immediate instinct was to go for Georg Büchner's *Woyzeck*. It was an obvious choice, since the main character is able to express himself only through violence. Unfortunately for Sarah, the Gate was already programming a season of plays by Büchner. Sarah always hated being thwarted in any way and it was with some difficulty and much reading through the nights that she came up with Bertolt Brecht's *Baal*. However, Sarah was once again to be frustrated. Brecht's estate managers proved very difficult to deal with; it is probable that they simply did not want anything to do with the kind of publicity Kane was liable to attract. The Gate gave up on it and returned to Kane, this time suggesting a Greek tragedy. Sarah had some initial reluctance; Greek tragedies were of little interest to her. But by now she was becoming keen to do something for the Gate Theatre. The Gate was a small, under-funded fringe theatre, specialising in producing new translations of European pieces. Sarah had very strong feelings that this type of theatre was essential to the development of new writers and directors and must be supported. She accepted the commission and straightaway decided upon Seneca. Sarah had seen and liked James Macdonald's Royal Court production of Caryl Churchill's version of Seneca's *Thyestes*. She turned to Seneca's *Phaedra*, which she read through once only. She then read Tony Boyle's translation and appraisal of *Phaedra*; in which Boyle says:

> Seneca's tragedy seems one in which to be human is to suffer .. to be alive is to be entrapped in evil ... to exist is to be located in the midst of ... perversity. The Prince, Hippolytus, is less the product of a noble vision than of a deranged psychology, as its connection with a ferocious misogynism reveals.

It is unsurprising that Sarah's final choice was *Phaedra*.

In seeking to update *Phaedra*, Sarah considered three classical versions of the story of Phaedra's sexual lust for her son-in-law Hippolytus. She was much influenced by Racine's version (*Phèdre*), just as that writer had influenced her writing of *Blasted*. Euripides' version (*Hippolytus*) she rejected:

> This supposedly beautiful young boy is, to my mind, totally unattractive and, other than the influence of the gods, I couldn't

see why Phaedra would fall in love with him. I didn't want the passion imposed by the external force of the gods. I wanted to give it to the characters, to make it a human tragedy, so I turned him into something quite different.

She returned to Seneca's version: 'There I was struck that it is about a sexually corrupt royal family, which makes it totally contemporary.' The Hippolytus Kane eventually created is ill-kempt, a loner and a layabout typically to be found in the 1990s era. The theme running through the play is that through being in the deepest of low spirits comes the ability to live in the moment, because there isn't anything else. Sarah wrote *Phaedra's Love* whilst she was in severe depression caused by the critics' savaging of *Blasted* and by problems with her relationships with partners. It seems she was looking for honesty and commitment from partners who were looking for short-term sexual relationships.

Certainly all of that came through in the play. At that time Sarah was more concerned with drafting *Cleansed* and, as a consequence, *Phaedra's Love* was written very quickly, probably within five weeks. This in turn led to her being uncertain whether the text would work. She was therefore quite decided that the play could only succeed with firm but sympathetic direction by a director who understood where the writer was coming from.

The play went into rehearsal at the beginning of April 1996; Sarah quickly fell out with the Gate's Artistic Director. She immediately turned to James Macdonald and asked him to direct. He had other commitments and thus was unavailable. Sarah did not hesitate; she would direct it herself.

Phaedra's Love opened at the tiny Gate Theatre in May 1996. The set for the play took up most of the theatre; the audience was cramped on benches in the middle of the theatre and around the edges. The early summer that year was unusually hot, which added to the audience discomfort. Fortunately the play only lasted 70 minutes. However, there was no interval.

In this play, Kane deals for the first time explicitly with love, which is to become the main theme of the rest of her work. It is Kane's way of presenting her thoughts about love that sets her apart from other playwrights of the 1990s. Savage violence, rape, gore, everything seen and explicit is her medium. *Phaedra's Love* was no different to *Blasted* in that respect. Highlights of this 'realism' in *Phaedra's Love* are the roasting of Hippolytus's genitals, a mob of actors rising out of the audience to tear Hippolytus apart and the hurling of his bloody body parts out into the audience. After seeing a production of the play, I was fortunate to be able to spend a little time in Sarah's company. I had a preconceived idea of what she would look like; medium height, muscular, long, flowing hair, glasses, with second-rate university written all over her. I have never been so wrong about anything in my life. Sarah was petite, with very short, spiky blonde hair, tomboyish, with trousers and baseball cap. She was instantly likeable with a wry sense of humour.

When I asked her why the violence and gore were so necessary to be seen on stage, when the previous writers of this myth had managed very well in depicting it off-stage, she said, 'The savagery and rape are there in the original texts; why should an audience pay good money not to see it when they can stay at home and not see it for nothing.' I said I was puzzled by noticing several European foreign accents amongst such a small London audience. 'They are mostly producers from Germany, Romania and Belgium,' she told me. 'I've already had several enquiries about productions of *Blasted* in Germany.'

Phaedra's Love was Kane's least successful play. It had none of the cutting dialogue and tense pauses that had been evident in *Blasted*. The quality of writing just was not up to the standard seen in *Blasted*. It never takes the audience on the emotional journey that was offered up in *Blasted*. It seems obvious now that the difference was that Sarah had spent a long time writing *Blasted*, whereas she had hastily thrown *Phaedra's Love* together to suit the Gate. The critics, in the main, seemed to think it was simply more of the same.

Charles Spencer (*Sunday Telegraph*) dismissed the play out of hand: he said he was 'seriously concerned about Sarah Kane's mental health. It's not a theatre critic that's required here, it's a psychiatrist'. Many would say that later events proved him to be correct.

Kate Bassett (*The Times*) said, 'Violence does not reach us by word of mouth. It is in our faces, almost literally... The trouble is that lashings of stage violence are not really shocking, just hard to believe.'

Michael Billington (the *Guardian*) was more mixed in his review, describing it as succinctly funny, but going on to say, 'Visually her play has undeniably power; intellectually it's hard to see what point it is making.'

Kathleen Stratton (*London Evening Standard*) was kinder: 'The play blows a range of dramatic raspberries at an unmistakable British society captured in galloping decay.'

For myself, the critics' reviews of *Phaedra's Love* demonstrate that it was all above their heads and Kane was simply years ahead of her time. In this play she seems at times to have flashes of psychic perception: for example, when Strophe asks Hippolytus whether he has had sex with Phaedra, the dialogue 'Did you have sex with her?' 'Sexual contact?' 'You know exactly what I mean' seems very like Bill Clinton being questioned about his affair with Monica Lewinsky. The play also echoes the subsequent death of Princess Diana when Phaedra's death elevates the queen to iconic status with the mob pouring out histrionic hostility towards the establishment. In the crowd scene at Phaedra's death, Kane uncannily foretells public sentiment at the time of Princess Diana's death with the remark, 'She was the only one had anything going for her.' The reviews which are closest to my own feelings are from David Greig: '*Phaedra's Love* contains some of Kane's wittiest dialogue. Perhaps the humour comes from its authorial detachment.' And from *What's On* magazine: 'Pure drama and it doesn't attempt to manipulate us emotionally and so earns our respect.' Nevertheless, I side with Mark Ravenhill who said, 'It was disappointing after the near perfection of *Blasted*.'

Now Sarah entered into a frenetic period in which she was much in demand. Those directors from Germany, France, Belgium and Eastern Europe, whom I had noted at the Gate, all wanted to put on productions of *Blasted*. Her style of writing, with few characters and settings, sparse language and lengthy pauses was much to their taste. Sarah was asked to travel to productions all over Europe; in Germany alone four productions took place during 1996. Most of them were not to Sarah's liking and she nagged away at herself and worried about them to excess. In August, Mark Ravenhill (*Shopping and Fucking*, *Sleeping Around*, *Handbag*) became Literary Manager for Paines Plough, a touring theatrical company, and almost his first task was to ask Sarah to be the writer in residence. She accepted and so commenced a friendship, which lasted until the end of her life. She was still suffering insomnia and continued writing through the nights; now she was drafting and re-drafting *Cleansed*. It was taking a long time to write and Sarah was experiencing wildly fluctuating highs and lows in her own feelings about the play. The Royal Court were not exactly helpful. They were in no hurry to produce the play, but were careful to renew their rights to it in 1996, so that Sarah had to press on with it. Her private life was by now in a cycle of turmoil. A combination of amphetamines, barbiturates and cannabis was taking a toll on her health. Insomnia was constant, and severe headaches frequent. Her emotional life was unsatisfactory; she was going through a period when she fell in and out of love frequently and quickly: mainly because she could not find in any partner that loyalty and constancy which was so important to her.

On the edge of a nervous breakdown, Sarah went to a writers' retreat in New York. She was in search of peace, away from the continuous (unsuccessful) pressure by the media to seek to discover what went on in the private life of 'theatre's *enfant terrible*'. While in New York, she found some Americans were interested in *Blasted* and she attended readings of the play.

She returned in better spirits and threw herself into script reading and teaching others at Paines Plough. It was almost her only income at the time. She completed her final draft of *Cleansed* and sent it to Mel Kenyon. Kenyon could add nothing to it, so they took it to the Royal Court. There it sat, in limbo, awaiting possible production.

The Gate Theatre wanted more of Kane and now asked her to direct a production of Georg Büchner's *Woyzeck*. She had wanted to do this since her teenage years and had come close to it for the Gate in 1996. The play had considerably influenced her writing of *Cleansed*; she was more than happy to accept. Some feeling of how Sarah's writing of *Cleansed* and direction of *Woyzeck* influenced each other may be gained from this extract from a public interview she gave to Dan Rebellato at Royal Holloway College ('Brief Encounter Platform') in November 1998:

Now Büchner's *Woyzeck* is an absolutely perfect gem of a play ... in that anything remotely extraneous or explanatory is completely cut and all you get is those moments of extremely high drama. And what I was trying to do with *Cleansed* was a similar thing but in a different way, and when I finished

16

Cleansed I was directing *Woyzeck* and I was playing around with all the different versions as he (Büchner) died before completing the play so nobody really knows the order he meant the scenes to go in. And I sat there with all the scenes with all these different bits of card, moving them around and I thought, 'Where have I done this before?' It was *Cleansed*!' And I wrote all the storylines – if you like the Rod and Carl story; the Grace/Graham story; the Robin/Grace story and the Tinker/Stripper story separately – and I thought, 'Where do they connect?' And so I was doing all this moving things around and going completely insane thinking, 'There's a scene missing – where's the scene?' Until eventually I had the thing that I wanted... And I think that in a lot of other plays there are things like, 'So he runs off and tells his father' or if you look at Greek drama a messenger comes on – all of which is a lot easier to take and gives you a chance to calm down. But I didn't want to give people a chance to calm down.

The production took place on an open set at the Gate in October 1997. It was done as an ensemble piece with lots of musical noise. As always with Sarah, the dialogue was sparse. The general view was that Kane had created from an already depressing play something even more dreary. The comments from her manager at Paines Plough, Mark Ravenhill (the *Independent*), seem significant: after reading *Cleansed* in August 1997 he had told Sarah, 'Brilliant, very Puccini', to which she had replied, 'Yeah, well, I'm in love,' but when in October 1997 he told her *Woyzeck* was just about the bleakest thing he had ever seen, she said, 'Yeah, well I fell out of love.'

Whether by coincidence or not, Sarah now entered into a period of her lowest depression and a lack of self-esteem so severe it could well be called self-hate. We can see reasons for this. *Woyzeck* is a dismal play, in any terms, and creating a new production of it is unlikely to uplift anyone's spirits. Clearly Sarah had reached another trough in her love life. Also there was the frustration and disillusionment of the Royal Court's failure to programme a production of *Cleansed*.

Suddenly, though, the clouds parted and the sun shone through. Ian Rickson took over from Stephen Daldry as Artistic Director at the Royal Court in January 1998. One of his early decisions was to stage a production of *Cleansed* at a grand West End theatre. He chose The Duke of York's Theatre in Shaftesbury Avenue. James Macdonald was again to direct her work. When Sarah received the news her mood changed dramatically. She was ecstatic and hyper. Depression disappeared, love and sexual problems were dismissed and she threw herself into rehearsals with James, designer Jeremy Herbert and a cast including Stuart McQuarrie (Tinker), Suzan Sylvester (Grace), Martin Marquez (Graham) and Daniel Evans (Robin). They had just four weeks to put the play together. Throughout the four weeks Sarah continued to revise the play, always cutting words and lines. Her objective, stark minimalism. Eventually, although the play lasts 90 minutes, the dialogue fills only 30 minutes and imagery occupies the rest.

The play opened on 30 April 1998 at The Duke of York's under the name 'The English Theatre Company'. It was a poor choice of venue: the theatre is vast and Kane's audience at that time was a very specific one. On the night I attended only about one third of the seats were filled and to my surprise about half of the audience were gays.

The play is set in a psychiatric institution where the inmates find love among one another. The central theme is: what is the most that one lover can truthfully promise another? The inmates are controlled by a sadistic psychiatrist (Tinker) who cruelly drives them to the extremity of pain to try to find out what power love has over them. There is a central plot where a sister (Grace) is searching for a lost brother (Graham); no doubt drawn from Shakespeare's *Twelfth Night*. Much of what caused revulsion in *Blasted* is repeated. There is nudity, sex and masturbation. A tongue is sliced off, an eyeball injected with heroin, a male inmate is raped with a broomstick, rats eat away at amputated limbs, breasts are sliced off and a penis is transplanted. Tinker cuts Rod's throat; Robin hangs himself. Yet the play ends in blinding sunlight with daffodils bursting into flower.

Of course most critics panned it. Charles Spencer (*Daily Telegraph*) said it was disgusting and he objected to it being staged. 'It has a dreary, linguistically impoverished flatness. It is a cynical attempt by the Royal Court to retain its reputation for cutting-edge theatre.' In the *Observer* Susan Clapp called it 'a howl of horror'. Georgina Brown (*Mail on Sunday*) said it was '... portentous drivel, exquisitely dressed in designer chic'. Sheridan Morley, writing for *The Spectator*, dismissed it out of hand, calling Kane '...a naughty schoolgirl, desperately trying to shock an increasingly bored and languid audience'. There were other more appreciative views. The *Independent* (Paul Taylor) said:

> *Cleansed*, beautifully mounted by Macdonald ... was like a cross between a play and an installation piece as it evoked an unremittingly harrowing institution designed to rid society of its undesirables. For the first time here, in my estimation, yearning for some loving, purifying alternative to the horror symbolised in the incestuous devotion between brother and sister, made a deeper dramatic impact in a Kane play than the atrocities.

John Peter, writing in the *Sunday Times*, observed:

> *Cleansed* is a nightmare of a play, it unreels somewhere between the back of your eyes and the centre of your brain with an unpredictable but remorseless logic. As with a nightmare, you cannot shut it out. You feel that somebody else is dreaming it for you, spinning the images out of some need that you don't want to think of as your own.

Kane had at first been delighted with the production, but she had at no time taken into account the size of the theatre and, when she saw how small the audience was in relation to the number of seats available, she resorted to her constant companion, depression. This was compounded by the reviewers again attacking her. Another rumoured broken love affair with Anne Mayer (at that time Press Officer at the Royal Court) may have been the final straw. An overdose of Valium gave her a brief stay in the Maudsley Hospital at Denmark Hill in south east London.

As was to happen so often in Sarah's life, an unexpected event occurred quite suddenly to take her mind far away from depression. With only four performances of the production remaining, Suzan Sylvester (Grace) sustained an injury to her back and could not appear. With no standby in the cast and without time, availability or inclination to get one, there was only one solution. Sarah took on the part herself, in one scene appearing nude with transplanted penis. Although always a better director than actor, she threw herself wholeheartedly into the role and gave four good performances. She was later to say that acting in the play suddenly made the piece much clearer to her than when she was writing it or attending rehearsals. Certainly it elevated her mood.

Now Sarah entered a period of frenetic activity beyond anything she had ever experienced. The pace was to quicken until it reached its peak and was to end in her death.

Productions of her works began to be performed all over Europe: Dublin, Berlin, Hamburg, Vienna, Copenhagen, Brussels. Sarah's attendance was much in demand and obviously required extensive travel. The Royal Court invited her to lead workshops and writers' discussion groups at their European summer schools in Bulgaria and Spain. She continued her work with Paines Plough in the most vigorous fashion, reading many dozens of plays and writing furiously. She struck up an intense relationship with Vicky Featherstone, the Artistic Director at Paines Plough.

While Sarah was writing the final drafts of *Cleansed*, she called at Vicky's office for a script discussion. Vicky was not there and, waiting for her, Sarah browsed through a copy of Fassbinder's *Pre-Paradise Sorry Now*. This was to give her the idea for a new play. Vicky at once asked her to write a short piece for the weekly lunchtime readings which Paines Plough were holding at the Bridewell Theatre near Fleet Street in the City of London. Sarah then wrote the first 20 minutes of what was to become *Crave* in three days. It was strongly influenced by T.S. Eliot's *The Wasteland*. In essence, the piece is four voices describing regrets, desires and hopes for the future within the context of their own psychological damage.

Sarah found four voices that she liked and at the readings she presented the play under the pseudonym Marie Kelvedon. Her motive was clear, she wished the work to be watched by an audience not biased by the reactions to *Blasted* nor by the Kane reputation.

The choice of name was obvious: Marie was her middle name, and Kelvedon the Essex town in which she grew up. The fictitious biography she invented for Kelvedon was less obvious: 'Expelled from St Hilda's College, Oxford, for acts in the dining hall involving evil and absurd concepts; served a prison term in Holloway; more recently she has worked as a taxi driver, a roadie with the Manic Street Preachers, and a continuity announcer for the BBC World Service. She now lives in Cambridgeshire with her cat, Grotowski!' Sarah had let her imagination run riot.

The readings took place in the late summer of 1997. Vicky Featherstone was impressed with the rhythmic and lyrical quality of the lines. She asked Sarah if it could be expanded into a full play; Sarah was sure it could and Vicky commissioned her to write it. One would have thought that, with the nucleus of the play written, Sarah would have extended and completed it in a matter of weeks. This was not to be. Sarah immersed herself in a great deal of deep thought about this piece and it was not until May 1998, whilst doing workshops with the New Dramatists in New York, that she completed it. Even then it only ran for 45 minutes. There is little narrative in *Crave* but the rhythm of the text demands concentration as the four voices become one. Kane uses as her reference many forms of love: maternal, abusive, compulsive, but essentially sexual. The longest speech is a poem in praise of the little everyday things of love. The play ends in a falling towards light. It seems obvious that Sarah was drawing heavily upon her personal experiences.

Paines Plough mounted the first production in the Traverse Theatre at the Edinburgh Festival in August/September 1998. Vicky Featherstone directed. For two months in Edinburgh Sarah and Vicky appeared to be blissfully happy together. Sarah always kept her love affairs strictly private and hardly anyone ever knew who her partners were. But when I saw her with Vicky at the festival, I thought I had never seen two people more in love.

With hundreds of shows on offer at the Edinburgh Festival, maximum publicity is vital to any piece. Now it was offered up as a Sarah Kane play, but publicity for the play was seriously blunted by Sarah's attitude. When Mark Ravenhill, for Paines Plough, asked her to do some publicity work for the production she refused; 'I'm not a brand name, I'm a person,' she snapped.

Nevertheless, *Crave* was well received by most of the critics. *The Times* called it 'strong meat. A dramatic poem in the late-Beckett style; sometimes a chamber quartet for lost voices.' David Greig said: '*Crave* is possibly Kane's best piece. It is an opaque, beautiful play, searching for answers with a liquid poetic voice.' Charles Spencer (for the *Daily Telegraph*), who had previously slammed *Blasted* and *Phaedra's Love*, now said of *Crave*: 'A fine, short, haunting and well-written play,' whilst Irving Wardle, writing for the Sunday version of the same newspaper said *Crave* established Kane as 'a commanding talent'. The general consensus was that

21

Sarah had moved away from the staged violence of *Blasted*, *Phaedra's Love* and *Cleansed* and had, in theatrical terms, been 'born again' (Nick de Jong, *Evening Standard*).

Crave moved from the festival to the Royal Court for four weeks, mid-September to mid-October. Simultaneously it toured Berlin and Dublin. In December it played three performances in Copenhagen and two in Maastricht. Sarah Kane attended nearly all of these productions. In the Copenhagen and Maastricht performances Sarah stepped in to play the role of Character C, a young girl.

The following quotation from her 'Brief Encounter' interview partly explains why she chose to see so many performances of this play:

> In some ways for me *Crave* has very fixed and specific meanings in my mind, which no one else could possibly know unless I told them. For example, who knows what 199714424 (Character B is speaking of lost faith) means? I'm the only person who knows – and the actors – and I have no intention of telling anyone what it means. So I can't possibly expect to see the same production of the play twice, thank God.

Although all four of Sarah's plays were now being produced throughout Europe, she still had not broken into the American market. *Crave* was the first of her plays to be produced in the USA but this was not until November 2000, some 21 months after her death. The production was mounted by the Axis Company, at the Greenwich Village Theatre in New York, under the direction of Randy Sharp. Ironically for Kane the spotlight was not upon her but upon the lead character: Debbie Harry (Blondie) making her debut in a major role on the American stage.

Throughout the writing and the productions of *Crave*, Sarah was suffering from drug abuse and its corollary severe depression. There is little doubt that whilst *Crave* was inspired by Fassbinder and T.S. Eliot, it was in large part based on Kane's personal experiences. The press release for the play, which I have no doubt was partially written by Sarah, describes the theme of *Crave* as 'the disintegration of a human mind under the pressures of love, loss and desire'. No one who knew her, even slightly, could deny that this applied to Sarah. Part of *Crave* deals with the effects of antidepressant and sedative drugs. At that time Sarah was taking several different prescription pills, changing them frequently. She was taking Setraline to stimulate her mind and body. To counteract this she would use Thioridazine, a tranquillizer generally used to suppress aggression and treat psychotic conditions; however, the recommended dosage is 30 to 800 mg and the 50 mg dosage, which Sarah was taking, would have had no effect upon her advanced condition. She had been taking the maximum dosage of Zoplicone (7.5 mg) as a sleeping pill and sometimes doubled up on the dosage. When I met Sarah at the Edinburgh Festival in the summer of 1998 she told me she had given up Zoplicone because it caused her to come out in a rash. From my own knowledge of the drug I told Sarah that I doubted it being the cause of the rash as this would be extremely rare. I also cautioned her about giving up this medication, as it is addictive and withdrawal can cause severe side-effects, not least of which is chronic insomnia. She was uninterested and it seems she soon returned to the drug as it is almost certain that she was using it whilst writing *4.48 Psychosis* at the end of 1998. Zoplicone is a short-acting sleeping pill, which lasts for exactly four hours; if one always took it just before 1 a.m., one would certainly always wake up just before 5 a.m.

Sarah found that when the short-term effect of Zoplicone wore off, she would awake and be unable to return to sleep. This is quite usual with this drug. Sarah would rise and sit there in her tiny Brixton flat on those dark, cold winter/spring mornings of 1998, consumed with despair about her life. She had completed *Crave* and now in those desolate night-time hours she began her early thoughts about a new play. These thoughts she would write down at random. Now came the summer and, with it, hope – the production of *Crave*, the Edinburgh Festival and Vicky Featherstone.

With the close of the Edinburgh production of *Crave*, Sarah began to create a collage of her random thoughts for her new play. The title choice was easy. It had to relate to those early morning thoughts when her mind had become distorted. *4.48 Psychosis* was to be her final play.

Through the autumn of 1998, Sarah was developing the play from her collage. Now she needed a structure to unify it. She decided there was to be only one central voice in the piece, with minor support from two other, nameless voices. Basically it was to be a narrative from a person whose mind has been severely damaged by deep depression. It would centre around the time of

4.48 a.m., that time in the darkness of the night when such people are most likely to kill themselves. Kane told Nils Tabert (Rowohlt Theatre, Verlag, who represents Kane's works in Austria, Germany and Switzerland), 'This is yet another play which is about the split between one's consciousness and one's physical being. For me that's what madness is about.'

With all her plays, Sarah, always a voracious reader, was much influenced by the work of other writers. *4.48 Psychosis* is no exception. Here she is influenced by, as ever, Samuel Beckett and by Antonin Artaud's work (usually referred to as 'The Theatre of Cruelty'), Martin Crimp's *Attempts On Her Life* and by Sylvia Plath (*The Bell Jar* and *Edge*). As we shall read later in this book, Plath's writing and suicide had particular relevance for Sarah Kane.

Although the central theme of *4.48 Psychosis* is about the severe mental disorder which causes the sufferer's contact with reality to become distorted, it is also about another of Kane's recurring themes – the fragility of love. A new theme is also introduced: the lack of interest of doctors in mental problems and their haste to resolve them with the over-prescription of dangerous drugs. Most critics have said that *4.48 Psychosis* is Sarah Kane's suicide note. A very few disagreed; as did her brother Simon. I think the latter are on weak ground. Consider the following lines, extracted at random from the play. 'I have resigned myself to death this year.' 'I shall not speak again.' 'At 4.48 when desperation visits I shall hang myself.' 'I have become so depressed by the fact of my own mortality that I have decided to commit suicide.' 'This is not a world in which I wish to live.' 'Take an overdose, slash my wrists, then hang myself.' The play ends, 'Watch me vanish; watch me, watch me.'

During the summer of 1998, through the Edinburgh Festival, and travelling extensively in Europe, Sarah had experienced one of the calmest and happiest periods of her life. Now, as autumn faded and winter moved in, she suddenly, and quite unexpectedly on her part, was hit by another period of depression. Strangely, this was the most severe she had ever encountered. She struggled, with little success, to overcome it. Determined to persevere with *4.48 Psychosis*, she found herself awake and writing at that time every morning.

By the dawn of 12 February, she had completed the first draft. On the morning of that same day she delivered it to Mel Kenyon. Anxious and uncertain whether the play made any sense, she rang Melanie several times that afternoon, desperate for a reaction. She asked for comments and detailed notes, something that was quite unlike her usual practice. Kenyon read *4.48 Psychosis* overnight and met with Sarah the next day. They discussed the play in depth; examining the role of doctor and lovers, the music, sex, how much humour she could get away with and how ambiguous she could afford to be, still leaving the play meaningful.

Sarah went away from her discussions with Mel Kenyon in a confused and depressed mood. Sleep would not come. She wrote into the early hours of the morning, revising and honing *4.48 Psychosis*. Ultimately she would dose herself up with Zoplicone and Temazepam and fall into a drugged sleep. But in that sleep dreams came, perhaps to tell her that she was sexually inadequate and that she had nothing left to give as a writer. She rose from a drugged sleep late on the afternoon of Monday 15 February. She gathered together the revised version of the play and delivered it to Mel Kenyon's office later that day.

It was probably at the Edinburgh Festival in the summer of 1992 that Sarah's thoughts had first turned to mental illness and suicide. Certainly it is evident from her plays and from her conversations with colleagues and friends that thoughts of suicide were increasingly with her from 1992 onwards. In the early hours of the morning of Tuesday 16 February 1999, she gave way to her thoughts. She swallowed 150 antidepressants (Prozac and Setraline) and topped them up with 50 sleeping tablets (Zoplicone and Temazepam). Astonishingly this was not the end for Sarah. The end to come was even more astonishing. By sheer chance, her flatmate, rising early for work, found her just in time and immediately took her to the nearest hospital, King's College at Denmark Hill. Here her stomach was pumped out and she appeared to make a rapid recovery. She asked to see Melanie Kenyon and Kenyon visited on Thursday 18 February. Kenyon says, 'We laughed about everything; and she was very calm and serene' (interview with Graham Saunders, *Love Me or kill Me*, November 2000). Certainly the hospital thought Sarah was in control of herself; she was released to go home that same day. However, the hospital and Mel Kenyon were wrong; Sarah's mind was in turmoil and she suffered a mental breakdown the next day. Desperate to ease her confusion she took a further cocktail of tablets, which was followed by a physical collapse. She was admitted back into King's College on Friday evening, 19 February.

In the early hours of Saturday 20 February 1999, Sarah was left on her own for about 90 minutes. At some time during that period, determined to commit suicide, she removed the laces from her boots, formed them into a noose, went to a toilet, locked herself in and hanged herself from the neck until she was dead.

The hospital has never satisfactorily explained why a suicidal patient was left unsupervised for a substantial period of time during those dawn hours of vulnerability. This despite questions from the police and the coroner and persistent enquiries from Sarah's family, led by her father Peter. It would, however, have mattered little if the hospital staff had been more vigilant; Sarah Kane was a very determined person; and upon suicide she was determined.

Following Sarah's death, James Macdonald and Mel Kenyon had several discussions about producing *4.48 Psychosis*. They both felt that the play could not be produced in the immediate aftermath of Sarah's death. But eventually they realised that the audience would always associate it with the author's suicide. Macdonald agreed to direct and chose Daniel Evans as the leading actor. The single voice he split between three actors, representing perpetrator, victim and onlooker. The play went into rehearsal for seven weeks; rather excessive for such a short play one would have thought. The first performance was at the Royal Court Theatre Upstairs on 23 June 2000. It lasted 75 minutes. The set, designed by Jeremy Herbert, was dominated by a mirror, which was enhanced by projections on to it of light and imagery. The real effect was to enlarge the stage and establish the set as a large attic room; the surreal effect was to present the action taking place from several different angles. The play ends with the lines, 'Please open the curtains', and the actors open the shutters to the windows, letting in the sound and lights of the London street outside.

Throughout the whole of the first run of the play, there was much tension amongst the audience. They were only too aware that the author had committed suicide. Their feelings were sharply focused by many of the lines, which seemed to be Sarah Kane's personal suicide notes; typical were these lines early in the piece when the patient is discussing a particular doctor who he believes has betrayed him: 'Nothing can extinguish my anger. Nothing can restore my faith. This is not a world in which I wish to live.' Some of the audience may have known that Sarah did have a relationship with one particular female doctor, who Kane believed ultimately let her down.

Following the Royal Court production, *4.48 Psychosis* played in 20 countries including throughout Europe and China. It was especially popular in Germany. In October 2004 it embarked on a six-city tour of the United States, starting in Brooklyn. Thus it achieved for Sarah an ambition which she had been unable to fulfil during her lifetime; acceptance by American theatregoers and critics. Today many colleges in the USA run courses on the appreciation of Sarah Kane.

With *4.48 Psychosis*, the critics did a U-turn. Matt Wolf (*New York Times*) thought it 'arguably Ms Kane's best play'. *The Scotsman* said, 'It has beauty and rawness ... a combination of unprocessed honesty and meticulous craft. Kane has the power to take material beyond endurance and shape it, burnish it, laugh at it, dominate it with her art.' Commenting on the closing lines of the play, Paul Taylor for the *Independent* said, 'The effect is strangely uplifting, like watching the final release of a turbulent spirit.'

Michael Billington, writing for the *Guardian*, said there was a huge contrast in audience reception between Kane's first play, *Blasted*, and this, her last, *4.48 Psychosis*. He wrote, 'In just over five short years, Sarah Kane moved from disrupter of the peace to dramatic icon. The new play is a sombre, poetic and subjective meditation on suicide.' This was the same Billington who had described *Blasted* as 'naïve tosh'. Susannah Clapp, for the *Observer*, was comprehensive: 'It is her most beguiling work: it's hard not to like a dramatist who describes a dream in which a doctor "gave me eight minutes to live; I'd been sitting in the fucking waiting-room half an hour". There is no attempt to suggest a colourful literary madness: it is a picture of the real thing.'

Unfortunately the critics' appreciation of Kane's work came much too late. It was their dismissal and disparagement of *Blasted* that had initiated that ever-intensifying depression from which eventually Sarah could not recover. However, we should not leave Sarah's death at a point where we ascribe the cause wholly to the journalists.

Why does a young, attractive female, with v.g.s.o.h. and four plays already shown in the West End of London and throughout Europe make a determined and successful bid to end her life at 28 years of age?

Shortly before her death, Sarah told her friend Mark Ravenhill, 'Most good playwrights write seven good plays and then something happens and after that they're crap.' There is a great deal of truth in that statement. But Sarah went on to say, 'I'm not far off my allotted seven.' Ravenhill sought to persuade her that she was only halfway there. But if you include *Sick* and her screenplay *Skin* then obviously *4.48 Psychosis* was the seventh. Sarah probably thought she had burnt herself out and had no more creative work left in her. Sarah's periods of depression were cyclical: her agent, Mel Kenyon, states unequivocally that the final bout of depression caught her by surprise and that it was so severe that she was unable to break out of it. Many critics believe that Sarah's depression was the product of despair of simple human existence. Some dispute this: playwright Anthony Neilson leads those who believe it was a chemical imbalance in the brain. In a letter to the *Guardian* dated 25 February 1999, Neilsen says Sarah battled against '. . . banal forces: crazy and irregular tides of chemicals that crash through the brain'. Circumstantial evidence leads me to believe that some of Sarah's depression and confusion was caused by the cocktail of prescription drugs that she was taking. We should also consider whether Sarah's disillusionment with her love life was an element of her suicidal thoughts. She was openly gay and had a number of short-term affairs; always seeking, but never finding, long-term love and loyalty. Yet it probably was not depression alone that caused such determination in Sarah to commit suicide. The 'free spirit' of her existentialism surely played an important role. It is known that Kane's suicidal thoughts were much influenced by her consideration of other writers. Probably the most significant of these was Sylvia Plath. Plath wrote shortly before her own suicide, 'The woman is perfected. Her dead body wears the smile of accomplishment.' We cannot be sure that Sarah felt fulfilled in death; but certainly her death was every bit as uncompromising as her creative life.

Suicide always poses a question, and the suicide of a writer leaves material over which the living can only ponder in search of answers. Sarah Kane guarded her privacy zealously and would never discuss sexuality or gender in relation to her plays. She told Aleks Sierz (*In-Yer-Face Theatre*), 'When people talk about me as a writer, that's what I am, and that's how I want my work to be judged – on its quality, not on the basis of my age, gender, class, sexuality or race. I am what I am – not what other people want me to be. I don't believe I have a responsibility to the audience. My responsibility is to the truth, however difficult that truth happens to be. What I can do is put people through an intense experience. Maybe in a small way from that you can change things.'

4.48 Psychosis was surely Sarah Kane's somewhat lengthy suicide note. It is to that play that we should turn if we seek further answers to her life and death.

Ernest Hemingway

The Conundrum Man

Ernest Miller Hemingway was larger than life and larger than death. Physically, intellectually, in his actions and his emotions.

At birth, he weighed in at a heavyweight 10 pounds. In his teenage years he grew to 6 feet and by the time he was 25 he weighed 240 pounds, was over 6 feet and had a chest span of 50 inches, a huge man for the early 1900s. For comparison purposes just consider that, during Hemingway's youth, the heavyweight boxing champion of the world was Tommy Burns, who stood 5' 7" and weighed 180 pounds.

A man of blatant masculinity, he lived life on an epic scale.

Photo: akg-images

31

Blood sports were his passion. Big game hunting, deep-sea fishing, bullfights, cockerel fights, boxing, he could not live without the adrenaline rush they gave him. He adored being in the spotlight and this led him to seek friendships with major film stars and championship boxers. His other big passion was women. But his emotional insecurity caused him to treat women badly. As a consequence, he had four wives and you can multiply that by a hundred and still not come near to the number of short-term sexual relationships he had with women. Trawling through his relationships with other men there is some cause to suspect that he may have been bisexual.

One of the most thoughtful and intelligent of American writers, Hemingway wrote 18 novels, about 150 published short stories and poems and, as a journalist, some of the finest reports ever recorded on the Greco-Turkish War, the Spanish Civil War and the Second World War. Unquestionably, he shaped the prose style of a generation. His Nobel Prize for Literature, awarded in 1954, speaks for itself.

In death he continued as in life. When he deemed the time right to exit he was in the hallway of his home in Ketchum, Idaho. He took up his double-barrelled shotgun, placed the barrels in his mouth and blew away his face and brains.

Aaron Hotchner was, for the last 14 years of Hemingway's life, his closest friend. In his book *Papa Hemingway* Hotchner says he cannot tell why this man, who seemed invulnerable and appeared to have everything, committed suicide. Hotchner insists no one can tell how this came to pass. I do not agree. We can examine Hemingway's early life, which was the foundation for his aggressive and possessive, yet insecure, adult lifestyle. We can consider the major events and relationships of his adulthood, and his reactions to people and events. We can retrace Hemingway's rapid decline leading up to his suicide and we can assess the conditions and events that contributed to it. From all of this the reader can surely draw out a valid opinion as to why Ernest Hemingway had suicide in mind.

It all began in Oak Park, a suburb of Chicago, Illinois, at 8 a.m. on 21 July 1899, when Grace Hemingway gave birth to her second child. She called him Ernest after her father whom she adored and thought the greatest man who ever lived, and named him Miller after her father's brother. His father had no say in the matter, which was usual in his relationship with his wife. Grace was a handsome woman, tall for her era at 5' 9" when women averaged 5' 4". A fine figure of a woman, she would today be termed 'busty'. Notwithstanding this, she was considered a tomboy. Grace had trained as an opera singer but failed in her first concert at Madison Square Garden and so her career never materialised. She was also handicapped by poor eyesight, being especially sensitive to bright lights.

In 1896 she married Clarence Edmond ('Ed') Hemingway, a medical doctor, specialising in obstetrics. Grace had delusions of grandeur and insisted on having a large house built at Oak Park and being attended by several servants. She also insisted on having a summer home built in North Michigan, with a separate cottage there for her sole use. After each summer holiday she would holiday for four weeks on Nantucket Island without Ed and taking only one of the children. She was truly a big spender. In fairness, we should note that she was the main breadwinner, giving singing lessons from home, charging at $8 per hour, a very high income indeed in the early 1900s.

At the time of Ernest's birth, Grace already had a daughter, Marcelline, born January 1898. Grace had wanted another girl; in fact her fantasy was to have twin daughters. She carried this over into real life, treating the two children in every way as twin sisters. Ernest was dressed in girls' clothes and referred to as Marcelline's twin sister. There are photos of him wearing a pink gingham gown and another labelled by Grace as 'summer girl 1901', in which he is wearing a picture hat and an ankle-length gown. He was given girls' dolls to play with. Grace insisted on him sleeping in bed with her and called him 'my Dutch dolly'.

Grace only ceased this charade just before his third birthday. At this time, his father had taken him on fishing trips and Ernest learned from him how to load and shoot a gun. On hearing this, Grace declared he was 'a real boy' and 'a proper little man'. But from now on she would be a strict disciplinarian with him, often punishing him with beatings with a hairbrush.

There is little doubt that Ernest suffered childhood anxieties over gender and that his night sweats, insomnia and nightmares in adult life are a throwback to his early childhood. Although Hemingway always maintained they were the result of bad war experiences, his short story 'Now I Lay Me' provides evidence of his early worries through the childhood memories within the main framework of a war story set in northern Italy.

Hemingway made it quite clear on numerous occasions throughout his adult life that he hated his mother. He constantly referred to her as 'that bitch'. He never wanted to talk about her or his childhood at Oak Park, but he was frequently to say that the best time the family ever had at Oak Park was when she was laid up with typhoid fever and they were free from her reign of terror. In 'Soldier's Home', he characterises her as Mrs Krebs, 'a monster'.

The feeling was mutual. Grace described Hemingway's writing as 'bastardising a noble art', and over his affairs with women she told him he was a monster for taking advantage of the feelings of gullible young girls.

In my view, his mother's character and actions were a primary factor in the emotions that Hemingway publicly displayed as a man. She certainly gave him a hatred of anything effeminate. When his brother, Leicester, was born in 1915, 16 years after himself, he expressed his astonishment and disgust that, although in an unhappy marriage, his mother had produced five children, the latest when in her mid-forties. It may have been this that made him constantly affirm that all women carried their brains between their thighs. Or he may simply have been blustering: no one doubts Hemingway's intelligence, but the sexual scrapes he got himself into might well qualify him as an example of the well-known maxim that men carry their brains in their balls.

Hemingway's father was a well-built man, 6 feet in height and barrel-chested. But he was a nervous man and weak in his dealings with his wife, who was aggressive and self-righteous. Thus he came to be utterly dominated by her. He was excellent at hunting, fishing and shooting. In this he was aided by exceptional eyesight, being able to pick out figures and buildings in concise detail at long distance. Clearly Ernest inherited his love of hunting, fishing and field sports from his father, but he did not inherit his father's good eyesight. All his life Hemingway had a defective left eye, which he blamed upon his mother. His father could be charming and often took Ernest on long walks and had lengthy and stimulating conversations with him. But Ed was a manic depressive, who in 1912 and 1922 had mental breakdowns, which resulted in him having to go away for 'rest cures'. Thus he was subject to sharp mood swings. He was also a strict disciplinarian. He could be engaging in some happy pursuit with Ernest when, suddenly perceiving something he believed wrong in his son's attitude, he would beat him soundly, often with a leather razor strop. Ed was unambitious and Grace was endlessly disappointed with him. A handsome man throughout his thirties and forties, Ed Hemingway deteriorated dramatically in his fifties. This was caused by physical problems with angina and diabetes and financial worries due to the collapse of his investments in Florida properties. There is little doubt that Grace's constant nagging had left him demoralised; Ernest certainly thought so, for he often accused her of hounding his father to death. On 5 December 1928, Ed Hemingway contracted a severe pain in his left foot. He suspected gangrene, which could lead to amputation. Depressed, he went to his bedroom and there he took up a revolver and shot himself dead.

Ernest hero-worshipped his father in the early days, as young children often will. Later this turned to disgust at his father weakly submitting to domination by his mother. Overall he had a good relationship with his father and was especially grateful for his father's loyalty towards him.

It is my opinion that Hemingway's relationships with his siblings had little impact on his future personality. There may be one exception to that view. He was dominated by his sister Marcelline, who was older, bigger and more advanced in learning than Ernest.

I think we can already see how Hemingway's family background and relationships shaped much of his later attitudes and actions. The suburb of Oak Park, where he spent his first 18 years, was also to influence his adult life. It was a deeply religious society and both his parents were strict Congregationalists. Standards of behaviour were high. Sales of alcohol were banned. In Oak Park there were no alcoholics, punch-drunk boxers, thieves, contract killers or matadors – the types whom he was later to seek out for the thrills their raw existence gave him. Standards were high too at Oak Park High, a school of some 1,000 pupils, and the regime was strict. Here Ernest conformed and worked hard. He did well academically, with grades averaging 90 out of 100. A strong swimmer, he captained the school water polo team. He was an all round sportsman of modest standards. Often he would spar at boxing with his peers; being taller and heavier, he would usually get the better of them. Sometimes he would beat them up quite badly. Now for the first time we see signs of the bullying and cruelty for which he was well known in his adult life. He contributed to the school newspaper and wrote short stories for its literary magazine. His manner was serious and he was invited to give a major speech on graduation day and invited to speak at the First Congregational Church.

During his schooldays, through age 15 to 17, he had a few dates with girls, but little success as he was bashful and at dances his size 13 feet made him somewhat clumsy. At most dances he accompanied his sister Marcelline at this mother's insistence. 1914 was a defining year for him. In that one year, he shot up from 5' 4" in height to 5' 10". It was at this time, when he was 16, that he had his first experience of sexual intimacy. Prudy Boulton was an Indian girl, just 13 years of age. Hemingway tells the story, under the guise of Nick Adams, in 'Fathers and Sons'. His relationship with Prudy may have succeeded because he did not feel threatened by her. She was younger, lower class and from a conquered race. By coincidence she later committed suicide.

Ernest graduated in June 1917. His parents were bitterly disappointed when he told them he had no intention of going to college. He was intensely interested in the First World War, which the USA had entered in the spring of that year. He wished to be drafted into the armed forces. As early as 1916 he had told his sister Marcelline, 'I can't let a show like this go on without getting into it.' I think the use of the word 'show' gives us some idea of how he perceived the action. He is too young to volunteer for drafting at that time, so he agrees to take a job as a journalist, which his Uncle Tyler is able to arrange with the *Kansas City Star*. He intends only to work for a few months, until he is old enough to apply for drafting. In Kansas City he experiences his first tastes of hard drinking and striptease joints. There were many whores working the town at that time and Ernest was later to boast that he had plenty of experience of them. In January 1918 he tries to enlist in the army, but is rejected due to his defective left eye. This is somewhat ironic in that his ability to see things in a way no one else could would subsequently make him famous. There now occurs a twist of fate, which is to play a significant role in shaping the future life of Ernest Miller Hemingway.

A colleague on the *Kansas City Star*, Ted Brumback, has a glass eye. Nevertheless, he tells Ernest that he is applying to the American Red Cross for overseas duty as an ambulance driver serving the American forces. Ernest sees this as the way forward and also applies. He is successful but the doctor who examined him recommended that he start wearing glasses. That he paid no heed to this advice is the first unassailable evidence we have of Hemingway's vanity. This vanity was to display itself frequently throughout his life and, as to glasses, he refused to wear them even towards the end of his life when his eyesight was failing badly.

He asked to be based in France, but was seconded to Italy. Later he was to lie in his humorous, bragging way by saying he had asked for Italy because he thought there was less chance of being killed there. More irony as Hemingway is posted to the front line of war at Fossalta.

On 8 July 1918, on his nineteenth birthday, he finds himself bicycling to the Italian (Allied) front-line troops to deliver cigarettes and chocolate. An enemy mortar shell bursts, driving shrapnel into his legs and knocking him to the ground, where he receives a severe blow to the head. It also badly wounds soldiers close to him. Despite his own injuries, Hemingway, with courage and determination, helps seriously wounded Italian soldiers back to the first aid post. He does not seek aid for himself until they are receiving attention. For this he receives the Italian Cross of War and the Italian Silver Medal for Valour. Hemingway was later to frequently tell one of his many infamous lies, stating that he had been riddled with machine-gun bullets, but had carried a wounded soldier back to the post on his back. The truth may be verified by inspecting the citation given by the Italian Government when the medals were awarded to Hemingway and this reports the facts exactly as I have described them. Hemingway uses this experience in the short story 'A Way You'll Never Be' and in his novel *A Farewell to Arms*.

He was hospitalised in Milan between July and November 1918. He did have several minor operations to remove shrapnel from his legs. Here he was attended by several nurses and as a big, handsome, wounded 'soldier' he probably could have had his pick. In fact it took him just two weeks to fall in love with one, Agnes Kurowsky. He believed his love was returned. Certainly between August 1918 and March 1919 she wrote about 60 letters to him and some of them seemed to confirm that there had been sexual intercourse between them, notwithstanding his wounded legs. Obviously it would have to have happened with Agnes on top. Possibly this is where Ernest's predilection for this type of sex originated. Ernest

37

wrote an equal number of letters to Agnes. It is not to be doubted that he was in love with Agnes, but his subsequent history shows that he fell in love, or his version of it, quite easily, and that one of his favourite pastimes was letter writing.

Agnes was posted to Florence and Ernest was discharged from hospital in November 1918. He remained in Italy to recuperate until January 1919, limping around from battlefield to battlefield, soaking up the atmosphere. He wrote many letters to Agnes during this time but responses slowed up. Sailing home to America, he confidently expected her to follow him. It was not to be, but it did provide him with a valuable lesson on the subject of naïvety. In March 1919, Agnes ended the affair, sending him a classic 'Dear John' letter. For most of his remaining life he would believe that she was the only woman he had ever really loved; but there was bitterness too as he later reveals in a sketch in *In Our Time*. In the end he blotted out her memory by using booze and other women.

Back home at Oak Park, he was accorded a hero's welcome. He milked it for all it was worth, giving speeches, embellishing his role and continuing to wear a bloodstained officer's uniform.

But he had now experienced death and love and these were the twin themes that would flow through his writing. He had matured rapidly. Yet what was he to do next? One couldn't live off one's war stories; anyway, people got bored with them. He sat in his room, chain-smoking, and began to write short stories, essays, even poems, which he sent to magazines. All he got back was a series of rejection slips. By 1921 he was doing his own share of rejection, turning his back on his sister Marcelline, who was ill at that time, and scarcely communicating with her for the rest of his life.

Generally in 1920 he was loafing around drinking, fishing and giving boxing lessons to his local pals. This created tension with his mother, who finally exploded, ordering him off their summer residence and writing him a long letter accusing him of corrupting his sisters, Ursula and Madelaine, and telling him he was overdrawn on her love for him. This marked the end of their relationship. Ernest did not care, as far as he was concerned his mother had been emotionally bankrupt all her life and so was hardly in a position to comment. He moved out to Boyne City, found cheap digs and took odd jobs to survive.

At this time he was dating Katy Smith, being much attracted to her maturity; she was 29 to his 21. When Katy suggested going to Chicago together, it seemed an ideal answer; he would look for work as a journalist. She would stay at the Arts Club and he would stay with her brother in East Chicago. No sooner had they arrived, than Katy invited her friend Elizabeth (Hadley) Richardson, whose mother had just died, to pay a comforting visit. Ernest fell in love with her the moment he met her.

It was not for her looks, for she was no great beauty. She was witty, intelligent and was a good listener, the latter being a great asset around Hemingway. He assessed her as cultured and refined. She was also the first woman he had met who regularly drank alcohol, much frowned upon at that time. As he was already well down that path, it suited him very well. They had an affinity in that their parents had similar characteristics. Possibly there was a brother/sister element, possibly a mother figure relationship, for Elizabeth was approaching 30 when they first met. Elizabeth found Ernest exciting and good-looking. They were both on the rebound, Ernest from rejection by Agnes, Elizabeth from the trauma of her mother's death.

Elizabeth's visit lasted three weeks and they saw each other every day. She returned to St Louis but they continued the courtship by letter, writing to each other daily for nine months. During that period, they met on only seven occasions. We should keep in mind that this was an era long before airline travel or even long distance telephone calls were commonplace. Whilst this long-distance courtship was going on, Hemingway continued to date Katy Smith and later was to state that they were lovers.

On 3 September 1923, Ernest Miller Hemingway and Elizabeth Hadley Richardson were married at Horton Bay Church in Michigan on a crystal clear day, with the sun sparkling off the waters of the bay. Both families attended.

In an effort at reconciliation, Grace offered them the Hemingway summer house for the honeymoon. Hadley later described it as a flop. Unfortunately, they both had upset stomachs and the weather was poor; Ernest exacerbated matters by showing off his ex-girlfriends, which Hadley thought vain and childish.

Hemingway had got a job as editor and journalist at the *Cooperative Commonwealth*, a small Chicago magazine. The income was meagre, but could suffice since Katy Smith's brother, YK, had offered them a rent-free apartment. The accommodation fell through, due to

Hemingway bad-mouthing YK's wife. Acting in desperation, Hemingway rented a fifth-floor flat in a rundown apartment block with no lift in North Dearborn St, East Chicago. It was awful accommodation, but Hadley played the dutiful wife and made it as comfortable as possible. Ernest spent very little time in it, going daily for long walks alone. At first they lived on Hadley's income from a trust fund, plus some capital she had inherited. Ernest saved his small salary against the day when they could depart to Europe, for he felt, rightly, that only there could he develop as a writer with the decent income that would lead to.

He had met the writer Sherwood Anderson at a YK party and, in November 1921, Anderson invited the Hemingways to dinner at his house. Hearing of Ernest's wish to go to Europe to write, Sherwood strongly advised Paris, of which he had much experience. It was cheap to live there, he said, and he would provide Ernest with letters of introduction to James Joyce, Gertrude Stein and Ezra Pound. Hemingway was convinced. He now contacted John Bone of the *Toronto Star* for whom he had written a few articles. Would *The Star* hire Hemingway as their European correspondent? Bone agreed; Hemingway would report on the war between Greece and Turkey for *The Star*. Perhaps Hemingway's audacity was the key factor. Thereafter everything fell into place very quickly. They left New York for Paris on the French liner *The Leopoldina* on 13 December 1921 and landed at Le Havre on 21 December. The letters of introduction from Anderson were in Hemingway's pocket. Within two years Hemingway would repay Anderson's kindness by disparaging him to Edmund Wilson of the *New York Tribune*, telling him: 'Anderson's work has gone to hell'; this in response to the mildest questions from Wilson as to whether Hemingway's 'My Old Man' plagiarised Anderson's *I Want To Know Why*, which it probably does. Shortly afterwards, Ernest produced a comic book seeking to rubbish Anderson's latest novel, *Dark Laughter*. Such was Hemingway's nature.

Their income made them fairly well off compared to most people in Paris at that time, but Hemingway wanted very cheap accommodation in Paris. He knew he would need most of the money they had to indulge what he thought of as necessities: drinking, gambling, fishing and skiing holidays in Austria.

He found an ugly, two-roomed loft apartment at 74 rue du Cardinal Lemoine in the working-class neighbourhood of Montagne

Ste-Geneviève. There was a tiny kitchen and a closet with a basin, pitcher and slop bucket, the latter to be emptied on to the landing and later carried down to the street.

In Paris, Hemingway lived an interesting and profligate life. He soon gave up the job with the *Toronto Star* to concentrate on writing short stories and a novel. By day he sat in the Left Bank cafes, drinking wine, staring at the blank sheets of paper and sometimes writing, and by night he often gambled at poker. He gambled too at the horse race tracks. He hired himself out to professional boxers for sparring at 10 francs per round.

On the more serious side, he spent time with Gertrude Stein, who helped his literary development a great deal, and with the poet Ezra Pound, who made many introductions for him and was his regular drinking partner. Hemingway made clear his gratitude to Pound in the Paris magazine *This Quarter* in May 1925. Pound also sparred with him, but since Ezra was neither a good boxer, nor as big as him, Hemingway was able to bully him. Ezra was to remain a long-term friend until about 1943, by which time Pound had lost his sanity and began to make pro-Fascist broadcasts on radio. James Joyce proved a great source of introductions for the young Hemingway and they too remained long-term friends.

This first year in Paris was difficult for Hadley, who was often left alone in the attic room. Friction and stress developed between them. This was increased when Hadley was travelling from Paris to meet him in Lausanne for a skiing holiday. She was bringing to him the drafts of all his writings, including the carbons, so that he could work on them. She had packed them into one case. During the course of the journey, she left the train compartment to buy a bottle of water. When she returned, the case was gone, never to be seen again. I feel sure that the thief, finding that he had stolen only a lot of old papers, threw them away. How rich he would have been if only he had held on to them. Hemingway said he was almost wiped out before he began. Only three stories remained, these being out to editors for consideration at the time. Further friction was to develop in February 1923, when Hadley told Ernest she was pregnant. Hemingway felt he was too young to have a child, and Ezra Pound exacerbated things by telling him at length that it would completely change his whole lifestyle, and not for the better.

Better news followed, in Ernest's view. Editor Robert McAlmon accepted his first book, *Three Stories and Ten Poems*. The three stories were those that had been out to editors at the time Hadley lost his work. They were 'Up In Michigan', which was sexually explicit and daring for its time, 'My Old Man' (surely taken from Anderson) and 'Out of Season', another Hemingway one-dimensional anecdote about a drunken Italian peasant trying to earn money by taking a gentleman to fish in a prohibited area. The poems were inconsequential. Three hundred copies were to be produced in August that year.

Ernest now considered the pragmatic problem of how to financially support a child. It would be better if he moved to Toronto and took up work again with *The Star*. Fortunately Hadley agreed, she felt she would receive better pre- and post-natal care in Canada. Just before they left, Ernest received news that Three Mountains Press would produce his book *in our time* (the pretentious absence of capitals was Ernest's idea). The stories were simply a group of concise descriptions of scenes of violence. He would receive no payment. But to Ernest they represented his second book in print.

They set sail for Canada in the spring of 1923. Hemingway's baggage was unusually heavy. He was smuggling in 100 copies of *Ulysses*, the book of his friend James Joyce, which the courts had banned as obscene.

At *The Star* in Canada, Hemingway found he had a new boss, Harry Hindmarsh. He was part owner of the paper, being the owner's son-in-law. He took an instant dislike to Ernest, assessing him to be a prima donna. Hindmarsh was probably right, and really what had Hemingway achieved at that point to justify his attitude? At all events, Ernest was given a number of rubbish assignments and soon got fed up. He was also bored with the people he was meeting in Toronto, who he deemed 'of no account'.

Hemingway's first child, a boy, was born on 8 October 1923. The Hemingways decided they were disenchanted with Canada and would return to Paris. The boy would be christened there; in the meantime he would be called 'Bumby'. It was to remain his nickname for his lifetime. Just before they left Toronto, Hemingway took delivery of 170 copies of *in our time*. More heavy baggage.

The Hemingways departed for Paris in mid-January 1924. Initially they used Ezra Pound's flat, whilst he was on holiday. They soon found a flat nearby at 113 rue Notre-Dame-des-Champs. The flat was not much better than their old one, but it was bigger and in a better neighbourhood. Hemingway immediately took up with all his old friends: Stein, Sylvia Beach, Pound, Joyce, Ford Maddox Ford and later a new friend who was to prove the pivotal person in establishing Hemingway's literary career, F. Scott Fitzgerald.

On 10 March 1924, 'Bumby' was christened John Hadley Nicanor in St Luke's Chapel in the rue de la Grande Chamiere. Even that occasion caused a quarrel between Ernest and Hadley. Ernest wanted Gertrude Stein as godmother. Hadley objected. She hated Stein's live-in lesbian friend, Alice B. Toklas, and anyway, how could a Jew undertake to ensure the child was brought up in the Christian faith? Hemingway had his way, as usual.

Ford gave Ernest some small work as a sub-editor on the *Transatlantic Review* and he spent his remaining time sweating over his stories, although allowing plenty of time for essential matters: drinking, gambling, fighting and having affairs behind his wife's back. They lived mainly on Hadley's income.

In December, the Hemingways sublet their Paris apartment and, at the invitation of a friend, Bertram Harman (the American artist), they spent most of the winter at the Hotel Taube in Schruns, Austria. They were to be joined by another friend, novelist Harold Loeb, but at the last minute Loeb had to go to New York to see his publisher. How fortunate for Ernest. Whilst there, Loeb spoke to various publishers and to Sherwood Anderson on Hemingway's behalf. Whilst at Schruns, Ernest received his first letter of acceptance from Anderson's publisher, Boni & Liveright. They would publish *In Our Time*. The advance would be £200. The contract would include options on his next two novels. The book was merely a collation of his previous two books, but a window to a wider reading audience through a well-established publisher. The book is also significant for introducing the reader to Nick Adams, who is Hemingway's double in many books to come.

Ernest is still only 25, but already his larger-than-life, hail-fellow-well-met character, together with his sense of humour and physical size and strength, have made him many friends who have now helped him to the starting line of his literary career. The next to enter is F. Scott Fitzgerald. When they first met in April 1925, Fitzgerald was a far more established author than Hemingway, with three novels to his credit with major publisher Scribners. He was 29 and far better known in Paris than Ernest.

Fitzgerald had wandered into the Crazy Bar in Montparnasse.

At the bar he saw Hemingway standing in company with Lady 'Duff' Twysden and her cousin, and lover, Pat Guthrie. Fitzgerald was only interested in the tall, muscular, good-looking guy Hemingway, who was talking in such an amusing way. Hemingway was only interested in 'Duff' (he was soon to start an intimate affair with her). But when Fitzgerald introduced himself, Hemingway, knowing his literary reputation and connections, turned on the charm. Fitzgerald ordered several bottles of champagne and, not being in Hemingway's class as a drinker, Fitzgerald soon got drunk and Hemingway had to put him in a taxi and send him home. It was to be a pattern in their relationship. Fitzgerald was always out to get drunk and Hemingway was always out to get laid.

From this first meeting onwards, Fitzgerald was in awe of Hemingway and always considered Ernest superior to himself as a writer and a man. This provides a good indicator of Hemingway's magnetism for, considering Fitzgerald's age and achievements at this time, it ought to have been the other way around. Fitzgerald set out to court Hemingway's company and they fell into a wild round of debauchery together. Anxious to curry favour with Ernest, Fitzgerald soon contacted his own editor, Max Perkins at Scribners, telling him Hemingway was a coming major author and that before long everyone would be talking about him. Scribners had previously been interested in *In Our Time*, and Perkins took note of Fitzgerald's endorsement.

At that time, critics were comparing Hemingway's style to Anderson and talking of him as Anderson's protégé. This upset Hemingway's ego and he decided to lash out at Anderson, casually dismissing all the help Anderson had given him when he first set sail from America.

Hemingway had been working on his first full-length novel, *The Sun Also Rises*, but now he diverted for a few days to write a short satire, *The Torrents of Spring* as a vehicle to deride Anderson's latest novel, *Dark Laughter*. Max Perkins, under prompting from Fitzgerald, called for a synopsis of *The Sun Also Rises*, and he liked it. The problem for Ernest was that he was under option contract to Boni & Liveright. Their main author was Anderson. Outraged, they rejected *The Torrents of Spring*, thereby forfeiting their option on the third book. Contract broken, victory to Hemingway. Max Perkins was not interested in *The Torrents of Spring*, but Hemingway made it clear he had to publish it if he wanted *The*

Sun Also Rises. Perkins agreed; another victory to Hemingway, by knockout. *The Torrents of Spring* was published in autumn 1925 to very little acclaim. *The Sun Also Rises* was to receive a very different reception.

In the summer of 1925, Hemingway and a group of friends and acquaintances decided to go to Pamplona, Spain, to see the fiesta and the bull fights and to take part in the bull run. Amongst the group were Harold Loeb, Duff Twysden and Pat Guthrie, Donald Ogden Stewart, Ford Maddox Ford, Bill Smith (his current drinking buddy) and F. Scott Fitzgerald. It was from this visit that *The Sun Also Rises* was created. It took Ernest about seven weeks to write. Everyone in the party was included in the story.

It is Paris in the twenties. They are portrayed variously as matadors, whores, drunks, bartenders and low lifes. Each spews out their grievances with the theme being eat, drink and be miserable for tomorrow we die. A significant omission in the characterisations is lesbians. Ernest had several close friends in Paris at that time who were extrovert lesbians, but he chooses not to include them. It was ahead of its time in painting the main characters as anti-heroes long before this became fashionable in novels. The prose is sparse but limpid. Much is left unsaid, in keeping with the style Hemingway is developing. It is Hemingway's attempt to write a popular novel; it is successful, selling 8,000 copies in the first three months and he has now reached a wide audience. Reviews are mixed, but overall very good. Conrad Aitken (*New York Herald Tribune*) said it achieved 'a quite extraordinary effect of honesty and reality'; the *London Evening News* called it 'a first novel by a genius'; *The Spectator* said 'remarkable, powerful, startling, disquieting'; Allen Tate, writing for *The Nation* magazine, felt that Hemingway was basically a short story writer and that he was trying in a forced way to write a novel. Tate said that Hemingway had failed in his use of human behaviour to create dramatic situations. According to Tate, the book reveals that Hemingway is not the emotional tough guy that he pretends to be. Ernest's friend, and fellow writer, John Dos Passos wrote, 'Instead of being the epic of the sun also rising on the lost generation, this novel strikes you as a cock and bull story about a lot of summer tourists getting drunk and making fools of themselves at a picturesque Spanish folk festival.' Dos Passos seems to have overlooked the fact that this is exactly what did happen at that summer 1925 vacation and that almost all Hemingway's writing was based on his observation of people.

The Sun Also Rises, published in October 1926, established Hemingway as an author who could name his terms for future works. It also established him as Scribners' star writer, ahead of F. Scott Fitzgerald. It also swells his ego to a huge level and it is now that he becomes unbearably arrogant.

Throughout 1925, Hemingway's marriage had been breaking down. Being left on her own a great deal depressed Hadley. She was also unhappily aware of his infidelity and his promiscuity. His affair with Duff Twysden in 1925 was common knowledge. Following a trip in April 1926 to the Loire Valley with Hadley and the Pfeiffer sisters, Jinny and Pauline, Ernest admitted, under pressure from Hadley, that he was having a love affair with Pauline Pfeiffer. Hadley also knew that Dorothy Parker (the American author) was crazy about Ernest and she suspected there had been something physical between them. She was also uncertain about his sexual preferences. Hemingway had been having a very close relationship with Scott Fitzgerald. Fitzgerald had been roundly denounced as homosexual by his wife and by Robert McAlmon. Zelda Fitzgerald had also accused Hemingway of having a homosexual relationship with her husband.

In September of 1926, Ernest walked out on Hadley to live with Pauline Pfeiffer. Hemingway had known Pauline only since March of that year, having first met her at Harold Loeb's apartment. Pauline was four years older than Ernest, small, ultra slim and chic. From that first meeting, she set out to capture Ernest for herself. Rather strange, as she was certainly bisexual; perhaps she felt some vibrations of kindred sexuality from Ernest.

Now for the first time Hemingway's mind is in turmoil. We must remind ourselves that this was not an era when it was acceptable for a married man to walk out on his wife and child to live with another woman. His parents were shocked and highly critical of his actions. Pauline also creates anxiety for him by making it clear that because she was a Catholic, she could only live 'in sin' with him for a short while until he got a divorce and married her. Hemingway was also suffering from writer's block. He had been trying to write another novel to follow up *The Sun Also Rises*, but had abandoned one, *Jimmy Breen*, after creating over 300 pages of manuscript. He is also suffering depression, which is exacerbated by his heavy drinking sessions. For the first time, his thoughts turn to suicide and in October 1926, he tells Pauline that if matters are not resolved by Christmas, then he will shoot himself.

By November, Hadley realises Ernest will not come back to her and she agrees to a divorce. On 27 January 1927, in Paris, the divorce is granted. Ernest and Pauline plan the wedding for May, but Pauline insists it must be a Catholic ceremony.

In March, Hemingway visits his old wartime friend Giuseppe Bianchi, now a priest, in Rapallo, Italy. He advises Ernest that to have a Catholic wedding, he will have to convert and will have to apply to the Vatican for an annulment of his first marriage on the grounds that it was not Catholic. All of this was undertaken and completed within six weeks, which I believe was the fastest time recorded that century. The annulment of his first marriage labelled Hemingway's son 'Bumby' a bastard in the eye of the Catholic Church. Pauline was delighted that Ernest had become a Catholic. She said, 'Confession will be good for him.' Hemingway was later to give Hotchner a different reason for his conversion. After divorcing Hadley, he found it difficult to have sex with Pauline. He took advice from doctors, and even undertook electrical shock treatment. Nothing worked. Finally Pauline suggested prayer. Ernest went to the local Catholic church and prayed; he returned home and they 'made love like we invented it. That's when I became a Catholic'. This, of course, was just another self-proclaimed Hemingway myth.

On 10 May 1927, Ernest Hemingway and Pauline Pfeiffer were married in Paris. By October Pauline was pregnant.

Meanwhile Ernest had temporarily abandoned the idea of a new novel and had collected together 14 short stories to be presented as a book with the inspirational title of *Men Without Women*. The work is distinguished by three of the stories. 'The Killers' concerns a heavyweight boxer who has double-crossed the Mafia and awaits, with resignation, the arrival of their hit men; it is later successfully made into a film. 'In Another Country' was Hemingway's favourite; it is the story of a major, wounded in war, who marries only to quickly lose his wife to pneumonia. This embitters him such that he advises everyone around him never to marry. The final story, 'Now I Lay Me', contains details of his childhood, with a destructive portrait of his mother, which shamed her and for which it seems she never forgave him.

Men Without Women is published by Scribners in New York in October 1927. Critics disagree about its quality. There were those, led by Percy Hutchison in the *New York Times Book Review*, who called the stories nothing more than high-class reporting by a journalist posing as a fiction writer. Some critics thought his talent had contracted rather than expanded with this book. Virginia Woolf, writing for the *New York Herald Tribune* (within days of publication) felt his vision of the relationship between men and women was not modern and his stories 'dry and sterile'. *The Nation* said 'painfully good ... no one can deny their brilliance'. *Town & Country* magazine (William Curtis) told readers, 'It is probably the best volume of short stories published since the days of Rudyard Kipling.' His constant admirer Dorothy Parker said, 'I do not know where a greater collection of short stories can be found. He discards details with ... lavishness.' For myself, this latter comment is one of my complaints about Hemingway's works. In my view, many of his stories lack detail in their ending.

The reviews may have been mixed, but readers were enthusiastic. By Christmas 13,000 copies had been sold, and rights had been sold to Jonathan Cape Limited, who published it in the UK early in 1928.

Ernest and Pauline honeymooned in the Rhone Valley. The trip lasted three weeks but, as with his honeymoon with Hadley, it was spoilt. Whilst swimming, Ernest cut his left foot, it became poisoned, swelled badly and he contracted a fever. They were forced to return to Paris, where he spent the next two weeks bedridden. This was to be part of a pattern with Ernest, who was accident prone all his life. He had barely recovered from this latest episode when 'Bumby' stuck a finger in Ernest's right eye, causing severe pain and watering to both eyes, and for several days Hemingway could barely see. Shortly afterwards, in March 1928, he was again injured by accident, although this time self-inflicted. Returning home to their Paris flat, drunk in the early hours of the morning, he visited the toilet, but instead of pulling the chain to the WC, he yanked vigorously on the cord to the skylight. The heavy glass, complete with frame, crashed upon his head, resulting in a gash requiring a dozen stitches and scarring him for life. Several more serious accidents due to drunkenness were to occur later in his life.

Hemingway now began to think of going back to America. Pauline's income from her parents and her trust fund were even more than Hadley's had been. Ernest's income was steadily rising. They could afford to have a good lifestyle in America and visit Europe at any time. Pauline wanted to have the baby in the USA. There was little to keep him in Paris permanently. Hadley had found another man. Hemingway had alienated most of his old friends: Gertrude Stein, Harold Loeb, Ezra Pound, Duff Twysden, even Fitzgerald, by using them as unattractive characters in his stories. In March 1928 they left for Key West, Florida.

By June they had moved on to Kansas City, Pauline having elected to have the baby there. Patrick Hemingway was born on 28 June 1928. When he was three months old, the Hemingways decided he was old enough to be left in the care of others from time to time and, in the following two months, they travelled widely around the USA. By December they had decided to return to Key West on a long-term basis. On 6 December, whilst travelling from New York to Florida, Ernest receives news that his father has that day committed suicide.

Clarence 'Ed' Hemingway had been under financial stress and in ill-health for some time. His income from his medical practice had been dwindling and, in a desperate attempt to improve his financial position, he had invested his life savings in Florida properties. Unfortunately the Florida property market collapsed. He had diabetes, which had grown worse; in December a wound in his foot turned septic, he feared gangrene and believed his foot would be amputated. This was the final blow to his morale. He took up a Smith & Wesson revolver and blew his brains out. Hemingway was numbed by his father's death. He told Max Perkins (Scribners), 'What makes me feel worse is that my father was the one I cared about.'

Ernest's only recourse was to throw himself into trying again to write a follow-up novel to *The Sun Also Rises*. He had resurrected *Jimmy Breen* and now used parts of it to create a story woven around war experiences in 1918 Italy. The title was to be *A Farewell to Arms*. He had found the title in the *Oxford Book of English Verse*, a poem written in 1580 by George Peele. He found it very difficult to get this novel together, rewriting parts again and again. Nearing completion, but still frustrated with the work, he called Max Perkins to his side to go over the final drafts. They spent about two weeks together and, despite the fact that they went deep-sea fishing every day, or maybe because of it, Ernest completed the novel. Before publication, Perkins had to delete several passages because they contained foul language unacceptable in those days. Although a war story, it is also a love story. Perhaps Perkins destroyed some of its earthiness, for the dialogue between the passionate lovers, Frederick and Catherine, is distinctly formal. *A Farewell to Arms* is Hemingway's personal and unflinching view of the world and life: 'The world breaks everyone and afterwards many are strong at the broken places. But those that will not break it kills. It kills the very good and the very gentle and the very brave impartially. If you are none of these it will kill you too but there will be no special hurry.'

The book was published late September 1929 to highly favourable reviews. In the USA T.S. Matthews, Henry Canby, Dorothy Parker and others gave Hemingway rave reviews. In England, *The Times Literary Supplement* said it was a novel of great power. Virginia Woolf would not review it, but her lover, Mrs Vita Sackville-West did, calling it 'a most beautiful, humane and moving book'. Other tributes came from Arnold Bennett and J.B. Priestley. I have not been able to find a poor review of the book. Readers received it with open arms; it sold 50,000 copies in the first two months and, by January 1930, sales reached 75,000. Before the year was out, Hollywood would come calling; they realised the violent action and tender love scenes with spare, taut dialogue could be good film material.

The movie moguls found Hemingway difficult to deal with. This may be seem strange in an era when writers were desperate to have their novels filmed. It may have been a deliberate ploy on Hemingway's part or because of his increasingly arrogant nature. It could simply have been that Ernest was too depressed to bother with film investors. He had been inactive for almost all of 1931 with a broken arm and damaged nerves in his right hand, which was a handicap to writing. This was the result of a car crash whilst returning from a hunting trip in Wyoming. It was particularly annoying to be slowed down in his writing at this time because in 1930 he had started writing his definitive work on bullfighting, *Death in the Afternoon.*

The Hemingways had planned to spend the whole summer in Spain, where Ernest would finish *Death in the Afternoon.* They did go to Madrid and, although Ernest spent more time watching the bullfights and drinking than writing, nevertheless he did complete the book. They may well have stayed on in Spain, except Pauline was again pregnant, and again wished to have the baby in Kansas City. Their second son, Gregory, was born there in November 1931.

In any event, it was the end of 1931 before the rights to *A Farewell to Arms* were sold and the film went into production. It seems Hemingway's reluctance was insightful. The film, starring Gary Cooper and Helen Hayes, was a flop. Hemingway was furious and blamed incompetent producers. He refused to attend the world premiere.

The Hemingways were once more back at Key West, now in a house purchased for them by Pauline's Uncle Augustus. But Ernest still found time to spend two of the early months of summer in Havana, Cuba, accompanied by one of his hangers-on, Joe Russell, a bar owner. In Havana, Ernest spent his mornings deep-sea fishing or sparring with the local boxers. Afternoons were for writing. Evenings were for drinking, gambling and sex with dancehall hostesses. He also found time for an affair with Jane Mason, wife of Grant Mason, the head of Pan American Airways in Cuba. Pauline, at home in Key West, was left with the baby. However, Ernest had to return for the publication of *Death in the Afternoon*. Max Perkins at Scribners thought it was a great book and it was rushed into publication in late autumn 1932, with more than 60 illustrations.

It may have been Hemingway's favourite subject, but it certainly did not interest the literary critics; reviews were modest to poor. Robert Coates, a friend from his early Paris days, found it boring and deplored Hemingway's mockery of T.S. Eliot, Aldous Huxley, William Faulkner and others. H.L. Mencken was offended by the book's over use of 'ancient four-letter words' and its 'gross cheapness'. In *The New Republic*, Max Eastman called it 'Bull in the Afternoon' and 'sentimental poppycock' and said, 'It is of course a commonplace that Hemingway lacks the serene confidence that he is a full-sized man.' Hemingway took this as a slur against his potency and tried to counter-attack Eastman in the same vein. That was rather stupid, since Eastman was a handsome man, well-known for his success with women over a long period of time. Later, in Scribners' offices, Hemingway physically attacked Eastman, but it seems Ernest got the worst of that encounter too. As to Coates' review, Hemingway called it a 'condescentious [*sic*] piece of phony intellectuality'. But there is no doubt he felt hurt by the adverse reviews. His feelings are best summed up in the opening lines of his letter to Max Perkins in June 1933 on the subject: 'I am tempted never to publish another damned thing. The swine aren't worth writing for. I swear to Christ they're not.'

Hemingway becomes extremely restless. He spends the winter fishing in Cuban waters and boxing with the local blacks. He now adopts the nickname 'Papa', which he insists that all his friends call him; does he think he is the father of all knowledge? From June to August he splits his time between the bullfights in Spain and the cafes in Paris. His only writing is for *Esquire* magazine. Now he enters one of the most difficult periods of his life, mentally and physically.

His marriage with Pauline is breaking down. He did not want the second child and is no longer sexually attracted to Pauline. He causes further confusion in his mind trying to deny this to himself. *Winner Takes Nothing*, a collection of short stories, is published. It is not a success and Ernest is becoming increasingly concerned about his writing ability. He wants to go big game hunting in Africa for two or three months, but cannot afford it. Although money has been coming in from his books and journalism, he has been profligate. Never one to be denied what he wants, Ernest becomes irritable.

Pauline persuades Uncle Augustus to pay for a two-month safari for them and the couple set off for Nairobi in September. Here Hemingway goes on a slaughter rampage, racking up 30 kills, including three lions. The animals may, in some mystic way, have had their revenge. Ernest was struck down with severe dysentery, was immobilised in the jungle and had to be airlifted back to Nairobi. The only good thing to come out of this is that he lost about 40 pounds in weight, which was necessary as he was bloated at that time. Later he was to use this incident in his short story 'The Snows of Kilimanjaro'.

The Hemingways sailed back from East Africa to New York via Villefranche. They broke the journey at Villefranche for ten days, whilst Ernest tried, unsuccessfully, to woo back the old Parisien friends he had alienated with his parodies of them. From Villefranche to New York, across the Atlantic on the *Ile de France*. Here he meets Marlene Dietrich and spends much of the voyage with her, the two often dining alone. They remained friends for 25 years, often meeting and frequently having lengthy talks long distance by telephone. Hemingway admired both Dietrich's beauty and her sexual ambivalence. Perhaps they shared the latter. Whether they were sexually intimate is a matter of conjecture; certainly Dietrich was Hemingway's 'type'. She was also his entrée into becoming a companion, if not a friend, to many great Hollywood film stars of the era.

Back in New York, he asked for a $3,000 advance from *Esquire* magazine, which he promptly spent as a down payment on a twin engine, 40-foot power boat, which he named *Pilar*. The boat was delivered to Miami at the beginning of May and Ernest spent the next six weeks fishing off Key West. He did write, but no new novel would come and he concentrated on writing an autobiography with the title *Green Hills of Africa*. At the end of June, he left Pauline in Key West and sailed off to Cuba, where he spent the next three months. Despite having got away from Pauline, his mind was not at ease. He was frustrated by his lack of success at deep-sea fishing. Gertrude Stein had published the biography of Alice B. Toklas and had woven in insults about Ernest, which infuriated him (he conveniently forgot that he had abused Gertrude first, even though she had been the first to help him in Paris). He had taken up his affair again with Jane Mason; but just as he was taking satisfaction from that, she informed him she would be off to East Africa in October to spend the winter with her 'good friend' Colonel Richard Cooper. Hemingway really had the hump. To add to everything, although his *Green Hills of Africa* book was close to completion, he was worried about the quality of it.

Scribners were worried too. They serialised it from early 1935, hoping to build up interest for publication in the autumn. They failed. *Green Hills of Africa* was published in October 1935 and received little interest and no acclaim. The *New York Herald Tribune* (L. Garnett) dismissed it as 'just another safari journal'. Edmund Wilson, in *The New Republic*, said 'Almost all we learn about the animals is that Hemingway wants to kill them', and, 'Hemingway's prose style goes to pot'. Much later, Aubrey Dillon-Malone summed up general opinion in his book *The Grace and the Pressure* when he described *Green Hills of Africa* as presenting Hemingway as a self-indulgent pub bore.

The 1933 safari had failed to produce another good book for Ernest. No inspiration for a novel was forthcoming and clearly his efforts to describe his travels and game hunting were poor quality literature. But the adventure did provide him with two top quality short stories in 'The Snows of Kilimanjaro' and 'The Short Happy Life of Francis Macomber'. Later, by intriguing coincidence, both were made into films and both starred Gregory Peck.

1935 is another difficult year for Ernest, but one that he copes with in typical bravado style. Naturally, he is depressed with the reaction to *Green Hills of Africa* and this is deepened by his struggle to create a new novel. He starts *To Have and Have Not*, an adventure story of smuggling in the Cuban and Florida waters. But creativity does not flow and he has to grind the story out laboriously. His marriage to Pauline is going rapidly down the tubes and he uses the book to spend almost all his time in Cuba.

Here long days are spent fishing with Max Perkins and he also has several boxing matches with the local Bimini blacks, which he wins. He also has a six-round 'no decision' contest with former heavyweight contender Tom Heeney. ('No decision' contests were popular among prominent boxers throughout the 1930s. The fight would be for a fixed number of rounds and could only be won, or more importantly, lost, by knockout or if the referee stopped the fight. A points decision would not be given.) Later Hemingway boasts that had a decision been given on points, then he would have been an easy winner. George Brown, a former boxer, trainer and New York gym owner and life-long friend of Ernest, did not agree. He was sure Heeney had deliberately gone easy on Hemingway. Heeney had not been long retired and, in 1928, had fought a close battle with Gene Tunney for the world heavyweight championship. Hemingway would not have been in Heeney's class and it is probable that Heeney was given a 'consideration' to enable Hemingway to boost his own already inflated reputation. George Brown had a low opinion of Hemingway's boxing ability. He pointed out that the Bimini blacks had little knowledge of boxing and would have been easy meat for Ernest. Brown had sparred with Ernest on several occasions and said that Hemingway used all manner of foul tricks, even though Brown punished him severely every time he did so. There is some irony in Brown's statement. Brown was the trainer of world middleweight champion Harry Greb, universally acknowledged as the dirtiest boxer of all time. Probably Hemingway picked up most of his dirty tricks from Greb.

Hemingway finds time to go bear hunting in North America, which relieves his mental stress a little. The bear hunting continues

54

in 1936. At one point in late summer he writes to boast to Max Perkins that he has killed a large number of bears that year, including 'three grizzlies in the past week'. He also tells Perkins that he is having terrible trouble trying to complete *To Have and Have Not*: 'It almost seems I have not got another novel left in me.' This at age 37! He also tells Perkins he is bored and desperate to go to Spain and be part of the unfolding Spanish Civil War, which had started in July. Perkins contacted John Wheeler, manager of the North American Newspaper Alliance and, in November, Hemingway was engaged as their war correspondent in Spain. Before the year was out, he was to enter into another important engagement.

In December 1936, whilst in Sloppy Joe's bar at Key West, his friend 'Sloppy' Joe Russell introduced him to Martha Gellhorn. Martha was 28, had blonde hair down to her shoulders and, according to Hemingway, 'long, shapely legs, which seemed to reach up to her shoulders'. Martha was already a very experienced journalist and the author of the acclaimed *Trouble I've Seen*, about her experiences as a Federal Emergency Relief Administration investigator during the Depression years. Hemingway was smitten and immediately turned on his charm full force. Ernest spent the rest of the evening with Martha. His wife, Pauline, was at home, serving dinner to Hemingway's guests, Charles and Lorrie Thompson. Hemingway did not return home until dawn. Martha Gellhorn was destined to become his third wife.

By spring of 1937, he was in Spain reporting on the Civil War. He returned to Pauline briefly in the summer, but by autumn he was back in Madrid at the Hotel Florida, reporting the war and living with Martha, who had already spent the whole year there as a reporter. *To Have and Have Not* is published in October 1937; Scribners describe it as a novel, but it is actually three short stories. 'One Trip Across' had been published in April 1934 in *Cosmopolitan*. *Who Murdered the Vets* (Veterans) was a political, communist-style attack on the capitalist Establishment and published in *Esquire* in February 1936. 'The Tradesman's Return' continued his attack on the Roosevelt administration. Reviews of the book were mixed, tending towards adverse and sales were modest. The mixture in the critics' appraisals can be summed up by the review given by Alfred Kazin in the *New York Herald Tribune*: the book as a whole was 'hardly up to snuff', nevertheless it was the work of 'a genuine artist who has worked his way out of a cult of tiresome defeatism'.

In a later review, Dillon-Malone said much of it was banal and lacked literary virtuosity. Even his own editor, Perkins, was unimpressed, but when he tried to express his views, Hemingway shouted him down, telling him to 'get Wolfe to write for you' (Thomas Wolfe); indeed Ernest came within an inch of hitting his long-time supporter. Hemingway was again irate at the lack of appreciation of his work by 'the philistines'. However, he was himself discontented with the book, so much so that he agreed to sell the film rights for the poor sum of $10,000.

To Have and Have Not had established Hemingway's left-wing sympathies and when he returned to Spain in spring 1938 to continue reporting the Civil War, he was popular with the loyalists. He spent most of the year there, living with Martha.

In October 1938, *The First Forty Nine Stories* is published to widespread acclaim, proving again that Hemingway is considered a better short story writer than a novelist. It was published in London shortly following its publication in the USA. The review in the *Manchester Guardian* was typical of reaction on both sides of the Atlantic: 'The author's exceptional gift of narrative quality gives the excitement of a well told tale to what is, in fact, a simple description of a scene.' The book sold well at that time and through the years to come. Nevertheless, it was simply a collection of previously published short stories and serves to highlight the fact that at this time Hemingway simply could not produce a novel.

He continued to write exciting, high quality reports from Madrid on the Spanish Civil War, and his statements that his life many times was in danger ring true.

Back home in the USA, early in 1939, he first located at Key West to sail his yacht *Pilar* and to seek inspiration for that elusive novel. Now he at least had the germ of an idea and a title. *For Whom the Bell Tolls* would be a fictional love story within the framework of the Spanish Civil War. He moved on to Havana to get the book underway. By May he had 30,000 words in hand and believed he would complete the work in two months. July came and went and Hemingway had dried up and the end of the novel would not come. He was also tormented by the knowledge that his second marriage had reached breaking point. He writes to Hadley, seeking comfort, telling her he felt oppressed on all sides by suicidal thoughts. At the end of August, he went to Wyoming to the ranch of his friends the Nordquists, principally to spend time with his three sons. Pauline immediately telephoned from New York to say she was flying down to join them. She was unwell when she arrived, but Ernest was in no mood to be sympathetic. Soon after her arrival he packed his bags and left Pauline for good. He phoned Martha, asking her to meet him and together they went to The Lodge at Sun Valley, Idaho.

Martha and Ernest were only at Sun Valley for three months. The Second World War had started in Europe and Martha left in November to report on the Russia–Finland war for *Collier's Weekly* magazine. After a month or so of gambling and general carousing, Ernest went back to Cuba. From there he sent Max Perkins drafts of *For Whom the Bells Tolls*. Max was most impressed and promised to send a contract. Martha was back; perhaps she was his muse, for he was now writing purposefully. By July 1940 the book is finished and Scribners are very enthusiastic. Hemingway travels to New York and from there he starts to send the corrected proofs to Scribners. A few days of time are lost in a typical Hemingway diversion. He is staying in a double room at the Hotel Barclay and invites Gustavo Duran to move in with him. Gustavo was a young Spaniard whom Ernest had met in the 1920s in Paris, where Gustavo was studying to be a music composer. They had met again in 1937 in Madrid, where Gustavo was by now an officer in the Loyalist army. There was much time-consuming conversation and drinking between them.

By the end of October 1940, *For Whom the Bell Tolls*, dedicated to Martha Gellhorn, was published to rave reviews. In November, 100,000 copies were sold. By the end of November, Pauline had divorced Ernest on the grounds of his adultery and Hemingway had responded by marrying Martha at Cheyenne, Wyoming on 21 November.

By spring 1941, Ernest was able to write to Hadley that half a million copies of *For Whom the Bell Tolls* had been sold; he told her, 'Book selling like frozen Daiquiris in hell'. Howard Mumford Jones, writing for the *Saturday Review of Literature*, for the *New York Times*, called it 'the finest and richest novel Mr Hemingway has written'. In England, the *Observer* newspaper said it was 'one of the greatest novels which our troubled age will produce'. This time Ernest knew Hollywood would come calling and he was ready for them. He would demand an enormous sum for the film rights and he would nominate which actors would play the hero and heroine. In the end he was to get nearly everything he wanted. He was paid $100,000 for the screen rights. He had met Gary Cooper for the first time at a dinner given by Dorothy Parker at Sun Valley in October 1940. Although Hemingway had disliked *A Farewell to Arms*, he thought Cooper had performed well as Frederick Henry, under difficult circumstances. He felt thoroughly comfortable with Cooper's presence at that first meeting and they quickly bonded together. Cooper had been big game hunting in Kenya and Tanganyika in 1931, making 60 kills including two lions. They swapped safari stories and drank together until daybreak. Now Hemingway was certain that he was ideal for the role of the hero, Jordan. Hemingway negotiated determinedly with Paramount to get Cooper the part, the deal not being concluded until July 1942.

In the meantime, Cooper and Hemingway had become close friends. Their companionship was to strengthen and to last for the rest of their lives. This was unusual for Hemingway, whose fiery temper and insulting behaviour ensured that most friendships were short-term. In November 1941, *Life* magazine carried a four page spread, incorporating 12 photos of the two men hunting, fishing, drinking and loafing around together. It was to be the constant pattern of their relationship. Cooper was 6' 3", slim and ruggedly handsome, with a charming personality and an easygoing nature. He was 39 to Ernest's 41 when they first met. At that time, Ernest was still a big and handsome man and his literary reputation was equal to Cooper's reputation as a film star. Both were magnets for women; when they were together they were often relentlessly pursued by beautiful women, often seduced by them; although I doubt either man was unwilling. Cooper followed Ernest's pattern by converting to Catholicism in order to marry his second wife. Ernest said of Cooper that he was the handsomest and most attractive man that Ernest ever knew or saw. That might seem a strange remark, unless you share the views of those who thought Hemingway was bisexual.

Hemingway wanted his friend and fellow hunter Howard Hawks as director for the film. Paramount were not having that. Their man was the solid and reliable Sam Wood and to him they would stick.

Hemingway also wanted the sophisticated actress Ingrid Bergman for the role of Maria. At first it seemed he would not get her either. Astonishingly the part of the Spanish heroine was given to

Norwegian ballerina Vera Zorina. It is difficult to understand how Paramount made that decision. Gary Cooper swore to Hemingway that he would get his star. At any event, by the end of the first month of filming, Zorina was declared hopeless by Sam Wood and Cooper and was sacked. Bergman was tested and got the part. Hemingway was delighted. He had been lusting after Bergman and wanted contact with her. This time however, he was outgunned by Cooper's powerful sexuality, which completely captivated Bergman. Cooper was to say of Bergman, 'I thought her the ideal of womanhood, in bed and out.' With the icy coolness that was the Swedish star's calling card, Bergman said, 'Gary Cooper was hung like a horse and could stay all night.' Both were married at the time.

The action of *For Whom the Bell Tolls* takes place in the Sierra de Guadarrama, north-west of Madrid in May 1937. It concentrates on the doomed struggle of a small guerrilla band of loyalists against the superior numbers and firepower of the nationalists. An all-action plot concludes with the surviving guerrillas having to cross enemy fire on horseback to try to escape into the hills. The hero, Jordan, is wounded and unable to ride on. He persuades his lover Maria to leave him and ride off with the others. Jordan remains with a machine-gun to delay the nationalists. As is usual with Hemingway, we are not given the end of the story; we are left to assume that Jordan gives his life for the cause.

As the film proceeds, Hemingway tries to interfere in the production. He is rebuffed by Sam Wood. Now he accuses Sam Wood of lack of planning and indecision in an effort to get Howard Hawks brought in. His efforts fail and Sam Wood completes. With the novel having strong political tones, Paramount feared the film would be banned in Spain. The US Government tried to get approval from the Spanish Government but failed. Screenwriter Dudley Nichols was called in with instructions to politically castrate the film. The result was a weak and muddled film. Hemingway was almost beside himself with fury and it was as a result of this that he would never screenwrite for the film industry. Ultimately the film was only saved from disaster by outstanding performances by the two stars.

What did emerge from this was that Hemingway was now friendly with several world famous film stars. He regarded them as his peers and himself on equal status with them. The next 15 years of his life would be spent principally in their company and the company of championship boxers. They provided the necessary support to his inflated ego that he so desperately needed. Martha had already been pushed into the background.

Ernest spends the whole of 1943 in Cuba, fishing and boozing and entertaining his film star friends. His sexual encounters, which are indiscriminate, range from film starlets and 'models' to Havana prostitutes. His hair has started to thin quickly; he responds by growing a thick beard, which he retains for the rest of his life.

America had entered the Second World War in 1942 and Martha was, in September 1943, sent by *Collier's* to be their European correspondent. Ernest had many offers from journals to be their correspondent and Martha begged him to come. He refused and stayed on in Cuba. When Martha returned on leave in March 1944, she again begged him to come to Europe. This time he agreed and accepted an appointment from *Collier's*. This cost Martha her position with *Collier's* because journals were only permitted to have one front-line correspondent. This was clearly an act of spite by Ernest, which spelled out the end of their marriage. It had lasted little over three years.

Hemingway flies to London for *Collier's*. He refuses to help Martha to get a seat on the Pan Am flight; 'I couldn't do that, they only fly men.' This is an outrageous lie. Martha later discovers that on the flight Ernest is ensconced with actress Gertrude Lawrence.

In May 1944, shortly after taking up his London post, Hemingway was having lunch at the White Tower restaurant when he spotted a 'well-upholstered' lady whom he immediately fancied. Her name was Mary Welsh, a journalist for *Time* magazine and she was having lunch with her current lover, Irving Shaw, also a writer. Hemingway had no hesitation in barging in and asking for a date. He always lined himself up with his next wife before getting rid of his existing one.

Mary was 36, pretty, with a good figure and glorious hair. She had married at 21 and divorced her husband within two years. Now she was married to Noel Monks, a journalist. But this marriage was failing and Mary, at that time, had several lovers.

The affair between Mary Welsh and Hemingway developed, despite being interrupted by another of Ernest's 'accidents'. This time he was in a car crash where he was not the drunken driver. He suffered a serious head wound and badly bruised and swollen knees. Martha arrives to visit him and tells him their marriage is over. Hemingway is nonchalant and continues his affair with Mary Welsh, although it is also interrupted by Hemingway's forays back and forth to France to report the war. Needless to say, in most of his reports he was the hero of the hour. Having said that, it must also be stated that he filed some of the finest end-of-the-war front-line reports of any journalist. By now Ernest is calling himself 'Dr Hemingway'.

The affair with Mary fluctuated between torrid and very cold, with Ernest being his usual abusive self. Nevertheless, when the war ended, Hemingway returned to Cuba, taking Mary with him. Ernest had divorced Martha on grounds of her desertion. Only Hemingway could have got away with that. What is more, he divorced her under Cuban law, which decrees that the innocent party has a right to everything belonging to their ex-partner. Ernest took plenty. Mary Welsh and Ernest Hemingway were married in Havana on 14 March 1946. Hemingway was in good form at the wedding party, but later that night he turned aggressive and abusive. Mary packed her bags, ready to leave him, but somehow, next morning, he charmed her into staying. Not that he cared. Within a month he had cleared off to Sun Valley, Idaho, to go hunting with Gary Cooper and Clark Gable.

On this trip Hemingway did not enhance his reputation with his friends. Driving along the Valley on one trip, Ernest indulged in indiscriminate slaughter of prairie eagles. Hemingway had a telescopic rifle mounted on a tripod in the jeep and, as they drove along, he picked off the eagles, which were perched on telegraph lines.

Now Hemingway brings Mary to live in Ketchum, Idaho. Things do not go well. Hemingway is in a bullying and controlling phase. This can never sit well with Mary. She is a first-rate journalist, she has capital and a good income and has experienced doting husbands and lovers aplenty. They have already become sexually incompatible. Matters are not helped by Mary having a burst fallopian tube and Ernest becoming somewhat impotent.

In 1946, 'The Short Happy Life of Francis Macomber' is made into a film, *The Macomber Affair*. Gregory Peck stars, along with Joan Bennett, In the book, Mrs Macomber walks free after shooting her husband. This would not do for Hollywood and they made enormous efforts to contact Hemingway to have him rewrite the ending. He determinedly avoided them. The film is rewritten and ends with the lady going to jail. Critics regarded it as the best screen adaptation of Hemingway's work. Hemingway did not.

Through 1947 to 1949, Ernest and Mary live between Idaho and Cuba and travel through France and Italy. In Venice, Ernest becomes infatuated with an 18-year-old Italian girl, Adriana Ivanich. She responds and they begin an affair, which lasts six years, but it is purely mercenary on Adriana's part. Hemingway is trying to create a lengthy novel. He has a title, *Across the River and into the Trees*, but the book will not come. In 1947, Max Perkins dies. It shakes Ernest badly.

In 1948 in Havana, Ernest gives an interview to a young journalist from *Cosmopolitan* magazine. The journalist, Aaron Hotchner, was not a significant figure, but the meeting in La Florida bar was very significant. Hotchner was terrified of meeting Hemingway and adopted an obsequious attitude. This went down very well with Hemingway. His life had just begun to enter a period when he felt the need of sycophants around him. Hotchner was to remain a close friend and comrade for the rest of Hemingway's life.

In 1950, the Hemingways are again based in Cuba. Ernest completes *Across the River*. Hotchner gets in on the act as Hemingway's agent and negotiates an $85,000 deal with Scribners for the serial rights. The book is published in September 1950. It is a boring tale of a garrulous old colonel, detailing the things he has liked best in life and the loveliness of his young mistress. The affair with Adriana, of course. The critics savaged it to a man. Maxwell Geismar, writing for *The New Yorker*, summarised their views: 'It is not only Hemingway's worst novel; it is a synthesis of everything that is bad in his previous work and throws a doubtful light on the future.' The reading public seemed to take the same view. Sales were poor and the book soon sank without trace.

Hemingway made furious outbursts at his publisher, but this was only to disguise his own deep despondency. It was now ten years since he had written anything worthwhile. During that time, his health had deteriorated rapidly. He had taken to heavy drinking from morning onwards. His early morning drink would be gin and tea and in the evenings he favoured strong Barcardi cocktails. He developed high blood pressure and high cholesterol. His eyesight and hearing were waning. He was becoming severely depressed. His jealousy of other writers became almost psychopathic. He wrote articles trashing old friends Scott Fitzgerald and James Joyce, who had helped him get started, and new writers like James Jones (*From Here to Eternity*).

1951 was a bad year for Ernest. At the beginning of the year his right leg and foot swelled badly and he could scarcely walk. In the spring he was diagnosed with cirrhosis of the liver and went through a traumatic time, trying, unsuccessfully, to cut his drinking down. In July his mother died. On 1 October, his second wife, Pauline died.

To Ernest Hemingway's enormous credit, he suffers all of this, and the failures of the last decade, and stands firm. Throughout 1951, he puts one last tremendous effort into what he knows will be his final attempt at a novel. Set in the Gulf Stream of Havana, *The Old Man and the Sea* is the story of a fisherman Ernest had known many years ago: an old man, Santiago, who wanted to reach for the stars and fight the big fish who would pull him out to where the sharks were, and they would leave the old fisherman with nothing but his dreams. In the end, it is not a novel, but an extended short story, running to about 27,000 words. But what a short story and what a comeback success.

Ernest is just completing the work in February 1952 when his publisher, Charles Scribner, dies. Nevertheless, the manuscript is sent to Scribners and publication is in September 1952. The preview received rave reviews by the literary critics. *Life* magazine paid $40,000 for the right to run the full text a week before general publication and sold five million copies in two days. The book hit the bestseller list immediately and remained there until spring 1953. In New York, Robert Gorham Davis, for *The Times*, wrote, 'It is a tale superbly told.' In London, the *Sunday Times* said, 'The best short story Hemingway has written', and the *Guardian* called it 'a quite wonderful example of narrative art'. There were those who felt that the book was over-praised and that much was attributed to the fact that the public never like to give up on their literary heroes; but there is no denying that Hemingway was now the comeback king.

It certainly is a successful year for Ernest. He sells the film rights for *The Snows of Kilimanjaro* to 20th Century Fox for $100,000. Darryl Zanuck was hired to direct. He immediately recognised that, as a short story, it would need padding out if it was to make a feature film. Casey Robinson was brought in as scriptwriter and simply went through Hemingway's works, lifting bits to weave in. Ernest was very bitter about this: 'I sold Fox a single story, not my complete works. This movie has something from every story I ever wrote.' It was then that Hemingway gave his now famous advice to authors: 'Let me tell you about writing for films. You finish your book. Now, you know where the California state line is? Well, you drive right up to that line, with your manuscript. First let them toss the money over. Then you throw your book over, pick up the money and get the hell out of there.'

Gregory Peck and Ava Gardner were picked to star in the film. Ernest really fancied Ava, rather unusually for him since she had jet-black hair, whereas his predilection was for blondes. On the other hand, she was a heavy smoker and drinker and swore like a trooper; just Hemingway's type. He did proposition her mildly, twice, but she was no more than sweetly polite and he backed off. She was married to a jealous Frank Sinatra at that time and Ernest was well aware of the crooner's Mafia connections. Ernest did tell Ava, 'The film is crap. The only two good things in it are you and the hyena.' Ernest was wrong. The critics loved Peck and said it was a peak point in his career; it also established Gardner as an international star.

In May 1953, *The Old Man and the Sea* was awarded the Pulitzer Prize, with a cheque for $35,000. Hemingway sold the film rights for $25,000 and, in an unusual move for him, agreed to work with the director; but only as the consultant on fishing and for an additional $25,000. Fred Zimmerman started as director, but could not cope with Hemingway's bad temper and foul mouth and was quickly replaced by John Sturges. The star, Spencer Tracy, was chosen with Hemingway's full approval. Ernest admired him and, more than that, he liked him. Tracy was, after all, a fellow alcoholic. The film was a flop, losing the film studio a lot of money. Experienced actor though he was, the rotund, affluent Tracy looked unrealistic in the role of a lean and hungry, poor, Cuban fisherman. Ernest took his money and ran.

Look magazine offered him $200,000 for a series of articles on East Africa. In August he took off with Mary for Mombasa, where he had arranged for his old friend Philip Percival to look after him.

The trip lasted three months and was a disaster for much of the time. Hemingway was at the height of his alcoholism and was drunk most days. One day, early in the trip, he became so drunk that, while being transported in a jeep, he fell out and dislocated his shoulder and cut his face badly. He shaved his head and dressed as a Masai warrior, walking around barefoot, covered only in a loincloth and carrying a spear. He carried on an affair with a native girl called Debba, locally regarded as 'unclean trash'. Hemingway regarded the affair as courtship and sex and states that he 'married' her and that, as part of the marriage settlement, he 'received' her 17-year-old sister.

In his saner moments, Ernest decided to view East Africa from a different perspective. He hired a plane with pilot to fly over Rwanda and Uganda to view its wonders from the air, accompanied by Mary. As they were viewing the Nile Falls, the plane suddenly struck a telegraph wire and crashed. Mary suffered broken ribs and Ernest took another severe shoulder strain. They were able to find a riverboat, which took them down to Butiaba, Lake Albert. Here they found Captain Reggie Cartwright, who had been flying around in his de Havilland looking for them since their crash had been reported. He offered to fly them to Entebbe. Shortly after take-off, the starboard engine caught fire, the fuel tank exploded and the plane crashed in flames. Passenger Roy Marsh kicked out the door on one side of the plane and he and Mary scrambled out. On the other side of the plane, Ernest chose to batter the door out by headbutting it several times. He did get out, but the injuries to his skull were severe and he suffered a crushed vertebra.

Eventually they were driven first to Entebbe and then Nairobi. In Nairobi he was surrounded by journalists from magazines that had already reported his death. His reaction was to dictate his own 15,000 word report for *Look* magazine. He began 'Death keeps crooking its finger at me. But I go on banging my typewriter anyway. When I go, I want to go fast.' He then flew onwards, to a beach camp on the Kenyan coast to meet up with his son Patrick to go deep-sea fishing. Whilst there, a big bush fire broke out. A drunken Hemingway insists on helping the local fire fighters; but he loses his balance and falls into the flames. By the time he is pulled free, he has multiple second-degree burns.

He now goes to Venice to recuperate. He is forced to spend several weeks in bed. He calls Hotchner from America to his bedside. From now on, Hotchner will be in his company much of the time until his death. From Venice they went to Milan, so that Ernest could visit Ingrid Bergman. When Ernest lusted, he lusted long. From Venice to Madrid for the bullfights. Here Ernest begins to show his first reported signs of memory loss. He cannot find some of his old café and bar haunts. Back now to Cuba.

Back in Cuba in October 1954, he receives news that he has been awarded the Nobel Prize for Literature: 'For his powerful, style-forming mastery of the art of modern narration, as most recently evinced in *The Old Man and the Sea* ... he also possesses a natural admiration of every individual who fights the good fight in a world of reality overshadowed by violence and death.' Publicly, Hemingway scorns the award, calling it the 'Ignoble Prize'. Privately he is thrilled and regards it as the coronation of his writing. In fact, no other book will be published in his lifetime. He accepts the Prize, but refuses to attend the awards ceremony.

During 1955–58, Ernest's health begins serious and rapid deterioration. The many blows he has taken to the head, through accidents, brawling and boxing, have left him suffering with splitting headaches, loss of hearing and memory loss. The latter was particularly galling for Ernest. He had always had a prodigious memory: he often said, 'Once I see something of interest, my memory photographs it and stores it away for future use.' This contributed to his outstanding ability to write about scenery, events and people in great detail. Now he could not even remember enough to boast with conviction: a typical example was a colourful story he told several times, relating to his lust for Mata Hari (the notorious First World War spy). 'One night I fucked her very well, but I found her very heavy in the hips and to have more desire for what was done for her than what she was doing for me.' Ernest was not in Italy until 1918; the old Ernest would have remembered that she was executed in 1917.

He now had serious liver problems due to his alcoholism. His eyesight, never good and worsened by his refusal to wear glasses, was now further impaired by an eye disease, which was drying out his corneas. He had by now become on the whole impotent. This may have been the result of a series of sexually transmitted diseases. Hemingway frequently boasted that he had been with many prostitutes and had what he called 'the clap' on numerous occasions. This may also have been the cause of his mental deterioration. He had been manic depressive over the past few years and now began to develop phobias and unreal paranoias. One paranoia that was real was that the FBI were watching his every move. This was completely discounted at the time by Mary and by his constant companions Hotchner, Gary Cooper, George Brown and Chuck Atkinson (an understanding motel owner from Ketchum). They were wrong. Recently, the release of some of J. Edgar Hoover's old files revealed that Hemingway was indeed being watched due to his suspected communist sympathies.

He is still trying to write, working on a story of his African adventures (*True at First Light*) and his memoirs (*A Moveable Feast*). The Hemingways continue to live in Cuba. Mary leaves him but comes back. They travel around France each year. In the autumn of 1958 Hemingway goes off to Ketchum on a hunting trip with Hotchner. Despite his mental illness, he retains his sense of humour. One day the pair find themselves trapped in the Valley by a snow blizzard. Gary Cooper, hearing of their plight, comes down, carrying with him some superb smoked goose and vintage Chablis. 'Got this locally,' says Cooper. 'These Mormon guys sure know how to live.' Hemingway responds, 'I'm practically one myself. Had four wives haven't I? Five if you include Debba.'

In the spring of 1959, Ernest and Mary sailed to Spain on the SS *Constitution*. Scribners, in the absence of anything forthcoming from Ernest, had decided to reissue *Death in the Afternoon* and had asked him to go to Spain to write a new piece to update it. *Life* magazine got wind of this and sent their representative to Madrid to negotiate a deal whereby Ernest would allow them to publish the piece prior to hardback publication. Hemingway contracted to a deal for a piece restricted to 5,000 words for $10,000. In my view, this deal was the first marker in the run up to the end of Hemingway's life.

Hemingway drove all around Spain in search of material until the end of September, exhausting himself and ignoring Mary. She left in October and, on arriving back in Ketchum, wrote to say she was leaving him. He replied and somehow persuaded her to stay and he quickly returned to her. They had a vacation in Ketchum; Hemingway invited the Spanish bullfighter Ordonez and his wife Carmen. It turned out to be disappointing and the Hemingways were pleased to return to Cuba at the end of January 1960.

Ernest beavered away at the piece for *Life* magazine, despite a continuous deterioration of his mind. He had some very real concerns about his position in Cuba as an American writer now that the dictator Castro had taken control of the government. Unfortunately once Ernest got immersed in his favourite subject, verbiage set in. By March, he was phoning Hotchner to ask him to liase and negotiate with *Life* magazine. He was already approaching 30,000 words and he would like to agree on 40,000 words and an 7 April deadline. This was vastly different to the original arrangement, but *Life* agreed it direct with Ernest, albeit on the basis of a watertight contract at 40,000 words, and they would pay $40,000. The rot now set in. Hemingway was totally undisciplined and by May he had 110,000 words and no idea how to reduce to 40,000. He called in Hotchner and, by the middle of July, they had reduced it to 55,000 words and Hemingway then swore his eyesight was gone and he could do no more. Hemingway then asked Hotchner to negotiate with *Life* for an increase to $75,000. He told Hotchner he had a tax liability for $35,000 that he could not meet. If he could get $75,000 he could bank his 'own' 40,000 and pay the tax man the other 35,000. So close was Hotchner's relationship that he knew Ernest had more than enough money put by to pay his taxes. It was just another mental aberration. Such was Hotchner's ability that he got $100,000 from *Life* and their selection from *A Dangerous Summer* was published in September 1960.

Immediately afterwards Hemingway goes back to Ketchum with Hotchner to meet up with Gary Cooper for another hunting trip. This illustrates Hemingway's physical courage, because the man can hardly walk. It is on this trip that he gives Cooper a piece of belligerent Hemingway advice that has been quoted more often than any of his written lines: 'Always stand in the back of the man who fires a gun and in front of the man who shits. That way you won't get shot or shit on.'

Ernest returned from that trip to find that he was quite unable to write anything at all. Believing he would never write again, he had all of his manuscripts confined to a bank vault. He knows he can no longer live in Cuba under the Castro regime, so he departs for Ketchum. He is not allowed to take any of his possessions with him.

He mentioned suicide to his friends, even demonstrating how he would shoot himself through the palate with a rifle. He also told Mary he wanted to commit suicide and she became very worried. She called in Dr Savier. At his first full examination, he measured Ernest's blood pressure at 250/125 (a normal level would be about 140/70).

Dr Savier had many long conversations with Hemingway, during which Ernest poured out all his fears and anxieties. His bank was siphoning off money from his account; he owed taxes and the Revenue was after him; his friend Bill Davis was trying to kill him. All of this was illusory. What was not unreal was that the FBI were watching him, that he would never be able to write again and that he wanted to commit suicide. Gradually Dr Savier convinced him of his need for psychiatric treatment. It took some doing, for Ernest had a contempt of psychiatrists and of 'wimps' who suffered with their nerves. Dr Savier suggested the world famous Menninger Psychiatric Clinic in Kanas. 'Out of the question,' said Ernest. 'People will think I am losing my marbles,' which he was. Savier then suggested the Mayo Clinic, in Rochester, Minnesota. They specialised in a wide variety of treatments. When news got out, it could be explained that he was being treated for hypertension. Ernest agreed to this; after all, he reasoned, treatment for hypertension was all he really needed.

On 20 November 1960 he was admitted to the Mayo Clinic, registering under his doctor's name. After initial consultations he was housed in the psychiatry section under the care of Dr Howard P. Rome. Aware of his patient's resistance to talk therapy, Dr Rome suggested a mechanical approach to the solution of Ernest's problems. Hemingway was impressed and agreed. 'Excellent,' said Dr Rome, 'let us begin the electrical shock treatment immediately.'

Electroconvulsive therapy had been found to produce good results in patients suffering from delusional depression. It had been found to have the side-effect of creating memory loss. With hindsight, it is difficult to justify this treatment for someone already suffering memory loss who was by profession a writer who relied upon his memory. In fairness, I should state that modern day antidepressant drugs, such as Thioridazine were not then on the market. Also the clinic records show that Howard Rome consistently prescribed electroshock treatment for most problems referred to him. Hemingway had received eleven treatments before being released on 22 January 1961. Hemingway's clinical records are not available for inspection, so I am unable to say whether Dr Rome considered him cured. In any event, Dr Rome had no authority to hold him against his will. My firm belief is that Hemingway discharged himself.

On his return to Ketchum, he immediately took out his manuscript of *A Moveable Feast* and spent a few days rearranging and revising it. He cannot settle and, before the month is out, he goes off hunting with Gary Cooper. It is the last time they are to see each other. Coop is shocked to see his old friend so thin and frail. Ernest is now down to 150 pounds. Coop has sad news of his own health. He reveals to Ernest that he has cancer and will have to have a tumour removed. Ernest is terribly shocked and from now on will worry daily about Coop and hope that his operation is successful. On returning to Ketchum, Hemingway takes up *A Moveable Feast* and tries for a few more days to work on it. In February, he writes to Louie Brague at Scribner's, telling him that he is working on the final chapter to the book. Momentarily it appears he has once again exorcised his demons through writing. This is not to be. He cannot do anything with his memoirs. When he is asked in late February to write a simple ten line eulogy to John F. Kennedy upon his inauguration, he spends many hours trying but fails. Upon giving up, he breaks down and cries copiously.

In her autobiography, *How it Was*, Mary tells us that throughout March Ernest was like a zombie, spending most of his time sitting in his favourite chair and staring into space. Sometime during the third week of April the first of Hemingway's suicide attempts occurred. Mary walked into the living room and found him with a double-barrelled shotgun in his hand and two shells near at hand. A letter addressed to Mary was on the mantelpiece. Ernest would not give the letter to Mary, but read extracts from it to her. It contained his last wishes and financial arrangements to be made after his death; clearly it was a form of suicide note. Mary telephoned for their local doctor, Vernon Lord, and kept Ernest talking until he arrived. Dr Lord immediately arranged for Ernest to be taken to the local Sun Valley hospital. There he remained, under sedation on sodium amytal, for a few days whilst efforts were made to get the Mayo Clinic to re-admit him. The problem arising was that Mayo would only take him back again if he came of his own free will. At first Ernest resisted, but on 24 April he agreed and a charter plane was immediately commissioned to take him to Rochester. Ernest said he would like to go back to the house first to collect a few things. The doctors saw no problem so long as he was accompanied. Dr Lord went with him, taking also a nurse and Mary.

Acting on some remarkable instinct, Lord decided they would be driven by a massive 17-stone friend, Don Anderson. This decision saved Ernest's life at that time. When they arrived at the house, Ernest made a sudden dash for the front door and bolted it behind him. Anderson rushed round to the side door and smashed it in with one charge. There he found Ernest at the gun rack, holding a shotgun, breech open, ramming two shells into the chambers and reaching for the safety catch. Anderson hurled himself at Ernest, knocking him to the ground. A violent struggle for the gun ensued, with Ernest demonstrating that he still had some physical strength. Ernest was only overpowered when Vernon Lord joined in. Ernest was then taken back to Sun Valley hospital and heavily sedated.

The next day they did depart for Rochester. Ernest was again heavily sedated. Nevertheless, shortly after take-off, he made an energetic effort to get a door open and jump out of the plane; only a strenuous effort by Anderson and Lord prevented him. Dr Lord then gave him a large injection of sodium amytal. Ernest appeared to become sleepy, but he was only feigning and, as they were flying over South Dakota, he made another attempt to jump out of the plane, again aborted by Anderson.

Dr Rome was waiting for him at the Mayo Clinic. After absurdly friendly greetings, Howard Rome arranged for Hemingway to be placed in the St Mary Special Security Section (known at St Mary's as the suicide watch). Dr Stone visited Ernest the next day to give him the good news that the electroconvulsive treatment would recommence straightaway. I have been unable to ascertain how many shock treatments Hemingway was given on this occasion. By the end of May, Hemingway complained bitterly that they had destroyed his memory and that he did not want any more. The shock treatments were not stopped until early June; if Hemingway had been having one per day, he would have had about 45.

About the middle of May, Hotchner gave Ernest the sad news that Gary Cooper had died after his operation for prostate cancer. Hemingway was devastated. Dr Rome notes in his diary that 'E H was in severe depression for several days after receiving news of the death of his close friend Gary Cooper.'

On 14 June, Mary was with Hotchner and took a conference call from Mayo Clinic. The doctor at St Mary's said Ernest had made considerable improvements and, in their opinion, he would benefit from a return to Ketchum. It later emerged that Hemingway himself had persuaded them that he was very much better and that a return to his home surroundings and work would complete the process. His memory may have gone, but obviously he was still able to dredge up an occasional burst of charm and cunning.

On 26 June Mary arrived at the Mayo to collect Ernest. He assured her he had no more thoughts of suicide. She had rented a car and Ernest's old sparring partner George Brown had agreed to drive them home to Ketchum. It was a trip of about 1,700 miles and Ernest asked for stops to rest several times along the route. They arrived at Ketchum on the night of 30 June.

On Saturday evening, 1 July, the three of them went out to dinner at a local restaurant. Whilst there, Ernest again became paranoid, insisting that two men at the bar were FBI, watching him because he owed taxes. They were not. Hemingway had not been cured.

Next morning, about 7 a.m., Mary tells us, she heard a gunshot and went out on to the landing from where she saw Ernest lying in the hallway, with a shotgun in his hands and most of his face and brains blown away. Mary tried to claim it was an accident; the *New York Times* headline read: 'Hemingway Dead of Shotgun Wound; Wife Says He Was Cleaning Weapon'. This was patently untrue. Hemingway was a firearms expert and would never have been cleaning a shotgun whilst both barrels were loaded. Furthermore, if, as Mary states, she heard the shot and then came out of her room, then she could not know whether it was accidental or deliberate. Mary was covering up, probably to avoid bad publicity, possibly to protect Ernest's death insurance. Evidence against Mary comes from Leonard Lyons, syndication journalist and long-time friend of the Hemingways. Lyons states, 'The first thing Mary did was to make several phone calls, trying to locate me. She found me at a Beverly Hills hotel. "Lennie," she said, very calmly, "I'm calling you because Papa has killed himself. Now what I'd like you to do is arrange for a press conference at your hotel –make sure all the wire services are there – and tell them I have informed you that whilst Ernest was cleaning his shotgun this morning it accidentally discharged and shot him in the head. Got that?"; only after she arranged all this with me did she phone Ernest's doctor and the police and tell them her version of what happened.'

Ernest Hemingway had committed suicide. He probably left a suicide note, but Mary says she never found it. It is my opinion that Hemingway called out to Mary and that, when she came out on to the landing, he shot himself in the most horrific way in her full view. This would have been a typically spiteful Hemingway act of revenge against a wife with whom he had been having vicious quarrels for several years, but whom he could not afford to divorce.

Why did Hemingway commit suicide? This is a question that has been raised for the past 40 years by more than 20 biographers, hundreds of articles, essays and theses; by the Hemingway Society and by the biannual Hemingway Review. Many of them conflict with each other over dates, places and events. Between them they cover several million words, yet all most of them come up with is that only Hemingway knows why he took the deadly act. I now pose some questions highlighted by this essay. I hope the answers which readers deduce will enable them to form a well-founded opinion.

Hemingway had close relationships with several men, including Scott Fitzgerald, Aaron Hotchner, Gustavo Duran, Gary Cooper. He also had relationship problems in all of his marriages; in public he wanted to dominate but in the bedroom he wanted his wife to be the dominant partner. Was he bisexual? He stated *ad nauseam* that he hated homosexuality and that he could never have a tactile relationship with any man. Why did he protest this so much? Did he have gender confusions: if he did, were these caused by his mother treating him as a girl in his early childhood and by the corporal punishment dealt out to him in his later childhood?

What effect did the death of Gary Cooper have on Hemingway's decision to end it all? They were the closest of friends for 20 years and Hemingway regarded him as a soul mate. Was there any sexual relationship between them? We know that Ernest was devastated over Coop's death. It may be that this was the last straw that broke Hemingway's spirit.

What contribution did his physical deterioration make to his mental deterioration? In his thirties and forties he was a huge, handsome, brawling womaniser. By his fifties, he had become a shell of that man. Balding, half blind, half deaf, impotent and suffering from diseases of the heart and liver. His inability to lead his former rumbustious life must have deeply affected his mind. In his forties he is manic depressive, but this develops through his fifties into morbid depression and mild dementia. It is possible that the fact that he had failed four times to make a good marriage, together with his belief that Agnes Kurowsky had been his one true love and his failure to capture Adriana Ivanich, was enough to make him commit the final act.

It appears Hemingway was always short of money. Gifts and borrowings were often necessary to provide the things he wanted. This despite all of his wives having their own capital and income. This despite Ernest earning more than $5 million in the last half of his life: equivalent to about $100 million today. Hotchner tells us that Ernest's all-consuming worry in his last months was his lack of funds to the extent that he could not even pay his taxes. If that really was the case, then what had Hemingway spent his vast income upon? Was it gambling? Is the answer to that mystery one of the keys to the puzzle of his suicide?

Was Hemingway schizoid? He was an excessively extrovert person, yet most critics agree that the predominant trait in his writings was reticence.

Castro's *coup d'état* in Cuba forced Hemingway to leave a country he loved. He had to leave behind his house, his yacht *Pilar*, his paintings and other treasured items full of memories. He told Hotchner, 'This is the blow that will kill me.' Was this the beginning of his rush towards suicide?

What contribution did electroconvulsive therapy make to Ernest's final decision? The ECT carried out on Sylvia Plath was described by Olive Higgins Prouty as 'disastrous'. Hemingway says it destroyed what remained of his memory, such that he would never be able to write again. Dr Vernon Lord had lengthy conversations with Ernest in the weeks prior to his death in an effort to determine the cause of his suicidal thoughts. He firmly believed that Hemingway's realisation that he would never be able to write again was the cause of his decision to kill himself. Writing was Hemingway's life and without writing he wanted no life.

Comparison of Hemingway with other acclaimed authors in this book may well lead the reader to a conclusion as to why Hemingway committed suicide. But Hemingway was a complex character, so there is no one single answer. Rather, there are several answers, which, combined, give us the solution. The answer to why Hemingway committed the act in the way he did is quite clear. There was only ever one way Hemingway wanted to take his own life. He always intended to blow his brains out.

Unfortunately we do not know what his final words were to us, his readers. Mary says she could not find the suicide note.

Sylvia Plath

Almost an All-American Girl

Ask the average reader what they know of Sylvia Plath and the probable answer will be: American poet and novelist, married to Ted Hughes, the Poet Laureate, and killed herself at 30 years of age. That answer would only scratch the surface of the story of Sylvia Plath Hughes.

Certainly Ted Hughes played a dominant role in Sylvia's life and death, but there was much more to Plath than her marriage to Ted Hughes. Sylvia Plath was not a poet or novelist in our standard understanding of those vocations. She was an autobiographer. Almost everything she wrote that was published – poems, letters, short

Photo: CSU Archv/Everett/Rex Features

stories, novels – was about herself or scenes and events where she was present.

Introspection: that is the key to Sylvia Plath's life and suicide.

Sylvia Plath was born on 27 October 1932 in Boston, Massachusetts. Her father, Otto, was German. Her mother, Aurelia, was born in Boston but both Aurelia's parents were Austrian immigrants. Sylvia, however, was from a very early age a typical all-American girl.

Otto Plath arrived in New York in 1902, at the age of 16, and although fluent in German and Polish and semi-fluent in French, he spoke no English. Studying voraciously, he worked his way through college and university. By 1926 he was teaching German and his favourite subject, Biology, at Boston University. In 1928 he was awarded his doctorate in Science. He developed an intense academic interest in bees, and when his book *Bumblebees and Their Ways* was published in 1934, it became and remained for many years the authority on the subject.

Otto was 47, married and separated, when he embarked on a relationship with Aurelia Schober, a slim, pretty, 26-year-old student in his German class at Boston. Aurelia was already a Bachelor of Arts and Letters and was studying for her Masters degree. The relationship developed, Otto divorced and married Aurelia in January 1932. Either Aurelia was pregnant at the time, or she conceived Sylvia within a week or two. Sylvia was born 27 October 1932.

Aurelia said later that, at the time of the marriage, she had taken it for granted that they would have equal rights within their partnership. She was greatly misguided. The relationship had begun as teacher and pupil; it would continue in the traditional German way, with the man being master in the household. Aurelia was a woman with great strength of will but she was no match for Otto. He made all financial decisions and all household purchases, including food. Aurelia was there to look after the children, attend to his physical needs and to assist him with his writing.

Aurelia carried out her wifely responsibilities dutifully. She also devoted herself to Sylvia, throwing overboard any routine and simply lifting and cuddling Sylvia whenever she cried and feeding her whenever she was hungry. In fact, Sylvia was over-coddled as an infant and this may well have had some impact on her character as an adult. This early over-attention continued at least until April 1935, when her brother Warren was born.

It was about the time of Warren's birth that Otto began to show the first signs of the illness that would precipitate his death and shatter Sylvia Plath's childhood. Otto began to lose weight, cough violently and become intensely irritable without reason. By 1937 he had deteriorated badly. Now he began to show signs of the severe depression, that had struck down his mother and sister. He also suffered from insomnia and exhaustion and the irritability became rage. Sylvia and Warren were allowed to see their father for only 30 minutes each day, in the evening after supper. Sylvia, aged five, would read him a poem, often one of her own composition, or dance for him.

Through 1938 and 1939, Otto's health continued to fail and now Warren was very ill with two attacks of bronchial pneumonia, chronic asthma and allergic reactions to almost everything. The Plath household resembled a private hospital. During this period, Sylvia was sent to live with her maternal grandparents at Shirley Point on Boston's Atlantic seashore. It was here that she developed a love of the sea that would continue throughout her lifetime.

Otto believed he had lung cancer and would not submit himself to hospital where the only known treatment was surgical operation, which was usually unsuccessful. By 1940 Otto was suffering severe leg cramps and persistent thirst. In August he had a minor accident, knocking his foot against a desk. The foot turned black and swelled badly. The local doctor was called and, resulting from routine blood samples, discovered that Otto had been suffering from long-term diabetes, which was now in an advanced state. Shortly afterwards, he developed pneumonia and was hospitalised for two weeks. The leg had turned gangrenous and a decision was taken to amputate it from the thigh. The operation was performed on 12 October. The operation was physically successful, but Otto was left with severe depression. From this depression he never recovered. On 5 November 1940, he took a handful of painkillers and sleeping tablets and went to sleep. He never awoke.

Sylvia was devastated by her father's death. She had adored and respected him. Throughout her life she fantasised about her relationships with him and often referred to him as 'my colossus'. Her first published book, *The Colossus*, was dedicated to him. When Aurelia went to tell her, 'Your father has gone, he is dead,' Sylvia asked, 'Gone where?' and when Aurelia replied, 'God has taken him,' Sylvia's immediate response was, 'I'll never speak to God again.' I do not believe she ever did. Typical of her outpourings about her father was a 1956 villanelle 'Lament' in which the father, who is killed by bee stings, walks on water like Christ. The keynote is that you could scour the earth and sky and still find it impossible to replace such a man. As to God, this is spelt with the lower case 'g'.

Aurelia decided Sylvia was too young to suffer the trauma of witnessing her father's funeral, so she was kept at home. It never occurred to Aurelia that she was denying her daughter the opportunity of a natural grieving outlet. It certainly occurred to Sylvia later in life: she blamed her mother for not allowing her to grieve properly for her father at the time of his death. It is highly probable that this was the cause of Plath's lifetime obsession with her father, as evidenced in so many of her poems: 'Daddy', 'The Beekeeper's Daughter', 'The Colossus', 'All the Dead Dears' and 'Electra on Azalea Path'. Plath also blamed her mother for her father's death. No matter how many compliments she paid her mother, Sylvia remained fixated upon the idea that, by marrying an older man, Aurelia had given her an old father who would inevitably die before the child had the full term of pleasure with him. Sylvia also believed that her mother ought to have insisted on medical attention for her father at an early stage and that, if she had done so, his life would have been saved. Certainly Aurelia was capable of having been able to take that action; she was a very strong-willed woman, as she was later to prove on many occasions.

Following Otto Plath's death, Aurelia found herself in financial difficulties. Otto had saved very little and his life insurance had been swallowed up with medical and funeral bills. The situation resolved itself in a strange way. Aurelia's father was made redundant and could find no further work. For economic reasons, Aurelia and her parents decided to live together. The Schobers rented out their house at Shirley Point and moved into the Plath house at Johnson Avenue. Sylvia was now able to spend much more time with her grandmother, grandfather and her uncle Frank. To some small degree, this mitigated the grief of losing her father. But it never went away.

Aurelia was prepared to work hard, live on a low income and make any personal sacrifice to ensure her children were well educated and prepared for the wider world. Sylvia had been one of the star pupils at her first public school, Warren Grammar, and now she moved into the fourth year at Newton School in Winthrop. Even at such a young age, she was fascinated by art in all its forms and aspired to be creative. Her first published poem was at the age of eight. The *Boston Herald* published a short piece of verse quite simply entitled 'Poem'. Significantly it was about Sylvia's own thoughts and visions on hot summer nights.

By the summer of 1942, Sylvia had begun to develop respiratory problems, which were to remain with her throughout her life. She started by having her tonsils removed, then soon developed mild asthma and severe sinusitis. Aurelia decided that the ocean did not agree with the children. There were also other problems to consider while they were living in Winthrop. Aurelia had secured a better paid, less stressful job at Boston University, but commuting was difficult. Most importantly, she did not want her children to grow up in the working-class environment of Winthrop. After much searching, she settled upon Wellesley, an upper middle-class community about 15 miles west of Boston City. Once resident there, Sylvia could qualify for a full grant to attend Smith or Wellesley College, two of the best schools in the state.

In the autumn of 1942 Sylvia was enrolled in the Marshall Perrin Elementary School. Wellesley did not prove to be the ideal location her mother had imagined. The Depression years had taken their toll and now the Second World War was in full swing with its attendant shortage of every commodity. The new house was smaller and Sylvia now had to share a bedroom with her mother; far from ideal for a girl coming into her adolescent years. Also she missed the ocean at Winthrop. She quickly found herself under pressure in the spring and autumn of 1943, when her mother twice fell ill for several weeks each time, an ulcer having haemorrhaged. This, combined with the difficulty of integrating into a new school, produced gradually mounting tension and depression within Sylvia. Towards the end of autumn that year she slit her throat with a carving knife. However, she chose to do it when her mother was near at hand. Aurelia rushed her to hospital; the wound was staunched and stitched, although the scar would remain for ever. Thus the first of Plath's several suicide attempts was thwarted. Aurelia kept it quiet and always maintained it was a cry for help rather than a suicide attempt.

Aurelia was determined that Sylvia would understand the sacrifices she had made for her and she made it clear to Sylvia that the family's whole future depended upon Sylvia's achievements all the way through high school.

Sylvia did respond and she worked hard that summer; she read prodigious amounts and ended the 1944 summer term with excellent grades. In the autumn of 1944 she commenced seventh year at Alice Phillips Junior High School. Here she began writing a great deal of poetry at an advanced level, often illustrating her work with her own fine drawings. Starting her teenage years, Sylvia began to enjoy a hectic social life, attending many events and usually escorted by boys. Now Sylvia, at 13, became seriously interested in boys, although they would always come second to her first love, writing. A string of young boyfriends followed, principals among them being Dick Mills, Perry Norton, Dick Cunningham, Philip McCurdy and Wayne Sterling. Sylvia was already growing into a lovely girl, with a vibrant personality.

In July 1946 she gathered together what she considered her best poems. Illustrating them copiously with her own drawings, she created an anthology called simply *Poems by Sylvia Plath*. At the age of 14 she had now been writing poems for nine years.

Sylvia completed her junior high school in the summer of 1947, collecting mostly 'A' grades. She had been very popular; her yearbook was signed by about 80 of her friends.

In the autumn of 1947 she joined Gamaliel Bradford High School. Here she was to encounter an English teacher who was to have a profound influence on the rest of her life. Wilbury Crockett was a softly spoken, grammatical teacher of the old school type. He commanded attention and hard work and repaid it with praise and encouragement. Sylvia was to refer to him in her letters throughout her life. She said that he had fostered her literary intellect and she nominated him 'the teacher of a lifetime'. Crockett had such an effect on Sylvia that first week at Bradford High that she began to write poetry again for the first time in five months. In October that first term Crockett read aloud to the class four of Sylvia's new poems. His favourite was 'I Thought I Could Not be Hurt', which was based on an incident when Sylvia's grandmother had accidentally smudged the paint on one of her watercolour paintings. Crockett said it showed a rare quality in its ability to describe deep anguish. He was presumably referring to the words 'dull and aching void', which she used to describe her feeling at the time of the incident. Here we see an early indication of the extreme emotional states that would play such a large part in Plath's death.

In November, Sylvia attended her first high school dance and this led to several formal dances and proms over the next six months. Her escort and boyfriend was Perry Norton, but she danced and socialised with many other boys. Now 15, Sylvia was tall for her age, around 5' 7", slim, attractive, tanned and with blonde, sun-streaked hair. She was very popular and had an active social life. This did not stop her working with a fanatical zeal upon both her poetry and her school syllabus. At the close of her first year, she received all 'A's for her academic studies.

For her second year at Bradford, she took English, Latin and French, American History, Maths and Art. She completed the year in July 1949 with straight 'A's throughout. This was quite remarkable because through that year a number of factors arose that might reasonably have been expected to disrupt her academic concentration.

Foremost amongst those distractions were boys. Sylvia had discovered them big time. During that year, she dated at least 20 young men. Principal amongst them was John Hall, whose body she considered 'perfect', John Hodges, Paul Hezlett and Bruce Elwell. With Elwell Sylvia had her first alcoholic drink, bourbon whiskey. Through these boys her sexuality was awakened, though she remained a virgin. At this time she began to encounter psychological and physical problems, related to her menstrual cycle, which were to curse her for the rest of her life; predominant amongst the effects were extreme fatigue, insomnia, feelings of suffocation, sinus infection and severe mood swings pre- and post-menstruation.

Through all this, Sylvia kept herself heavily involved with high school life. She was editor of the school magazine, chair of the poster and decorating committee and member of the school orchestra. Throughout the autumn and winter of 1949, Plath wrote a great many poems. Amongst the best of these were 'The Invalid', 'East Wind', 'Lonely Song' and 'Gone is the River'. These she sent to various magazines; *Seventeen*, *Mademoiselle* and *Ladies' Home Journal* being the foremost. All this work was rejected.

At this time Sylvia was contemplating which colleges she would apply to after Bradford. Money would be a dominant factor. Clearly she had to apply for Wellesley College because she was certain to receive a town scholarship. However, Sylvia's preference was for Smith College, one of the USA's top women's colleges. Smith offered excellent courses in English and Art and awarded a generous number of bursaries. Another advantage, from Sylvia's viewpoint, was Smith's distance from Wellesley; some 100 miles. Sylvia's discovery of the physical attractions of young men persuaded her it was time to cut the strings that tied her to her mother. Aurelia, who never missed an opportunity to make Sylvia aware of the sacrifices she was making for her, was inclined to support Sylvia's preference for Smith. Not only would it provide a premier education for her daughter, but would also give Aurelia some much needed time and space.

Sylvia applied for admission to Smith College in November 1949. Supporting Plath's application were references from Wilbury Crockett and the Principal of Bradford High, Dr Samuel Graves. Graves said, 'Sylvia is a superior candidate for college. Her capacity for thoroughness is clearly evident. May college mean some "fun" for her, as well as intellectual accomplishments.' This wish was to be well and truly granted, as we shall see.

In May 1950, Smith College accepted Plath's application. The Director of Scholarships added the good news that she had won a scholarship grant of $850. This would cover her tuition fees, but she would still have to find $750 a year for room and board. Aurelia's annual salary of $3,650 simply did not enable her to cover that cost. Wellesley's Smith Club (ex-Smith College graduates) came to the rescue with a scholarship of $450. Her mother would somehow find the balance of $300. Sylvia would go to Smith.

This good news rounded off an excellent spring of 1950 for Plath. In March she received acceptance for publication of her first two pieces of paid writing. *The Christian Science Monitor* paid $5 for 'A Youth's Plea for World Peace' (written jointly with Perry Norton). *Seventeen* would pay $15 for her short story 'And Summer Will Not Come Again', and they would support it with Sylvia's photograph and biography. 'And Summer Will Not Come Again' is a story of a teenager's unrequited love and her boyfriend's unfaithfulness (based on John Hodges). It is significant that for this story Plath drew inspiration from a poem by Sara Teasdale, who, by strange coincidence, had committed suicide at the time of Sylvia's birth.

In April she surprised herself by auditioning successfully for the leading female role of Lady Lasenby in the school's senior production of J.M. Barrie's *The Admirable Crichton*. The play was enthusiastically received. Sylvia ended the spring of 1950 in high spirits.

At the end of the senior year at Bradford High, there were 158

82

graduates. Sylvia received straight 'A's and was first in class. Under her schoolbook portrait her character sketch reads:

> Warm smile. Energetic worker. Co-editor of *Bradford Magazine*. Boogie pianist. Sociable and Socialist. Future writer. Those rejection slips from *Seventeen*. Acceptance. Oh for a licence.

Now, in the summer of 1950, Sylvia has to confront the problem of earning enough money to cover her personal expenses at Smith. The lower paid temporary jobs, such as waitress or shop assistant, simply would not pay enough. Sylvia opted for a $25 a week job as a field hand at Lookout Farm, Natick, about five miles from home. The work was exhausting and, when she returned each night, Sylvia would eat and then collapse into bed. It was not all work though. Working in the fields, she often found herself talking to Ilo, a big, muscular, blond Russian. He was studying for an Art degree and they talked of Raphael, Picasso and Michelangelo. Ilo gave Sylvia a present of one of his sketches of the farm. Sylvia's own interest in drawing was re-awakened. One afternoon, in late summer, they were unable to work in the fields due to torrential rain. Ilo lived on the farm, in a small space in the loft above the main barn. He invited Sylvia to view a drawing he had just completed. Once in the tiny room, Sylvia took only a few moments to view the sketch. As she turned to leave, Ilo closed the door, switched on some loud music and the real motive of his invitation became clear. He forced himself upon Sylvia, squeezed her body tight to his and French kissed her fiercely. Sylvia was startled; with great difficulty she struggled free from his grasp and left.

Sylvia may have escaped Ilo, but she could not escape the wider issue of sex. Two days later she was dating a boy named Emile and her diary reads: 'I dressed slowly, smoothing, perfuming, powdering. This is I, I thought, the American virgin dressed to seduce. I know I'm in for an evening of sexual pleasure. We go on dates, we play around, and if we're nice girls, we demur at a certain point. And so it goes.' She dances and kisses all night with Emile and when he leaves she tells her diary: 'He kissed me goodnight, I know that something in me wanted him, for what I'm not sure.'

With the publication of 'And Summer Will Not Come Again', she acquires a rather different type of male friend. Ed Cohen reads the story in *Seventeen* and is so impressed that he seeks out Sylvia's address and writes the first letter of what is to become a lifetime of intimate correspondence between these two equally sensitive people.

September 1950 sees Sylvia Plath commence her college education at Smith. She would study English and Art, her two favourite subjects, plus French Literature, European History and Botany. All Smith students were required to take Physical Education. As a scholarship student, Sylvia would have to maintain a mean average of B+, otherwise she would lose her financial aid; this put a great deal of stress upon Sylvia to work very hard. Discipline at Smith was strict; students had to check in and out of campus; curfews of 10 p.m. weekdays and 12 p.m. or 1 a.m. at weekends had to be observed, dinner was formal each night, with dress to be 'appropriate attire'. All students were required to adhere to strict social standards.

Most of the first year students at Smith dated regularly with boys from Harvard and Yale, but when visiting the girls, the young men were not allowed beyond the common areas of the colleges and certainly were banned from staying overnight.

Sylvia dated very little during her first year, feeling under pressure to study hard. She did, however, keep up a very flirtatious correspondence with Eddie Cohen. Eddie made most of the running, making it clear that he was keen on Sylvia and that he planned to visit her soon. For her part, Sylvia was very responsive. She did, however, make it clear to Eddie that she would not follow the path of other Smith students. They were just filling in time and assumed that they would conform to the norm of getting married when they left college. That was the way life was, Sylvia said, but she would not get married so quickly, she did not want to be dismissed so easily.

In November, Mary Mensel, Director of Scholarships, revealed to her that her scholarship sponsor was the best-selling author Olive Higgins Prouty. Sylvia immediately wrote to Prouty to thank her. The letter was enthusiastic and grateful. In it she described her first impressions of Smith. She also told of her ambitions for a career in writing and discussed her main current influences, Sinclair Lewis, Sara Teasdale and Virginia Woolf. In closing she said: 'I just want you to understand that you are responsible, in a sense, for the formation of an individual, and I am fortunate enough to be that person.' Prouty was impressed and told Sylvia: 'There is no doubt that you possess a gift for creative writing.' She invited Sylvia to visit her during the Christmas half-term. Sylvia did visit, for tea, and each made a deep impression upon the other. Prouty told Plath that an author could find all the characters they would ever need to write about from within themselves, their family and their friends. This advice came to influence Sylvia for the rest of her life. Equally, Sylvia made a strong impact on Olive Higgins Prouty, who detected deep emotions within her. Prouty was to remain a sponsor, supporter and sometimes crutch to her for the remainder of Sylvia's life.

In January Sylvia returned to Smith. She was surprised to learn that her friend, Ann Davidow, had dropped out, having not returned from holidaying at home in Chicago. Sylvia recalled a conversation with Ann before Christmas in which Ann had said she did not feel she could succeed at Smith and that she was seriously contemplating suicide. Sylvia wrote to Eddie Cohen and asked him to visit Ann in Chicago. Eddie replied that he would look Ann up 'provided that she has not stuck her head in an oven'. In fact Ann Davidow did not commit suicide and Sylvia continued to correspond and confide in her for the next dozen years. Strangely, Eddie Cohen's words were to return to Sylvia in the last hours of her life.

Sylvia took her first semester exams and the results were good: all 'A's except, disappointingly, B+ in English. *Seventeen* published more of her writing that term, including 'Den of Lions', based on her affair with Emile. That semester, Sylvia discovered fully the power of her attraction for young men. Several of her peers fell in love with the tall, sensual, vivacious, intelligent, artistic young Sylvia. Principal among many was Dick Norton. Sylvia had known him for some years, as they had been neighbours in Wellesley. Dick was a science student in his last year at Yale; he would soon be moving on to Harvard Medical School. In January 1951 he invited Sylvia to visit him at Yale. Tall, blond and good-looking, he made a strong impression on Sylvia. She stayed so long that she missed the last train back. She arrived back at Smith so late that she was confined to campus for seven days. Later Dick invited her to a Yale prom, where they danced close together until dawn. The relationship was to continue until December 1952, and it was a lovers' relationship, although Sylvia retained her virginity. Marriage was discussed and there is no doubt that Sylvia had fallen in love with Dick. But the autumn of 1952 brought two shocks for her: Dick admitted to her that he had been having a sexual affair with a waitress, and he also told Sylvia that he had been diagnosed with TB, so he would have to go to a New York sanatorium for lengthy convalescence.

Sylvia was badly shaken. Dick had seemed to her like a young god. Sylvia did visit him at Christmas time, but she could no longer bear to be touched by him and she broke off the affair. She stayed on for a further few days, as a guest of Dick's friends, the Lynns, but she was to experience another type of break. She went to the nearby Pisgah mountain slopes and tried skiing for the first time. Using the advanced skier slopes, she came rushing down and crashed into a bank of ice and snow. Result – a fractured fibula to her left leg. Despite detailing almost every incident of her mature life in letters and diaries, Sylvia never revealed why she took to the advanced slopes that day. Could it have been another self-harm or even suicidal attempt?

Returning to Smith College at the end of December, her leg was encased in plaster. She found it very difficult to move around, particularly from floor to floor, and when bathing. Her social life, especially dating, was very restricted. She did date, however. Eddie Cohen had made a special trip to meet her for the first time, with all the anticipation of the closeness between them that their many letters had promised. It was a minor disaster. Eddie just was not Sylvia's physical type. He was shorter than her and his looks were plain. Sylvia, conscious of being 5' 9", could only be attracted by tall men and they had to be handsome and strong too. Eddie failed the tests and returned home disillusioned. But they still wrote frequently to each other. As early as January, Sylvia was writing at such length to Eddie about her 'severe depression' that he felt deeply concerned and advised her, in the most friendly and helpful way, to obtain psychiatric help.

The plaster was to remain on for two months. Initially her depression was deep, but it was interspersed with bright spells. The administrative board at Smith granted her permission to substitute poetry studies for some of her hated compulsory science studies. She now found another very suitable boyfriend, Myron Lotz, a Yale student, also a professional baseball player. A handsome giant, he was much to Sylvia's taste and she even contemplated marriage. But not sex. For several years she had fought her sexual urges;

86

often she had fantasised having violent sex in a rape context, but still she retained her virginity.

Another boy Sylvia dated, and was seriously attracted to, was Gordon Lameyer. A senior student at Amherst College, he was another neighbour from Wellesley. Tall, slim, handsome, steeped in knowledge of English literature, he was to survive much longer than most of Sylvia's admirers. Certainly longer than Myron Lotz, with whom she all too rapidly became disillusioned.

By the end of February, the leg was healed and Sylvia entered an upbeat period. The results of her second year finals came through – straight 'A's, including the dreaded Science. In April came a letter from *Mademoiselle* magazine that Sylvia had been praying for: 'Happy to announce you have won a *Mademoiselle* 1953 Guest Editorship from June 1st through June 26th'. Plath's only real worry now was about money. She would have to earn enough over the summer holidays to carry her through her final year at Smith. The $150 *Mademoiselle* would pay would barely scratch the surface of her needs. Further, she had applied for a place on Frank O'Connor's fiction writing course, to begin in July, at Harvard summer school. She simply would have to earn the money she needed from her writing; a story she intended to write in Frank O'Connor's class would, she hoped, provide the bulk of it.

In fact her assignment with *Mademoiselle* was to start earlier than she anticipated. In May, the magazine required her to write an article on young American poets and to interview writer Elizabeth Bowen. A hectic month for Sylvia included her 1953 finals at Smith, the results of which included 'A's in Creative Writing and in Modern Poetry, a first in class and two 'open' prizes for poetry.

On 1 June she arrived in Manhattan for the 26-day editorship with *Mademoiselle*, which was to be a catalyst in her life. She tells the story of her experiences in her only major novel *The Bell Jar*. There were 20 guest editors, 17 of whom were to be accommodated in the Barbizon, a women-only hotel, for the next four weeks. They had much in common: students from the best universities and colleges in the USA, bright, motivated and enterprising. Yet, as Sylvia got to know them throughout that month, she found that she was different to all of them in two ways: first, they were able to express their emotions publicly (Sylvia had always kept hers for the written page); second, they did not feel the same pressure to succeed academically that Sylvia always felt burdened with.

Assigned to assist the Managing Editor, Sylvia's main tasks were to write critiques on famous authors, a feature on rising poets, editorial on the August issue and writing rejection letters. There were fashion shows, promotional launches and functions, film and theatre premieres, art exhibitions, cocktail parties and dances. As guest editor, Sylvia was wholly involved. Long before the end of the month, she was totally exhausted. Her physical exhaustion was compounded by mental stress. Two spies, Julius and Ethel Rosenberg, were due to be executed by electrocution on 19 June and for some reason, never explained, Sylvia had given an inordinate amount of thought to the event and had become excessively concerned about what she thought to be a wicked way to deal with human beings, whatever their guilt.

She was also stressed out with worrying what the outcome was to be of her application for Frank O'Connor's Harvard summer school class in creative writing; inwardly she felt confident of acceptance, but she tried to offset this in her letters and conversations by expressing doubts that her résumé would be good enough. During her final week she writes to her brother Warren; she is dating the most brilliant, wonderful man in the world, the simultaneous interpreter Gary Karmirloff. Tragically he is two inches shorter than Sylvia so for her the relationship cannot work, but she says she will spend the rest of her life seeking his second self. She and the other guest editors have been very ill with food poisoning from crabmeat served at one of the promotional luncheons and the aftermath is that she is lethargic.

It is a weary Sylvia who is met at Wellesley Station by her mother and grandmother. On the way home her mother tries gently to break the bombshell news that she will not be going to Frank O'Connor's creative writing summer school. 'The course is full, you will have to re-apply next year,' Aurelia told her. Sylvia knew the truth; she had been rejected. No reason was given, and to this day it is difficult to understand the decision, given Sylvia's achievements at the time.

Exhausted, depressed and disillusioned, Sylvia found herself unable to read or write and could not make any progress with her end of year thesis (on James Joyce). For a short while she disguised her depression, especially to Gordon Lameyer, with whom she spent most of her time and to whom she would always be the 'carefree, golden girl'. But with Gordon's departure in mid-July, to join the navy, she plunged into a steep downward spiral. Her true moods are revealed in her diaries. She says she is 'plunged deep in her own private whirlpool of negativism' and retreating 'into a masochistic mental hell where jealousy and fear make you want to stop eating'. She cannot sleep and does not want to cope. She has visions of killing her mother and herself. On the last day of July, Aurelia notices unhealed scars on Sylvia's legs. Sylvia tells her she wanted to see if she had the willpower to commit suicide. Sylvia breaks into hysterics, 'Oh, Mother, the world is so rotten. I want to die. Let's die together!'

Following this outburst, Aurelia arranges for Sylvia to consult a psychiatrist, Dr Peter Thornton. On 27 July, after three sessions with Sylvia, Dr Thornton formed his diagnosis. Sylvia was suffering from extreme emotional depression and would require immediate treatment by electroconvulsion therapy (ECT). Dr Thornton's view was that without this treatment Sylvia would suffer a total nervous breakdown. Aurelia was not inclined to seek a second opinion, particularly in view of financial considerations. Sylvia was enrolled for a course of ECT at Valley Head Hospital. Her first treatment was on 29 July. Metal probes were fixed to her head and massive electric shocks were shot through her body. No anaesthetic was given and the result was that she came close to being electrocuted. The sessions continued, with at least eight treatments being given over the next three weeks. Sylvia indirectly gives some description of the treatments and their impact on her in *The Bell Jar* and in a short story, written shortly afterwards, 'Tongues of Stone'. Despite these insights from Plath, it is difficult to assess the damage these electric shocks did to Sylvia's psyche. Certainly her two serious attempts at suicide came after these shock treatments. We do, of course, have for comparison purposes the ECT treatments that Hemingway suffered and the effects which it had upon this great author. Olive Higgins Prouty was in no doubt that they were the direct cause of Plath's first serious suicide attempt.

One clear side-effect of the electric shocks was to develop Sylvia's usual pattern of restless sleep into complete insomnia. She had been taking sleeping pills for some time and had become addicted, but now she became immune to them. Aurelia was worried about them and kept them locked in a metal box. On 22 August Sylvia made another half-hearted attempt at suicide. She swam far out into the Atlantic Ocean with the intention of drowning herself; but her willpower was insufficient and could not force her body to comply with the deadly wishes of her mind.

By 24 August Sylvia had reached an all-time low. The academic year had exhausted her; New York and *Mademoiselle* had disillusioned her; O'Connor's rejection was degrading; the electric shock treatments had disturbed her mind. Whilst her mother was out, she bust open the box with the sleeping pills. She left a note for Aurelia saying that she had gone for a long walk to clear her mind and would not be back until the next day. Sylvia then went to the cellar, taking only some water, the pills and a blanket. In the cellar she crawled into a small space under the front porch and pulled over a pile of firewood to cover the entrance. She then began slowly to take the pills; she had taken 40 before she passed out.

Returning home, Aurelia found the note and spent the next few hours phoning around friends, trying to trace Sylvia and fearing the worst. Eventually she phoned the police, who searched the house from top to bottom with no result. That evening Aurelia and Warren searched Boston for Sylvia, but without success. The next day the police mounted a full-scale search of the Wellesley area, again fruitlessly. The newspapers nationwide now began to publicise the mystery of the missing Miss Sylvia Plath; describing her as the beautiful, top-ranking Smith student. It was not until the evening of 25 August that Aurelia checked the tablet box and found it broken. This seems strange, since it is clear that Aurelia suspected the possibility of suicide within a couple of hours of finding Sylvia's note. In any event, the discovery did nothing to assist matters.

On Wednesday 26 August, Sylvia's grandmother went down to the cellar to do the laundry. Whilst there, she heard a groan from behind the firewood stack. She called for Warren, who immediately took the wood bundle apart. There they found Sylvia, semi-comatose and covered with her own dried vomit. In that vomit lay about half the pills that she had taken. There is little doubt that being able to take so many pills before she passed out had saved Sylvia's life. Her stomach rejected such a large quantity and sicked some back up. As Warren sought to raise Sylvia from her bolt-hole, she struck her face on the concrete cladding; ironically this injury was to cause her far more problems than the overdose.

She was removed to Newton-Wellesley Hospital and placed in

the care of Dr Francesca Racioppi. She regained consciousness and stabilised, but the cut to her face became acutely septic and had to be treated with maximum dosages of penicillin. It was made clear to Aurelia that Sylvia required expert psychiatric treatment and that a suitable consultant should be called in. The problem for Aurelia lay in the cost; she simply did not have the money. Fortunately this problem was solved by Olive Higgins Prouty. Prouty and her husband had both had nervous breakdowns and she felt great sympathy for her protégé. She immediately offered to pay Sylvia's medical bills and also engaged her own psychiatrist, Donald McPherson, to consult on the case. Obviously Aurelia had to accept Prouty's offer, but Aurelia was a proud woman and decided that Dr Erich Lindemann, Senior Psychiatric Consultant at Massachusetts General Hospital, should be called in. He declared that Sylvia should be transferred to the Massachusetts General psychiatric facility and this was done on 3 September.

On 9 September Lindemann met with Olive Higgins Prouty and stated there was no permanent mental damage but Sylvia had suffered a nervous breakdown, due to stress, and should make a full recovery. On 12 September Prouty called in Dr McPherson to give a second opinion. He wrote to Prouty, indicating a temporary schizophrenia: 'This is not at all a hopeless situation as many recover completely with or without treatment. The time factor is unpredictable. Insulin and shock treatment are often indicated and seem to be of real value in this kind of trouble.' Lindemann and McPherson concurred that Plath should be moved to a private sanatorium and suggested McLean Hospital, part of the Massachusetts General complex.

Prouty was most unhappy. She was certain electroshock therapy had been a major contributor to Sylvia's problems. Further, she wanted Sylvia to go to Silver Hill, a country club type institution where Prouty herself had received treatment and where Sylvia's bills would be met from a trust fund to which Prouty was a contributor. Understandable, since Prouty had assumed responsibilities which Aurelia could not meet. But Aurelia still wished to make decisions and agreed with Lindemann that Sylvia would go to McLean. This decision had some very mixed results.

Sylvia remained at McLean until mid-January 1954. She quickly deteriorated. She became lethargic and bored, frequently complaining that she had nothing to do. Sylvia also complained that she was suffering premenstrual problems. Initially she was given insulin injections. Later she was treated with the drug chlorpromazine as a sedative. The most common side-effect of this drug is lethargy. Another side-effect is irregularity of periods. It is therefore almost impossible to understand why it was administered to Sylvia in her condition. Her moods had no integration; they swung between severe depression and wildly manic. She lost her ability to communicate. Her old tutor, Wilbury Crockett, visited her several times in October; he said she had 'lost touch with words'. Indeed it was mainly with his help that she recovered her literate skills by the end of November.

On the plus side, Sylvia's psychiatrist at McLean was Ruth Barnhouse. Dr Barnhouse was 28; she had eloped and married at 18, had two children, divorced and married an eminent doctor. Although from the Tiffany (jewellery) family, an Ivy League woman from Columbia, she had lived a life far removed from that of her peers. She was able to relate to Sylvia and Sylvia felt she had at last found a doctor she could trust. Ruth Barnhouse would remain a trusted advisor for the rest of Sylvia's life.

Barnhouse engaged in daily psychotherapy sessions with Plath. Early on, Barnhouse identified one of the problems causing Plath's abnormal behaviour. Sylvia was suffering from severe sexual frustration. She was a physically attractive young woman who attracted much attention from young men and she had strong desires to have sexual intercourse in every conceivable way. That she had not fulfilled them, and remained a virgin, was in part due to what she perceived as the moral code of her era and in part due to confusion in her mind about the role of sex in human life. For the past three or four years she had lived with the stress of arousal and unfulfilled sexual tension. Ruth Barnhouse encouraged her to liberate her sexual desires and actually told her to experiment with sex at her earliest opportunity. That Plath had confidence in Barnhouse may be illustrated by the speed with which she took that advice.

Allowed visits home for Christmas and New Year, Sylvia renewed her friendship with Philip McCurdy. They went dancing at a local club on two occasions and each time when Philip drove Sylvia home they had sexual intercourse in his car. Sylvia's virginity was gone and with it all her psychological fears of the act and its aftermath. She then decided that there would be no more sex with

Philip; they would continue as 'just good friends'. If ever a man was used!

It may be that this act finally banished Sylvia's depression. Certainly Sylvia showed dramatic improvement during the first two weeks of January. Barnhouse put this down, in large part, to electric shock treatments, which Barnhouse had initiated, as a last resort, a week before Christmas. She had only three treatments but it is true that Sylvia showed a marked and rapid improvement in the week before her home visits. Barnhouse felt that Sylvia had a guilt complex, which created a desire to be punished and that, having received her electrotherapy 'punishment', the guilt blockage had been removed. My own view is that Sylvia was so terrified by the re-introduction of the treatments that they literally shocked her out of her lethargy and depression. No doubt it was the combination of three events at the same time, electroshocks, release to visit home, and sexual emancipation, that created the breakthrough. At any event, Sylvia improved so quickly that she was released by McLean in mid-January to go home and to continue as a special student at Smith College.

Returning to Smith on 1 February 1954, Sylvia met with a great deal of sympathy and was given a lightened work schedule. She would, however, have to attend the college psychiatrist once a week. The winter and spring passed relatively uneventfully. She did accept an invitation to visit Ilo in New York, which seems strange considering her harvest picking experience with him. Anyway, this ended badly, with Sylvia leaving abruptly for home when he again tried to press his physical attentions upon her.

By spring she had taken up writing poetry again for the first time in a year. Her poetry began to be published again. Much of it was in the Smith Review, but, significantly, *Harpers Bazaar* published 'Doomsday'.

May 1954 was an eventful month for Sylvia. She received a scholarship from Smith sufficient to cover her expenses for the next year. She had met Scott Campbell, Assistant Director at Harvard summer school, at a dance in March; he encouraged her to apply again for a scholarship. In May she received news that this had been awarded. Her end of term grades were announced: straight 'A's in American Fiction, European History and Russian Literature. In April and May she dated with Richard Sassoon (relative of Siegfried) and his college room-mate Melvin Woody at the same time, whilst exchanging many letters and discussing marriage with Gordon Lameyer, with whom she said she was in love. Truly the golden girl was back with a bang.

At the Harvard summer school, Sylvia took courses in The Nineteenth-Century Novel and in German. She had for companionship her friend Nancy Hunter. Both girls had boyfriends, in Sylvia's case Gordon Lameyer, but they agreed together that they would date other men that term.

Nancy was the first to score. Her date was Edwin, a Harvard research professor. The date was dinner at this flat and afterwards he made strong attempts to have sex with her; in Nancy's version chasing her all around the flat. She escaped and would have nothing more to do with him, although he telephoned several times. Sylvia fielded those phone calls and, when Edwin asked her out, she said yes. They quickly became involved to the extent that Sylvia had the key to Edwin's flat. However, their first experience of intercourse together ended in disaster, with Sylvia suffering a vaginal tear, which required hospitalisation to stem the bleeding. Sylvia said that Edwin raped her; in the light of her own experiences, Nancy believed her. The significant fact is that although Sylvia blamed Edwin for the incident, she went back to dating with him within a few days. We can only conclude that she was drawn towards men who would abuse her. As Sylvia Plath's story unfolds, we shall see whether our conclusions are justified.

As the Harvard summer school ended, she was again dating Gordon. They were intimate sexually in August and September, but never after that, although they remained friends and in communication for most of Sylvia's remaining life. She also spent time with a Hans, a young married professor from Harvard.

Her final year at Smith began in October. Like all final graduation years it was tremendously eventful; yet for Sylvia it unfolded with a familiar pattern.

There were lovers: she was still in love with Gordon Lameyer, she always would be in a way for the rest of her life; but for now she threw him over for Richard Sassoon, with whom she had a torrid affair, three times visiting New York for passionate liaisons with him. That she was drawn to Sassoon is intriguing, for he was the first of the two men who were to treat her with physical and emotional brutality. Sylvia says that Sassoon slapped her around, and from their letters it is clear that he spanked her and that he threatened to beat her. Ultimately he would abuse her by deserting her in Paris at a time so critical in her life that she would be left emotionally fragile. There were of course other boyfriends that year, including Philip McCurdy (back on the scene) and Peter Davison, a young editor son of a poet.

There was academic work. She would take classes in Shakespeare, German and the Twentieth-Century American Novel. As the year unfolded and work pressure tired her, she would drop German. Later in her life she would be tormented by thoughts that the one subject she had dropped was her 'colossal' father's favourite. For her thesis she would study Dostoevsky; she would concentrate on *The Brothers Karamazov* and the short novel *The Double*. The thesis would be entitled 'The Magic Mirror. A Study of the Double in Two of Dostoevsky's Novels'. She would also have to concentrate on applications for scholarships, for she was determined to continue her studies after graduation. Long talks with her old tutor and friend Wilbury Crockett had determined her to apply for Fulbright scholarships to Oxford and Cambridge Universities. A Fulbright scholarship would pay all travel, accommodation and living expenses. As a fallback she would also apply for a Woodrow Wilson fellowship at Harvard. These applications do show that within only 12 months of being suicidal, Sylvia Plath's mind had returned to full confidence in her ability to achieve the highest academic honours.

Then there was the poetry and the short stories. She was back writing voluminously. *Harper's* published 'Go Get the Goodly Squab', *Mademoiselle* featured her poem 'Parallex', an early indication of her preoccupation with her periods and of her belief that the most ordinary human events are influenced by nature. They also commissioned a review of 'The Mid-Century Novel'. Further they paid her for the poem 'Two Lovers and a Beachcomber by the Real Sea'. Her beautiful poem 'April Aubade' appeared in *The Christian Science Monitor* and *The Atlantic Monthly* printed 'Circus in Three Rings'. Naturally, *The Smith Review* supported her, commissioning an article on Alfred Kazin (author of *A Walker in the City* and *On Native Grounds*). They published her short story 'In the Mountains' but it received little acclaim. It is really just a description of her feelings when she visited Dick Norton at his tuberculosis sanatorium in December 1952, at the time when she ended their affair. *The Smith Review* also featured her short story 'Superman and Paula Brown's New Snowsuit'. The 'Superman' story is another incident from Plath's life. She is about ten years old when she is accused, and found guilty, of a nasty act, which she did not commit. It marks the change in Sylvia from a child, who has fantasy dreams about life, into a youth who, for the first time, understands what real life is like.

In January she is interviewed for her Woodrow Wilson fellowship. She is not accepted. Her access door to a top American university is now closed. Her remaining chance rests upon her first choice, Cambridge University. Supported by letters from authors Mary Ellen Chase and Elizabeth Drew, and the all-important one from Dr Ruth Barnhouse concerning her mental stability, Plath's application goes forward.

As May 1955 ends, Plath's life at Smith College is drawing to a close. Now all the great news comes in a rush. She is accepted by Cambridge. A Fulbright scholarship, which will pay for everything, is awarded. She obtains her degree: First-Class Honours. All her enthusiasm for life, so dominant in her early years, has returned. Less than two years previously, she had been at death's door. Little over a year ago she had been in a mental institution where desperate measures were being used to try to break through her depression. Sylvia Plath has made a fairytale comeback. But as we review the final seven years, we shall find that the remainder of her life was far from a fairytale.

She would not depart for Cambridge until September. July and August were to be months of leisure and recuperation. She dated and slept with Peter Davison several times and with Richard Sassoon. She went out with Gordon Lameyer and dated with Hans Kohn, the Harvard professor she had met in summer 1954.

On 14 September she packed her bags and her beloved bicycle and set sail on the *Queen Elizabeth II* for her voyage to England. First things first; she immediately struck up a friendship with a young man called Carl Shakin. Just as quickly, this turned into a shipboard affair. After they landed in London, on 20 September, they stayed together for a few days, but on 25 September Sylvia more or less dropped Carl and, until the 30th, she dated Bruce Cantor, an ex of her friend Sue Weller. On 1 October she left for Newnham College, Cambridge to begin the Michaelmas term.

Arriving in Cambridge, she found to her delight that the ratio of men to women was ten to one. Certain that her social life was assured, she moved to considering what lectures she would attend

CONYNGHAM, ANNETTE COLLEEN

Expires: 10 Nov 2019

RYDE

Reserved Item

Branch: Ryde
Date: 24 Oct 2019   Time: 8:59 AM

Item: Silence in the mind
      3483420

Expires: 10 Nov 2019

and what degree she would take. She settled upon Seventeenth-Century Poets, History of Literary Criticism and English Moralists. The PhD course required too much detailed study, she thought, so she would take a BA programme. Her dating programme started immediately. Mallory Wober, a tall, well built Indian; Nat La Mar, a published writer and friend of her brother Warren; David Buck, a young Christ College English student; and John Lythgoe, a biology student, were the main men. Richard Sassoon was studying in France, but paid a visit. Sylvia realised the only man she wanted was Sassoon. She agreed to visit him in Paris.

Arriving at Christmas time she saw all of the Parisian highlights with him and they then went touring. Through the French Alps, on to Nice and Monte Carlo, then into Italy to San Remo. Sylvia was happy; she had now found a dominant lover with whom she felt she could spend the rest of her life. They arrived back in Paris on 8 January. Sylvia now had to return to Cambridge. Imagine how devastated she was when Richard told her he intended to see other women whilst she was away. Indeed he confessed he was already in a serious relationship with another girl.

Back at Cambridge, Sylvia was depressed and unhappy but, with her second term starting, she turned her thoughts to the coming challenges of academic work and creative writing. Two thoughts would not go away: she would never become an important writer, so perhaps fate intended her to marry, have children and keep home and write in her spare time.

Sylvia's depression deepened during February, peaking during the last week when she received poor reviews of her poems, which had been published in the university magazine, *Chequers*. By chance, that week a group of current and ex-Cambridge writers and poets had decided to produce a rival magazine, *St Botoloph's Review*. To launch it they were holding a jazz party at the Women's Union. Sylvia decided to attend, recognising that she needed some stimulus to lift her depression. That night she had a dinner date with Nat La Mar, but she also accepted a date with Hamish Stewart, who would take her to the party afterwards.

As soon as she arrived at the party, Sylvia left Hamish. She wanted to be introduced to Ted Hughes, whose poem 'Falgrief's Girlfriends' in the *St Botolph's Review* had deeply impressed her. The moment she saw him she knew this was a man she wanted. Tall, at 6' 1", dark, broad-shouldered, handsome. Exactly her physical type; 'huge', she called him. They danced, they kissed, he was rough, he tore her hairband from her head and ripped out her earrings, she bit his neck so fiercely that he bled. Thus began the torrid romance of two of the twentieth-century's greatest poets.

It did not immediately develop intensely. Hughes was interested, indeed he paid a couple of drunken visits to her college without finding her there. However, Sylvia wanted to find out more about him before going further. Her friends told her he was 26, born and bred in Yorkshire. His father was originally a carpenter, later a small shopkeeper. Ted had fulfilled national service in the RAF and then went to Cambridge, where he graduated from Pembroke College in 1954 with a 2:1 in English. Afterwards he worked for short periods at various manual jobs, but was now a script reader for London film company J. Arthur Rank. He appeared to have few clothes and little money. Although living in London, he returned constantly to Cambridge. He was a leading light amongst a group of poetically inclined young men, mainly homosexuals. Ted was described as a serial seducer.

At this time Sylvia still felt that she was in love with Richard Sassoon. She was still dating Hamish and writing affectionate letters to Gordon Lameyer. In March Gordon invited her to Paris. Sylvia accepted and, at the same time, arranged to visit Richard Sassoon at his apartment in rue du Vivier. Hughes' best friend, Luke Myers, invited Sylvia to visit him and Hughes in London while *en route* to Paris. On 25 March Sylvia met Ted at the tiny Bloomsbury flat. They immediately set to lovemaking, which lasted until daybreak on the 26th. It was physically violent; Sylvia records that her face was battered and bruised and her neck was raw and wounded. Weary as she was, nevertheless Sylvia travelled to Paris the next day with only one man in her thoughts, Richard Sassoon. Arriving late, she booked one night at a small hotel. Next morning she went to Richard's flat. He was not there. The concierge told her he had gone away and would not return for a month. Obviously Richard did not want her. We should note this was the first time such a thing had happened to Sylvia. She wept bitterly for a while. Pulling herself together, she decided off with the old and on with the new. She spent the next seven days and nights enjoying all of Paris with three different men: Tony Gary, whom she had met in England when queuing for the French ferry, Giovanni, an Italian journalist she had encountered at the hotel on her first night in Paris, and

Gary Haupt, a friend from Cambridge University. Sex was on the menu, but little was consumed. For example, Sylvia and Tony were naked in bed, exploring each other's bodies, but Tony took fright, dressed and left.

Gordon arrived on 5 April and they left together for Munich the next day. From Munich to Venice and Rome. Already the relationship had broken down, being ruptured by several quarrels. In Rome they went their own ways, Sylvia being escorted by a friend of Gordon's, an Oxford student, Donald Cheney. On the 13th, Gordon took Sylvia to the airport, bought her a ticket and said goodbye in a manner that clearly indicated that their affair was over. Apart from two occasions at social gatherings, Sylvia never saw Gordon again.

Arriving in London, Sylvia rushed straight to Ted's flat. They went to bed immediately and spent the whole of the night and the next morning in sexual intercourse. In early April Ted went to Cambridge to spend more time with Sylvia. He stayed in her room at Whitstead. The affair was now full blown. This did not change Ted's ways; he continued to join his friends in wild drinking parties. Sylvia did not attend, but it is fair to say she was not much of a drinker anyway. Sylvia described Ted as arrogant and violent, with a booming voice and as 'a breaker of people'. Nevertheless, having lost Gordon and Richard, both of whom she had loved and discussed marriage with, Sylvia was now very vulnerable. Ted fitted her ideal of physical and intellectual type. Those ways that she did not like, she felt she could change. She reasoned that he was rebelling against the restrictions of his early village life and that if he lived in America its vastness and freedom would have a dramatic effect on him. They soon began to talk of marriage.

Aurelia was not so happy. A penniless poet from a working-class English family was not what she had in mind for her golden girl for whom she had made so many sacrifices. Olive Higgins Prouty was even less happy, actually fearful. She wrote to Sylvia: 'You don't really believe, do you, that the characteristics which you describe as bashing people around, unkindness and cruelty, can be permanently changed in a man of 26? Your own experiences with several men with whom you thought you were in love are warnings, don't you think?'

In fact, she did not. Sylvia and Ted had made their minds up to get married as quickly as possible. Aurelia planned a visit to

London in June to meet Ted. Acting on impulse, Sylvia Plath and Edward James Hughes obtained a licence and were married on 16 June 1956, enabling Aurelia to attend the ceremony. They were married at the Church of St George the Martyr in Queen Square, Bloomsbury; very close to the long-time residence of her archetypal literary heroine Virginia Woolf. The only other person attending was their witness, the church sexton. Ted had not bothered to tell his parents or his relatives. Indeed he was so casual about the event that he turned up in the old, black, corduroy jacket he wore every day.

The whole of the summer was spent on honeymoon, although, with little money, they had to live frugally. The remainder of June and July and most of August were spent in a quaint, unspoiled fishing village in Spain. It has changed a great deal since 1956; readers know it as Benidorm. Most of their time was spent walking and writing together. Their main topics of recreational conversation were the occult and black magic, which subjects Ted had studied in depth. In the last week of August, they went to Paris for two weeks. Already substantial cracks in the relationship were beginning to appear. The everyday detail of the honeymoon in Sylvia's diaries is at times too much and becomes mundane. But it does seem that she was near blameless in the early change in the tide of their relationship. Ted's sudden black moods, his gross untidiness and his unclean habits were all in direct contrast to Sylvia's way of life. They led to quarrels and raised barriers between them. She had been warned; but, incessantly interested in her own inner life, she appears to have been incurious about his. In early September they returned to England and, having no money, stayed with Ted's parents in Heptonstall, Yorkshire until the new Cambridge year began.

In October, with Sylvia's final year underway, they moved into a small flat in Eltisley Avenue, Cambridge. In November she applied for a post to teach English at Smith College from September 1957. She was fully determined that they would live and work in the USA once she had her Cambridge degree. In addition to studying for her finals, Sylvia spent a great deal of her time typing Ted's poetry and forwarding it to magazines. This left her little time for her own writing, but 1957 began with several pieces of her work being published. *The Atlantic Monthly* prints 'Pursuit', her poem about a panther. Plath feels the panther stalking her down. She tries in every way to stop him but he keeps pace with her every movement and closes upon her. She will be one of the many women he has ravaged and he will cause her death. Most reviewers believe the panther referred to is Ted Hughes.

Poetry Magazine publishes a small portfolio of her poems, including 'Channel Crossing' and 'Verbal Calisthenics'. Granta publishes her short story 'The Wishing Box' to a wide readership. This story concerns a woman's jealousy of her husband's creative mind. More shades of Ted Hughes perhaps. Her efforts on Ted's behalf paid a jackpot dividend at the end of February when The Poetry Center in New York judged his volume of poems *Hawk in the Rain* winner of a national contest. They were both overjoyed for they felt that this was the breakthrough that would lead to recognition of Hughes as one of the great poets of his era. As we now know, their instincts were correct.

In March, Smith College approved Plath's application to teach English from autumn 1957 at a salary of $4,200 per annum. Sylvia immediately accepted. The first quarter of 1957 had started exceptionally well for Sylvia. Now she had to study strenuously for her final exams. For the first time in her life she was behind in her academic studies. She sat her exams in May and, when the results were announced, she had achieved a 2:1. That result may seem very acceptable, but we should view it against Sylvia's previous exceptionally high academic record, which suggests she should have obtained a First Class Honours. Was the difference between the two degrees the result of the time and attention she gave to Ted Hughes? Were spaces in her mind, where learned facts should have been stored, taken up by fantasies from the many evening hours spent at the Ouija board with Hughes?

Sylvia was homesick and, soon after receiving her degree, she and Ted set sail for New York. At the end of June, Aurelia arranged a reception party for them at her Wellesley home. About 70 guests attended. They were mostly wealthy upper middle-class professionals. The antithesis of Ted, but people Sylvia had known and been close to all her life. Among the guests were Gordon Lameyer, Philip McCurdy, Bruce Cantor and Peter Davison; all ex-lovers of Sylvia. This may be an appropriate moment for us to pause and ask ourselves why did Sylvia choose to marry someone from such a different background from her own? Was it purely physical lust or perhaps because poets are irresistibly drawn to each other?

After the reception, the couple left for a holiday at Eastham, Cape Cod, where Aurelia had rented a cottage for two months as a wedding present for them. They decided the holiday would be a combination of writing and keep fit. In the mornings they would write and in the late afternoon they would cycle and swim. Ted, encouraged by the publication of *Hawk in the Rain*, worked hard on a second volume of poems. Sylvia, however, was having problems. Certainly she tried to write. But she had not written any poetry for several months. She had tried to work on a novel, but it simply would not come together. She composed one new short story, 'The Troublemaking Mother', in which she reveals something close to hatred for her mother, and a long poem, over 500 rhymed lines of dialogue between a couple around a Ouija board, simply entitled *Dialogue Over a Ouija Board*. Instinctively she knew neither would be published. Sylvia ended the holiday with another bout of depression. She was already looking to Ted to play the multi-roles of father, mother, husband and lover.

In September they left Cape Cod and took a small apartment in Northampton. At the end of the month, Sylvia began teaching at Smith College. It did not go well. The brilliant scholar, so admired by her tutors, was now a junior tutor and treated with little respect by her seniors. She also found it a great deal more difficult to talk to students about a story than to write one. The depression increased and the writing dried up. By October she was hearing an inner voice telling her, 'You can't teach, can't do anything. Can't write, can't think.' Finally, in December, she broke down with viral pneumonia. Meanwhile, Ted was writing and publishing successfully. Further, the University of Massachusetts was so impressed by his writings that they offered him a position teaching English from spring term 1958. Sylvia recovered physically by January but remained stressed emotionally.

Sylvia now decided she would not carry on teaching at Smith after spring term 1958. In part this was because she felt overworked and believed this was the cause of her insomnia and resulting tiredness. She desperately wanted to get back to her writing and she and Ted had decided to spend next year in Boston together, writing. Also she was jealous of the attention that young Smith girls paid to Ted; she knew from her own experience that many young students were always looking for affairs with tutors or senior students. Sylvia's jealousy and Ted's flirting had already caused friction between them. Having made her decision, Sylvia felt a great weight lifted from her mind. Her poetry began to flow again. At the end of March she wrote eight poems within eight days: 'The Dream', 'The Disquieting Muses', 'On the Decline of Oracles', 'The Ghost's Leavetaking', 'Snakecharmer', 'Perseus', 'Virgin in a Tree' and 'Battle Scene'. She believed they were amongst the best she had ever written. All were inspired by her innermost source of inspiration – paintings.

Sylvia finished her last class at Smith in May 1958. Ted had arranged to pick her up from college. He never arrived. After waiting some time, Sylvia went looking for him. The psychic intuition, which studying the occult and using the Ouija board had developed, suddenly burst forth and Sylvia found herself at the pond road where students were apt to go for snogging sessions. There she saw Ted walking, almost arm in arm, with a young, heavily made-up girl. Her face was upturned, gazing into Ted's eyes. As Sylvia approached, the girl ran off in guilty fashion. When Sylvia questioned him, Ted said they were simply walking together. Sylvia did not believe him and they argued fiercely. Ted then admitted to fucking her. Whether this was the truth or said in spite we cannot know. His reputation would suggest the former. The quarrel was kept up for several days and culminated in a fierce fight in which Sylvia scratched Ted's face so badly his skin was marked for a week and he hit her so hard that she saw stars. Sylvia's anger made her recognise the violence in herself. In her diary she calls it 'hot as death blood'. In that anger, she admits, she could kill herself or someone else.

As with most quarrels between partners, the strength of it died away. They carried through with their plan to give up teaching and settle in Boston to write. In September they found a two-roomed flat at Beacon Hill, close to Louisburg Square, at $100 a month. During their first month in Boston, Ted earned about $1,000 for his poetry. Sylvia was thrilled to earn $338 from *The New Yorker* for her poems 'Mussel Hunter at Rock Harbor' and 'Nocturne'. 'Mussel Hunter' had been written whilst on 'honeymoon' at Cape Cod and is interesting for its observation of a dead crab and its speculation upon its suicidal thoughts and its deviation from the crowd. No doubt she was expressing her own suicidal urges and her belief that she and Ted were defiantly separating themselves from the herd. *The New Yorker* was the magazine she most wanted to be published in and she was overjoyed.

As was usual with Sylvia the joy was short-lived. She was having another spell of writer's block. Furthermore, despite the income, they were, for some obscure reason, short of money. In October Sylvia took a position as a secretary at the Massachusetts General Hospital psychiatric clinic, where she had been a patient in the summer of 1953. It was this work that inspired one of her best short stories, 'Johnny Panic and the Bible of Dreams'. The job was said to be part-time, but 30 hours a week, plus looking after Ted and typing and despatching all his work, was quite enough to prevent her from writing. Such little free evening time as she had was spent with Ted, consulting the tarot cards or calling up the spirits from the Ouija board. Another bout of depression arrives and she decides to return to Dr Ruth Barnhouse for psychoanalysis. Significantly, Barnhouse gives her permission to hate her mother.

The financial situation continued to worry Plath into the spring of 1959. She calculated they had only enough money to last until September. Ted had applied to the Guggenheim Foundation for a grant of $5,000. News came through late in April that it had been granted. This was immediately followed by an invitation for Ted to read and lecture at Yaddo, an artistic community in New York, for eleven weeks from September; pressure relieved.

Sylvia now began to attend Robert Lowell's creative writing classes at Boston University. There she met Anne Sexton, a poet and artist with whom she developed an immediate rapport and who was to become an important influence in her life. They had much in common. Sexton was from Wellesley and had attended the same high school as Sylvia, albeit three years earlier. She was a beautiful and vibrant young woman who, like Sylvia, had experienced many boyfriends and lovers. Although she was already married with two children, men were much attracted to her. As a poet, her work had already been published. She had been in psychotherapy for some time and had already made at least two suicide attempts. Little wonder that Plath was drawn to and influenced by her. Sexton had a car and after classes they would go to Boston's best hotel, the Ritz-Carlton, where they would eat bowlfuls of free snacks and guzzle several Martinis. Indicative of Sexton's personality is the anecdote she often told of those visits. 'I would always park illegally in the LOADING ONLY ZONE, telling the hotel commissionaires, "It's OK, because we are only going in to get loaded!"' Their friendship continued after Sylvia returned to England and they were still writing to each other in the last year of Sylvia's life. Anne Sexton committed suicide in 1974. When we come to examine Sexton's life and death, comparison of these two young female American poets may provide some possible answers to the enigma of why so many writers commit suicide.

Free from financial worries, her writing block released, and with the company of a congruous friend, one would think Sylvia was now content. Not at all. She now decided that she longed to have a baby. So desperate had she become that she visited a gynaecologist to have her fallopian tubes unblocked. She believed the procedure was a failure and became more depressed.

In July they borrowed Aurelia's car and set off on a tour across America, with a target to arrive back at Yaddo in September. Now Sylvia found she was pregnant. They travelled east to west, to California and back to Wellesley. At Sewanee, Tennessee, Luke Myers' home town, their Cambridge friend hosted a party for them. There Sylvia met up with Monroe Spears, editor of *The Sewanee Review*. The *Review* had recently published Plath's poems 'Point Shirley' and 'The Ghost's Leavetaking'. Now Sylvia pressed on him her short story 'The Fifteen Dollar Eagle', a rather inconclusive essay on the art of the tattooist. By the time the Hughes arrived back at Wellesley, Spears had accepted the story for publication. This softened Sylvia's disappointment at rejection by Little, Brown and Company of her collection of poems, *The Bed Book*. The book had been intended for children; the characters are different types of bed in human form, the main characters being Stay-Uppidy Sue and Wide-Awake Will. It is a fair example of the difference between the late 1950s and today's era to speculate that such a book written in contemporary style would be published with enormous success.

Whilst at Yaddo, the rejections of Plath's work continued. A major irritation to Plath was that one of her ex-lovers, Peter Davison, now editor at *The Atlantic Monthly*, kept rejecting her work. She was sure this was not on merit but because of their previous relationship. Encouragement came from London publishers Heinemann, who indicated an interest in publishing a collection of her poetry. Determined and optimistic, Plath decided to try a new direction to stimulate her writing. Robert Lowell and Anne Sexton would provide inspiration and she would try to evolve a 'confessional' style to her poems. She and Hughes had regularly hypnotised each other, believing their best work came from deep within their imagination. Now Sylvia would try mind control, stream of consciousness activities and concentration exercises, all directed by Ted. The results appeared for Plath with surprising speed. The poetry began to flow and, after warming up by completing several minor poems in late September into early October, by the end of October she had produced a collection of seven poems as a volume, to be called *The Colossus and Other Poems*. It was a mixture of old and new poems; 'Two Lovers and a Beachcomber' had been published in 1955; 'The Colossus' and 'The Manor Garden' were her latest efforts.

'The Colossus' describes a daughter's unsuccessful attempts to restore a disintegrating statue that is her father. It was, in poetic terms, the most mature piece of work she had produced to date. She was later to describe it as her most intellectually satisfying poem. In two weeks, at the end of October, she wrote 'Poem For a Birthday', a kaleidoscope of seven pieces of poetry; note the entrance of the mystic number seven again. 'The Stones' was the most important of the pieces. The poem is narrated by a hospital patient. The patient is severely injured and her body has to be stitched together. Old-fashioned catgut stitches are used. Plath describes the hospital as 'the city of spare parts'. After suffering emotional and physical trauma, the patient is pronounced 'as good as new'; but the stitches still itch. One can see the corollary with Plath's own life. Hughes regarded it as her most significant poem to date. Later he would write that it was 'unlike anything that had gone before in her work ... the birth of her real poetic voice and the rebirth of herself ... we can see the peculiarity of her imagination at work and we can see how the substance of her poetry and the very substance of her survival are the same'.

Ted had for some time been trying to persuade Sylvia that they should return to England. She had some reluctance; but introducing Ted to the USA had not worked as well as she had hoped and she had her own frustrations with writing and work. Now there seemed prospects that Heinemann would publish her work in England. The baby was on the way and Sylvia rather favoured it being born in the UK. Gradually she allowed herself to be persuaded, on condition that they would return to Boston after two years.

Sylvia was suffering another long period of insomnia, often only being able to sleep if Ted hypnotised her. When they visited Aurelia at Thanksgiving, to say goodbye prior to their departure for England, she thought Sylvia looked tired and ill; but on 12 December, the day of their departure, Aurelia wrote that Sylvia looked so young, her hair in a long braid down her back, a little wool cap on her head, looking like a senior schoolgirl.

They departed New York for Southampton on 13 December 1959. Sylvia was full of optimism. A new baby, a new style of poetry, a new adventure with Ted; Sylvia looked upon it as a new beginning to her life. In fact it was the beginning of the end of her life. She was never to return to America and within three years she was dead by her own hand.

Arriving in England, they spent Christmas with Ted's parents in Yorkshire. In January they went flat searching in London, never an easy task. Eventually they found a small, unfurnished, third-floor, one-bedroom flat in Chalcot Square, NW1, quite close to Regent's Park, available on a three-year lease. With the baby on the way it was too small, but the rent, at £10 per week, was so cheap that they signed up to move in on 1 February. They had to borrow furniture from friends, which illustrates the state of their finances. This, notwithstanding the Guggenheim award, the income from their poetry and the money earned working in the USA.

Late in March, Faber published a collection of 41 poems by Ted Hughes under the title *Lupercal*. It received excellent reviews and sold so well that it was into a second printing within two months. It also won the £500 Somerset Maugham Award. Finances were temporarily eased.

Large quantities of correspondence began to pour in for Ted. He would not deal with it, thus Sylvia felt obliged to do so. She was now nearing the full term of her pregnancy. Exhaustion was overtaking her.

Their first child, Frieda Rebecca, was born on 1 April at home in their flat. Ted hypnotised Sylvia to minimise the pain.

For the next three months, Sylvia's time was consumed with attending the baby, cooking, cleaning and dealing with Ted's correspondence and his diary. She did no writing and, as was usual when this happened, she fell into depression. However, following a two-week vacation to Ted's parents in Heptonstall, Sylvia returned with her appetite to write renewed, and was able to create four new poems in September and October. At the end of October, Heinemann kept their promise and *The Colossus and Other Poems* was published.

Little notice was taken by the critics. However, in December, Alfred Alvarez, poetry editor for the *Observer* newspaper, who had met Sylvia when interviewing Ted in March, included a significant review in his article on the Hughes: 'The Poet and the Poetess'. He wrote, 'Miss Plath neither asks excuses for her works nor offers them. She simply writes good poetry. She is not, of course, unwaveringly good. At times ... the language goes off on its own and she lands in blaring rhetoric. At other times she hovers close to the whimsy of fairy stories. But it would be a strange first book that had no faults; *The Colossus* has more than enough excellent poems to compensate for them.' In happier mode, Sylvia now fell pregnant again.

To Yorkshire for Christmas. They now make plans to holiday in Italy. A quarrel between Ted's sister, Olwyn, and Sylvia, combined with bitter rain and influenza means they return to London earlier than intended. Sylvia is now suffering with appendicitis. She is somewhat cheered by a positive review of *The Colossus* by John Wain in *The Spectator*. Although he suspects some plagiarism, he says 'Sylvia Plath writes clever, vivacious poetry which will be enjoyed by most intelligent people capable of having fun with poetry ... this is a first book and the surprising thing is how successful Miss Plath has been in finding an individual manner.' For some incomprehensible reason she takes a part-time job as a typist with *The Bookseller* magazine.

Towards the end of January, a major quarrel ensues between Ted and Sylvia. Hughes had been working for the BBC and was invited to a lunch meeting by Moira Doolan, Head of BBC Schools Broadcasting. He returns late in the evening. Sylvia has spent several hours in brooding and suspicion and eventually tears up all his manuscripts, drafts and notes. She also destroys his treasured *Complete Works of Shakespeare*. Both are furious for their own reasons and they attack each other physically. We have no more details of this great quarrel from Sylvia's letters or journals but we do have clues from Plath's short story 'Day of Success', which is obviously based on this confrontation. Whether this incident was the cause of Sylvia's miscarriage on 6 February is not possible to tell. Though she had certainly forgiven Ted by that time. She had written to Anne Sexton on 5 February and within the letter she says that Ted is 'wonderful'.

Sylvia's grief over her miscarriage is not in doubt. Yet it sparks off her writing again; in the last two weeks of February she creates seven new poems. The most significant are: 'Parliament Hill Fields', in which she describes the emotional tug of war between the grief of losing one child and the joy of having another still living; 'Zookeeper's Wife', in which she expresses violent, female revulsion against the raw physical desires of the male, a poem clearly aimed at Ted; 'Morning Song', which was Plath's conclusive statement on the condition of motherhood.

The miscarriage had aggravated her appendix problem and, at the end of February, she was taken into St Pancras Hospital at King's Cross for surgery. Whilst there, she was able to read new notices appearing of *The Colossus*. In *The London Magazine*, Roy Fuller is another who complains of plagiarism; but Howard Sergeant's review in the spring edition of *English Magazine* is kinder; he says, 'Miss Plath is unusually reserved and precise ... what few defects there are in this distinguished first volume are due more to her sudden descents into fantasy than to any failure of craftsmanship.' She also now receives news that Knopf are interested in publishing *The Colossus* in the USA.

Despite the double pain of miscarriage and appendectomy, Sylvia is very much in creative mood. Within the next few days she writes two new poems, 'Tulips' and 'I Am Vertical'. Strangely, both take the death wish as a theme. In 'Tulips' all she wants is to be empty, to lie with her hands upturned, enjoying the peacefulness that is what the dead shut their mouths upon like a communion wafer. 'I Am Vertical' states her preference for the horizontal position and says that she will be of more use when she lays down for the last time. She also makes significant progress on her novel *The Bell Jar*.

In April the significance of the poem 'Zookeeper's Wife' becomes apparent. Sylvia is again pregnant.

Interest in Plath's work is growing. *Critical Quarterly* publishes 'I Am Vertical' and 'Private Ground'. In the same periodical, A.E. Dyson reviews *The Colossus*, saying, 'It establishes Miss Plath among the best of the poets now claiming our attention; the most compelling feminine voice, certainly, that we have heard for many a day.' The BBC records Plath giving a half hour reading of her poems for their series *The Living Poet*. Later she reads her poem 'Tulips' live for the BBC from the Mermaid Theatre.

In June Aurelia visits and looks after Frieda whilst Sylvia and Ted take a short holiday in France. During that holiday they discuss the fact that it is no longer possible for them to live in the tiny Chalcot Square flat. They both need space to write and they now realise that a second baby will arrive by the end of the year. Ted wants to live in the country; Sylvia does not, she prefers the social life of a big town. But with the high price of houses in London beyond their means, she sees there is little alternative. Upon their return, they spend several days house hunting in Devon. The only property they find that is within their budget is a small estate at Court Green in the small hamlet of North Tawton. It consisted of a run-down, two-storey house of about ten rooms, a two-roomed cottage and a small row of broken-down stables. The grounds covered about one hectare, laid out as fruit orchards in need of substantial attention. No price was agreed, indeed the Hughes were not really in a position to make a commitment, since they had only about £2,000 in savings. They returned to London and, at the beginning of August, Aurelia returned to Boston. In the middle of the month, the owners of Court Green wrote offering to sell at £3,600. The Hughes considered this an offer too good to miss. They withdrew their savings, borrowed £1,000 from their parents and £600 from their bank. The deal was done in cash and they wanted to move immediately.

August was certainly an eventful month for Sylvia. On the 16th, she signed the contract with Knopf for publication of *The Colossus* in the USA. On the 18th, the *Times Literary Supplement* carried a belated review of the book, in which they said Sylvia was 'elusive and private' and that it was 'as if what the poems are about is very much her own business ... this first volume is a stimulating one but combining as it does fine surface clarities with a deeper, riddling quality, it is a teasing one'. Sylvia has continued to work at her novel *The Bell Jar* and this month she completes the first draft. During this month Sylvia's doctor confirms she is four months pregnant.

They have house hunted and now they are moving from London to Devon. Before they can move they need to sublet their lease on Chalcot Square. From several applicants, they choose David Wevill, a young Canadian published poet, and his German wife, Assia. The Hughes were much taken with them and invited them to visit North Tawton in the future. Sylvia and Ted moved to Devon on 31 August.

September was a busy settling-in month. By October Sylvia had settled into a routine of writing every morning at a tremendous pace. In that month she completed four poems, the most successful being 'The Moon and the Yew Tree', based on a yew tree growing close to the stables. Heinemann in London and Knopf in New York agreed to accept *The Bell Jar* for publication. Elizabeth Anderson of Heinemann was concerned that much of the novel might be considered autobiographical and be upsetting to Plath's family and friends, who would recognise unkind caricatures of themselves within the novel. Plath understood this and it was decided to issue the book under the *nom de plume* Victoria Lucas.

In November Sylvia receives the stunning news that the Eugene Saxton Foundation has awarded her a grant of $2,000 (say about $50,000 today) to write prose fiction. Sylvia decides to send them *The Bell Jar* in instalments, so that she would appear to be complying with their requirements. Heinemann obligingly postponed publication until January 1963.

On 17 January 1962, the Hughes' second child, Nicholas, was born. Again the delivery was at home. Again Ted hypnotised Sylvia, as he had been doing regularly since their marriage. This time the healthy boy weighed in at ten pounds, a mighty weight for that era. For some reason, never identified, Ted did not take to the boy; naturally, this worried Sylvia.

In April she had another of her manic bursts of writing poetry. In that month she wrote eight poems. The most significant is 'Elm', a dramatic expansion of a short poem she had written in April 1962 into a soliloquy in which the speaker, an elm tree, speaking as a woman, discovers that her love affair is ending. The break up of this affair spells death for the woman. The message is clear: when love ends, life ends. This poem is a good example of Sylvia's psychic powers. At this time, there was no outward sign that the Hughes marriage was anything but loving. Yet within a few months, the affair was ended and so was Sylvia's life.

In the middle of May, the Hughes had visitors who were to prove the catalyst for a disastrous change in Sylvia's life. David and Assia Wevill, who had taken over the Chalcot Square flat, now accepted the Hughes invitation to visit them in Devon. David was a mild-mannered, pleasant young man, ten years younger than Assia. He was Assia's third husband. Assia was a strong-willed woman with a beautiful face, although not with a figure to match. Her record of previous affairs with poets establishes that she understood that particular breed of artist. Assia set herself out to entice Ted. When the foursome went walking on the moors, Ted and Assia dropped back and Sylvia noted they were almost arm in arm. Later, when Assia was in the kitchen alone, helping to prepare lunch, Sylvia heard Ted come in and go straight to the kitchen. After a few moments, Sylvia followed and found them too close together for Sylvia's comfort. Her worst jealousies were aroused when she came down to the kitchen next morning to find Ted and Assia again close together. In later years, Assia revealed that she had lifted her nightgown and wrapped her bare body around Ted on that occasion. Although Sylvia had not seen that, she had seen enough and asked the Wevills to leave. Before they left, Ted slipped a note to Assia saying, 'I must see you in London tomorrow.' After their departure, Ted and Sylvia quarrelled fiercely. Something of Ted's character may be gauged from the fact that he accused Sylvia of outrageous behaviour. Ted left the house the next day, saying he was going to London for two or three days. In fact he went straight to Chalcot Square. Assia had contrived to get her husband out of the way. Immediately upon Ted's arrival they engaged in urgent and violent sex.

Ted returned to Devon, but now began to make visits to London every week. He had rented a small flatlet and here Assia and he would make love. It was clear that the Hughes marriage was breaking down. Despite this, Sylvia continued to write to her mother that this was the happiest and richest time of her life. How much she was hiding is revealed when she deliberately drove her jeep off the road and crashed in an adjacent airfield; she was later to tell Alfred Alvarez that this was a suicide attempt.

At the end of June Aurelia arrives at Court Green to visit for a month. This causes Sylvia to attempt to keep a lid on her grief; but it mounts up towards explosion point. On 9 July she takes her mother to lunch and shopping in Exeter; here she is still telling her mother that Ted is a wonderful husband and that she has all she wants; a home, children and her writing. They return to the house to find the telephone ringing. Sylvia reaches it before Ted. It is Assia, asking for Ted. Sylvia hands the phone to him, but when the conversation is finished she tears the telephone lead from the wall. This was to signal the beginning of the end of their marriage. Next Sylvia makes a bonfire of whatever traces she can find of Ted: letters, drafts of poems, the human dust from his desk, even some old clothes that reeked of his body. It is a witch's bonfire. She is trying to exorcise Ted from her system.

After 4 August, when Aurelia returns to the USA, Sylvia is left to cope with her disintegrating marriage alone. On 15 August, the Hughes put a brave face on the situation and accept an invitation to visit Olive Higgins Prouty for two days, who is staying at the Connaught Hotel in Berkeley Square, London. During this visit, they agree to attempt a reconciliation; they will accept an invitation from fellow poet Richard Murphy to spend a few days in Galway, Ireland.

Sylvia's health was deteriorating. Respiratory problems and severe PMS, both of which had been constantly with her from her teenage years, were worse than ever. Insomnia and headaches were ever present. She was having a serious period of writer's block and she did not feel she could face another winter in Devon. Maybe they would spend the winter in Spain, alone. On 27 August she wrote to her mother:

I am going to try to get a legal separation from Ted. I do not believe in divorce and would never think of this, but I simply cannot go on living the degraded and agonized life I have been living, which has stopped my writing and just about ruined my sleep and my health. I feel I need a legal settlement so I can count on so much a week for groceries and bills and the freedom to build up the happy, pleasant life I feel it in myself to make and would but for him.

Contrast this with 'the wonderful husband' Sylvia had described to her mother in Exeter only seven weeks earlier. The impact of finally facing the fact of Ted's affair with Assia had been devastating for Sylvia.

* * *

To Galway on 11 September, to sail the Atlantic Ocean off the west coast of Ireland. Perhaps peace between them would come. It was the last throw of the reconciliation dice. It was not to succeed. On 16 September, Ted, without explanation, abandoned Sylvia and left for London. On the 18th, Sylvia returned to Devon. Here she found waiting for her a letter from Dr Ruth Barnhouse and a telegram from Ted. Barnhouse told her in the strongest terms to petition for a divorce immediately. In his telegram, Ted said he would be returning to Devon in about two weeks. In fact he did not appear until the end of September, when he arrived unannounced to collect his personal belongings. It is not surprising that Sylvia, who still had some spirit left in her, told him it was inconvenient and he should return another time by appointment.

Sylvia had a conference in London on 25 September with solicitors Harris Cheetham. She had by now discovered that Ted had been drawing sums of cash out of their joint account, indeed all of the $7,000 of their recent earnings was gone. Sylvia had suspected that most of it had been spent on Assia. No one knew Ted's new London address, but the solicitors undertook to find him and pursue a maintenance settlement. In fact they succeeded.

Ted returned on 4 October to collect his things and to see the children. He stayed for seven days. During that time he created enormous stress for Sylvia. He physically attacked her, demanding money from her; she refused. He then did a U-turn and agreed with Sylvia that he would pay £1,000 per year maintenance for the children, nothing for Sylvia. Next he informed Sylvia that Assia and he were living together. This was because he wanted a real woman (presumably this meant a woman who had three previous husbands) and that he had wanted to leave Sylvia for some long time previously. He would now agree to a divorce. Sylvia was further distressed when Ted informed her that Assia's husband, David Wevill, had attempted suicide because of the situation. Ted then packed all his belongings and left for ever. Those who think this was the beginning of the end for Sylvia are quite wrong. She wrote to her mother the next day and said that she was so relieved that, after driving Ted to the station, she returned to Court Green and sang and danced through the house in the happiest mood. She wished only that Ted would have told her earlier that he had long wished to leave her; that would have given her time to find a man more worthy of her to share her life with. In the event, Ted had abandoned her. It was reminiscent of Richard Sassoon in 1956.

Released finally from Ted, Sylvia now enters into one of her frenetic periods, writing poetry at a furious pace. In the one month of October 1962, she wrote 30 poems, the most interesting being 'Daddy', 'Lady Lazarus', 'Medusa' and 'Ariel'. Speaking directly to her dead father in 'Daddy', the narrator unleashes a wild anger against him and her husband. She says her husband claimed to be her father, but was, in reality, a vampire who drank her blood. He is now dead. Everyone in the village hated him and now they stamp upon him. Although she loved her father, she sees him as Fascist. She is completely disillusioned with both men, as we see in the final line of the poem: 'Daddy, daddy, you bastard, I'm through.' One can speculate here that she is through with her husband, through with her life-long adoration of her father and through with the lifestyle she has led. In 'Lady Lazarus' the speaker is a 30-year-old woman, who believes she is directed to make a suicide attempt once every ten years. In this poem the unsuccessful attempts at suicide are not failures but rather a victorious resurrection. Their representatives are Lazarus and the Phoenix, rising from the dead and the ashes respectively. The poem is a wild lyric, at once dark and mocking, yet bright and blazing with similes (her skin is like a Nazi lampshade) and metaphors (a paperweight is her right foot). Many critics have said it is autobiographical.

'Medusa' relates how a young woman is being persecuted by a monstrosity. In fact, it is simply a vicious attack upon her mother, Aurelia. Sylvia well knew that Medusa is also a name given to a species of jellyfish, *aurelia*. 'Ariel' was written on 27 October, her birthday. It is a faultless lyric. In it, Ariel is a horse, ridden by the poem's narrator. The ride is into 'the cauldron of morning', the rising sun. The destination of the journey, and its certain end, in death, is fixed.

October had been Sylvia's most prolific writing period to that date in her life. November was to be barren. This is not surprising. Ted's departure had allowed her to release her every emotion. Now she decided she could not live alone in Devon; she would return to London. Much of early November was spent in flat-hunting. Eventually she found a maisonette to let at 23 Fitzroy Lodge, NW1. Amazingly it bore an English Heritage blue plaque, declaring that William Butler Yeats, one of Sylvia's literary heroes, had lived there. It was on two floors, having three bedrooms and a balcony garden. She lost no time in negotiating for a five-year lease. This was completed in London on 3 December and, after arranging for a gas cooker to be fitted and for the electricity to be connected, Sylvia returned to Devon.

On 12 December Sylvia moved to London, but Court Green, Devon, was to be retained. At Fitzroy Lodge, she arrived to an uncomfortable start. The electricity was not turned on and the gas cooker not fitted. In leaving her maisonette, she forgot her entrance keys and locked herself out of the house. Now occurred a most illuminating first meeting with the tenant of the other maisonette to the house, Trevor Thomas. Seeing him leaving the house, Sylvia rushed up to him in delight saying, 'Oh, wonderful! You have keys and can let me in. I'm moving in to the flat upstairs and I've locked myself out and the babies are crying.' Thomas suggested she called the police and walked away. To Sylvia's great credit, she dealt with all the problems and, despite having influenza, she got on with decorating and furnishing the flat.

She wrote only three poems in December. In addition to the problems of settling in to the flat, she had to spend a great deal more time with the children since she had been unable to find an au pair. She was also diverted by Ted, who, now that she was in London, took to dropping in to see the children.

Sylvia had renewed contact with some old friends from Chalcot Square days and had made some new friends. Thus she was not alone over the Christmas period. On Christmas Day she and the children had afternoon tea with Catherine Frankfort and her family. In the evening they went to dinner with Helder and Suzette Macedo. For Boxing Day, back to the Frankforts. These kind invitations relieved Sylvia's despondency a little, but she remained depressed. The weather compounded her depression. It began to snow heavily on Boxing Day and this developed into one of the coldest and longest spells of severe weather on record; it lasted until February. Sylvia was one of many who suffered burst pipes and had to draw water from a standpipe in the street. Worse still, her burst pipes had been caused by snow leaking through the roof. She had no heating and there were frequent failures of electricity supply.

Sylvia may have had some thoughts about a possible reconciliation with her husband. In the last days of December, she invited Ted to dinner. She wore her best dress, styled her hair and applied her make-up carefully. She was looking her best for some time and Ted told her so. Having complimented her, Ted straightaway cross-examined Sylvia upon two matters that had been troubling his mind. He had been told she had been taking large quantities of antidepressants; was it true? Sylvia told him she had only taken what the doctor had prescribed. In fact she had been overdosing only on phenobarbitone and not excessively because her doctor, John Horder, had restricted her supplies. Ted then accused her:

116

'Alvarez [Alfred] says you made a pass at him.' By this he meant Alvarez stated that Sylvia suggested they became lovers. Sylvia answered, 'No.' Upon this point I do believe Sylvia. It is true that she had visited him in London whilst flat-hunting and since she had moved to Fitzroy Lodge and that he had visited her. Equally, it is true they were intellectuals on a similar wavelength and had other things in common – poetry, divorce proceedings, both had made suicide attempts. Sylvia would certainly have respected him as a leading poetry critic of his era. However, he simply was not Sylvia's physical type, so the suggestion seems most unlikely. Readers will have noted that all Sylvia's boyfriends and lovers were tall, well built, handsome, clean cut young men. Alvarez was none of that. He was short, flabby, fortyish, had receding hair and a beard. Sylvia was conscious of her own height and always disliked short men. Sylvia probably did say to Alvarez that she was thinking of taking a lover. If she did, then probably it was so that the comment would reach Ted's ears. That Alvarez should interpret that as an invitation from Sylvia to him betrays, perhaps, overweening conceit on his part. Alvarez says that Sylvia sent him many letters, but he weakens his own credibility by stating that he destroyed them.

That late December evening spent with Ted was to be the last time she was to be close to him and ended any hope of reconciliation between them. In the 2003 film *Sylvia* (Gwyneth Paltrow and Daniel Craig) that encounter is portrayed with Ted staying the night and making passionate love with Sylvia: in the morning Sylvia asks him to leave Assia, but he says he cannot because she is having his baby. There seems little direct evidence to support the screenwriter's portrayal, but there is plenty of indirect evidence and it does have the ring of truth about it.

In the first week of January, Heinemann published *The Bell Jar* under the *nom de plume* Victoria Lucas. Reviews were very good. The *Times Literary Supplement* said, 'Few writers are able to create a different world for you to live in; yet Miss Lucas in *The Bell Jar* has done just this. Miss Lucas certainly can write and the book is convincing. There is a dry wit behind the poetic flashes and the zany fiascos of her relationships.' L.D. Learner wrote for *The Listener*, 'This is a brilliant and moving book.' He praised it for its criticisms of American society. Perhaps that is why Knopf turned it down and, indeed, no American publisher would touch it at that time. The BBC's review, printed in *The Listener* on 31 January, heaped praise upon it and gave it a strongly recommended rating.

Unfortunately these encouraging reviews came too late to lift Sylvia's mood. Early in January Sylvia was suffering from PMDD (premenstrual dysphoric disorder, the most severe form of PMS), together with sinusitis and flu. The children were also suffering with flu. Sylvia at last had managed to find a German au pair, but, although this helped to give her time away from the children, it was negated because Sylvia simply could not get on with her. All this, together with the service problems caused by the severe weather, drove Sylvia towards the lowest ebb of her life.

Now we begin to see clear signs of manic depression. Suddenly, at the end of January, Sylvia's mood changes dramatically. She begins to write furiously, seeking to complete a second collection of poems under the title *Ariel*. In seven days between 28 January and 5 February 1963 she completes two poems already in progress and writes ten new poems. Of these 'The Munich Mannequins' and 'Edge' are particularly significant. In 'The Munich Mannequins', Sylvia characterises childbirth as incompatible with perfection; the shop window mannequins, baldly naked, want nothing but themselves. Perhaps Sylvia is thinking of Assia, or maybe she is feeling that bearing children has held back her own perfection. She recalls her visit to Munich with Gordon Lameyer. Had that trip proved to be the reconciliation both intended, instead of a disaster, perhaps she would have married Gordon and settled down in America instead of marrying Ted Hughes and embarking on a journey to nowhere.

'Edge' was the last poem Sylvia wrote. Many critics consider it her finest. Alvarez said, 'It is a poem of great peace and resignation, utterly without self pity.' The edge is the edge of death. Only in death is the woman's body perfected. Only then is her journey ended and her mission accomplished. The poem shows us so much of Sylvia's innermost thoughts as she prepares for suicide, and contemplates whether she should take her children with her. The moon, perhaps the world, looks on unmoved.

On 5 February her mood swung rapidly back to full depression. Her last letter to her mother, dated 4 February, says that she is suffering from loneliness and grim problems. But she also tells Aurelia of her upcoming work, her thoughts about intended visits from friends and her plans for the future; it is clear that on the

4th she had not made an irrevocable decision to commit suicide. On the 5th she did make that decision as the poem 'Edge', written that day, indicates.

From now until her death, Sylvia would see Dr John Horder every day. On 6 February she went to him with a severe throat and chest infection. He immediately recognised that Sylvia was suffering from chronic depression. He knew the symptoms very well; he had suffered from it himself. He had already referred her to Dr Kathy Dalton, a specialist consultant for PMS sufferers, who was to see her on 22 February. Now he referred her to a National Health psychiatrist. The waiting list was shorter then than now; nevertheless, it would be a month before Sylvia could be seen. That would prove to be three weeks too long. In the meantime, Dr Horder prescribed phenelzine, an antidepressant of the monoamine oxidase inhibitor type. Dr Horder knew that this drug took about two weeks to take effect: what he could not know was that Sylvia Plath would be dead within five days. Dr Horder later refused to reveal the name of the psychiatrist. Perhaps he felt some guilt over Sylvia's death.

By the afternoon of Thursday the 7th, Sylvia's nerves were close to breaking point. A fierce quarrel erupted with the au pair and Sylvia physically attacked her. The au pair quit, leaving Sylvia alone with the children. Sylvia phoned Dr Horder and told him she was very sick with her respiratory infection, PMS and was unable to sleep; to compound things she had no one to look after the children. Horder said he would arrange for her to be admitted to hospital as soon as possible and he would arrange for a nurse to come to Fitzroy Lodge to look after the children. Next, distraught almost to the point of hysteria, she telephoned friend and neighbour Jillian Becker (author of *Hitler's Children*) and asked if she and the children could stay with the Beckers for a few days until Horder could find her a hospital bed. Jillian told her to come straightaway. Sylvia and the children arrived at Barnsbury Square, North London in the late afternoon. Sylvia had brought nothing with her so Jillian had to rush back to Fitzroy Lodge and collect everything necessary for the children and, at Sylvia's request, cosmetics, perfume and a party dress. I think we can gauge from this Sylvia's state of mind and body on 7 February.

In the early hours of the morning of the 8th, Sylvia awoke the Becker household screaming out for help. Jillian sat with her for two hours, during which Sylvia bombarded her with a tirade against Ted and the entire Hughes family. Why had she made the mistake of marrying him? Dick Norton, Gordon Lameyer, Richard Sassoon had all loved her and wanted to marry her. She felt now that she could have been happy with any one of them, but never with Ted. At 5.30 a.m. she took an antidepressant and went back to bed. In the morning she ate a hearty breakfast and she seemed to Jillian a little improved. Notwithstanding, Jillian telephoned Dr Horder, and Sylvia made an appointment to see him that afternoon. That day Sylvia took four baths; she was almost certainly taking an amphetamine type respiratory stimulant for her chest and throat infection; this type of drug often causes profuse sweating.

After seeing Dr Horder, Sylvia drove back to Fitzroy Lodge. Her neighbour Trevor Thomas saw her at 7 p.m., sitting alone in the car in front of the building with a vacant expression on her face. Although they had not been getting on well as neighbours, Thomas was concerned for Sylvia's well-being. He approached and asked whether Sylvia was all right and whether he should call Dr Horder. Sylvia said no; she had seen Horder earlier and she was fine, she was just day-dreaming. 'I'm going away for a long holiday, a long rest,' she told him. She then returned to the Beckers, where she ate dinner and then left to drive back to Fitzroy Lodge to meet Ted.

The meeting was brief. Sylvia left her car at the flat and took a taxi back to the Beckers. What took place at that meeting we shall never know. Ted refused to say anything beyond that he had not stayed long. There has been speculation that Ted hypnotised her and left her believing she had to kill herself. Whatever did happen created an immediate change in Sylvia's personality. This was clearly noticed by Jill Becker, who said her actions were more purposeful, as if some important matter, which had been disturbing her, was now settled.

The next day passed uneventfully. Sylvia again attended Horder. At night she took her sleeping pills, awoke in the middle of the night, aroused Jill and confided in her at length, mainly about dreams she was having, and then went back to sleep.

Next day, 10 February, Sylvia ate a huge lunch and then retired to bed for a long nap. Awaking in the early evening, she declared it her most restful sleep for some time. Now she said she felt better and wanted to return home; the Beckers tried desperately to dissuade her, but she was adamant. Eventually Gerry Becker was persuaded to drive her and the children back to Fitzroy Lodge. She cried bitterly all the way. Here we see the manic depression in action again. At first the mood is positive. She sleeps and eats very well and is certain that she wants to return home. Almost immediately this is followed by a bout of depressive sobbing.

Gerry tried to get her to return with him, but she refused and he left her about 7 p.m. Dr Horder called shortly afterwards. He saw no cause for immediate alarm and suggested Sylvia attend surgery the next day. Sylvia then fed the children, put them to bed and sat down to write letters to America. Later she spent some time pacing up and down the living-room. Just before midnight, she called at Trevor Thomas's door, asking if he could let her have some postage stamps. He noted that she looked drugged and distracted. Could it not wait until morning? No, Sylvia said, the letters must be posted tonight. Thomas produced the stamps but declined payment. Sylvia insisted, 'I must pay you or I won't be right with my conscience before God, will I?' Sylvia then asked what time he left for work in the morning. Thomas said about 8.30 a.m., but why do you ask? Sylvia's reply was, 'Oh, nothing, I just wondered that's all.' Thomas then shut his door. About half an hour later, just as he was about to go to bed, he noticed the common entrance light was still on. Opening his door he found Sylvia still standing there with a vacant look on her face. I'm calling Dr Horder for you, he told her. 'Oh no, please don't do that. I'm just having a marvellous and most wonderful vision,' Sylvia replied. Thomas closed his door and went to bed. However, he was kept awake until about 5 a.m. by the sound of Sylvia pacing the floor above him. About this time, the noise ceased and Thomas finally slept. It must have been at that time that Sylvia went out to post her letters and left a note saying 'Please call Dr John Horder' pinned to the children's pram, which was in the common hallway. She then made a plate of bread and butter and two cups of milk, which she left in the children's bedroom. She then opened the window and left the room, sealing the door off with towels and tape. She went into the kitchen and sealed that room, again with towels and tape. At about 6 a.m. on Monday 11 February 1963 Sylvia Plath turned the gas supply to the cooker on to maximum level. Placing a towel on the floor of the gas oven, she rested her head upon it and gassed herself to death.

Sylvia Plath Hughes died still married to Ted. As a result of this, all rights in her estate became the property of her husband Ted Hughes. Despite enormous pressure from those interested in Plath's work, Ted would only release Plath's work piecemeal over a period of the next 20 years. He earned a great deal of money from this process, which seems to me like taking a pension rather than a lump sum. *Ariel* was Sylvia's final work; it was a collection of 41 poems. Ted Hughes allowed his own selection of 27 of those poems to be published in 1965. Half a million copies were quickly sold. *The Bell Jar* he allowed to be published under Sylvia's name in 1967. In 1970 Ted announced that Plath's unfinished novel *Double Exposure* had been destroyed. This is not surprising; in this novel the heroine discovers that her perfect husband is a serial adulterer. The title of the novel was intended to reflect the theme that re-examination of events frequently reveals more than one first thought. Two further selections of poems were published in 1971, *Winter Trees* and *Crossing the Water*. In 1975, in the USA, and in 1976, in the UK, a selection of Sylvia's letters from 1950 to 1963, running to 500 pages, was published, as selected by Aurelia Plath. In 1977 Faber & Faber published *Johnny Panic and the Bible of Dreams*, a selection of 31 short stories and other pieces, edited by Ted Hughes. In 1977 Ted sold the film rights to *The Bell Jar* to Avco Embassy Pictures (Jerry Brandt and Michael Todd) for $100,000. The book, whilst in principle was a fiction novel, was in practice autobiographical. The film deviated so much from the book that it flopped disastrously; even attracting a successful lawsuit from Jane Anderson, Sylvia's fellow patient at the McLean institution.

Collected Poems, containing 224 poems, written by Plath between 1956 and 1962, was published in 1981. Again edited and introduced by Ted Hughes. Although Hughes' haphazard editing and serious omissions in this collection received adverse reviews from the critics, the book won the Pulitzer Prize the following year. In that year *The Journals of Sylvia Plath* was published in the USA; edited by Frances McCullough, with Ted Hughes as consulting editor, it is somewhat disappointing in that many of the entries are deliberately omitted. A much fuller version, containing about twice the amount of material, was published in 2000 after Ted's death in October 1998; edited by Karen Kukil, it runs to 732 pages.

Any way you look at it, the fact is Sylvia Plath's reputation was gained through the publication of her writings posthumously. Today she is recognised as a feminist iconoclast, whose works are as fresh and relevant as when she first wrote them. We know so much about her because most of what she wrote about refers to herself, her experiences and her relationships with others.

Many critics, scholars, those who knew her and readers of Plath's works believe Ted Hughes was the catalyst for Sylvia's death. They reinforce their opinions by pointing out that Assia also committed suicide. Is that a fair judgement? Certainly the impact of her emotional, psychological and artistic relationship with Hughes was enormous. Her academic standards fell for the first time in her life. She spent so much time devoting herself to Hughes and working to get him published that she was unable to put sufficient time into getting her own work published and inevitably deep frustration followed. Hughes was physically violent towards her. He hypnotised her and taught her black magic. Ultimately he deserted her for another woman. This shocked her profoundly and weakened her ego badly. Hughes was much more concerned for himself than for his wife, as was proven after her death. His remarks at the reception after her funeral are significant: 'Everybody hated her. It was a fight to the death. One of us had to die.' But there were important causes, other than Hughes' ill-treatment of her, that contributed to Sylvia Plath's death.

It is clear that Sylvia Plath had suicide in mind from the age of eleven onwards. In the ten years from 1943 to 1953 she makes at least three suicide attempts. Two of them might have been cries for help, but the 1953 attempt was deadly serious for she could not have expected to be found. Yet for the next ten years she made no suicide attempt.

What are the other factors that led to Sylvia carefully executing her own death? We should take into account that the possessiveness of Aurelia and her mother's ambitions for her daughter had been a burden to Sylvia from her teenage years onwards. That it was with her to the end may even be seen in Sylvia's final letter to Aurelia on 4 February 1963. It is relevant to consider the latent effect of the electroshock treatment given to her in her early years. Although her exam results and her sexual activities in the years immediately afterwards suggest, on the one hand, that she recovered well from the treatment, on the other, her nightmares and her later poems show that she had frequent, horrific flashbacks to the experience.

We must not underestimate the effect of her poor physical condition in February 1963. She had suffered from PMDD for 15 years and at that time it was as bad as it ever had been. Doctors John Horder, Kathy Dalton, Glenn Blair and Catherine Thompson, together with biographer Ann Stevenson and writer Kate Moses, all believe it to have been a major cause of her suicide. But can anyone believe that the suicide of this attractive 30-year-old mother of two children, an impeccable and ruthless poet, novelist, autobiographer and short story writer, was primarily due to PMS? Severe PMS played its part, but was only one element in this complex tragedy. Continuing with Sylvia's physical condition, we note that she was suffering with the remnants of a long bout of flu and a serious respiratory infection. This was exacerbated by exceptionally bitter winter weather.

As to her mental state, we should consider to what degree the depression, from which she had been suffering for many years, was inherited from her father's family in which it was endemic. Sylvia's manic depression had begun in her teenage years and had grown progressively worse until it could be diagnosed in her final weeks as bipolar II, where the mood swings are sudden and extreme. One of the most disturbing similarities between bipolar II and PMDD is the potentially lethal nature of both illnesses. Dr K.R. Jamison, an expert in the field, states in her book *Manic Depressive Illnesses*, 'Patients … with manic depressive illnesses are far more likely to commit suicide than individuals in any other psychiatric or medical risk group.' Studies by Dr Jean Endicott (New York State Psychiatric Institute) and by Dr Kathy Dalton have produced evidence that in PMS sufferers a significant percentage of suicide attempts take place during the luteal phase of the menstrual cycle. Perhaps the most frightening thought is that Sylvia Plath was suffering from bipolar disorders *and* PMDD simultaneously.

Evidence suggests that Sylvia Plath was overdosing on an amphetamine type respiratory stimulant at the time of her death. One side-effect of this could be hallucinations. Surely that was what was happening when Trevor Thomas saw her on the evening of 8 February and the night of the 10th.

With hindsight, we can now see that it is a combination of factors that led to Sylvia's death. The parental background, focussing on the obsessive mother and the early death of a depressed father. The moral tone of the era in which she lived her early life and which forced her to suppress her sexual desires. Her marriage, perhaps on the rebound, to another brilliant poet, who overshadowed her and finally deserted her. The parapsychology, which he taught her. Her mental and physical illnesses, exacerbated by one of the most bitter winters in living memory.

The 12 final poems, written shortly before her death, define a philosophy of knowing and being oneself whilst rejecting all established authority and institutions. From this philosophy, death provided the only dignified escape. It is to those final poems that we should look for an understanding of the suicide of Sylvia Plath Hughes.

Thomas Lovell Beddoes

The Nearly Man

Thomas Lovell Beddoes, the Poet Laureate who never was. His story is one of what might have been. A man of great promise in his youth, he should have gone on to be the greatest dramatist and poet of his era. But from his late teenage years he suffered severe depression, which led to his mind becoming progressively unstable until his suicide at the age of 45. The consequence was a period of more than 20 years during which Beddoes had nothing published. It was not until long after his death in 1849 that the manuscripts of much of his best work were gathered together and published.

His plays and poems were written and talked about for a hundred

By kind permission of The Master, Fellows and Scholars
of Pembroke College in the University of Oxford

years after his death, but few readers today know of his work. Yet examples of his poetry can still be found in the latest edition of *The Oxford Book of English Verse,* and the two following extracts give some flavour of his macabre style whilst also illustrating his delicate touch with lyrics and his wistful, nostalgic manner with his poems.

Taken from the lyric 'Song From the Waters' written circa 1827.

The swallow leaves her nest,
  The soul my weary breast;
But therefore let the rain
  On my grave
Fall pure; for why complain?
Since both will come again
  O'er the wave.

The wind dead leaves and snow
  Doth hurry to and fro;
And, once, a day shall break
  O'er the wave,
When a storm of ghosts shall shake
The dead, until they wake
  In the grave.

The refrain for this lyric was 'wild with passion'.

The second example is two verses taken from the poem 'Dream Pedlary', written in the spring of 1830.

If there were dreams to sell,
  what would you buy?
Some cost a dying bell;
  Some a light sigh,
That shakes from life's fresh crown
  Only a rose-leaf down.
If there were dreams to sell,
  Merry and sad to tell,
And the crier rang the bell,
What would you buy?

But there were dreams to sell
  I didst though buy;

128

Life is a dream, they tell,
  Waking, to die.
Dreaming a dream to prize,
  Is wishing ghosts to rise;
And, if I had the spell
  To call the buried well,
Which one would I?

Thomas Lovell Beddoes was born 30 June 1803 in Bristol. His father was an eminent physician who is still noted in medical history for his experiments in the discovery and development of laughing gas. Dr Beddoes was an unattractive man, short and grossly overweight, reticent, outwardly aggressive. Naturally, he had few close friends. The closest perhaps was Samuel Taylor Coleridge. He brought a strong poetical influence to the household. This effect was intensified for Thomas by his mother's background. She came from the wealthy Irish literary family of Edgeworth. Her father Richard and her sister Maria were both authors. The Beddoes household was much dominated by the tools of the medical and chemical professions together with a strong literary influence ranging through books on practical education, parental guidance, poetry, drama and novels.

Beddoes inherited much of his father's character and was deeply influenced by the accoutrements of anatomy and surgery, which he found himself surrounded by from a very early age. However, his father died when Thomas was five years old and now he came under the literary influence of his mother's family.

In 1808, the widowed Anna Beddoes took her eight children to Edgeworthtown in Ireland, home of her brother Richard Lovell Edgeworth, where they spent the entire summer. Here they joined the 22 children, product of Richard's four marriages. In his younger days Richard Edgeworth was known as an arrogant moralist and philosopher but also a ladies' man and a gallant gentleman. By 1908 he had become a cynic, a man whose thoughts were dominated by logic and reason. He ruled his household as an absolute tyrant. Thomas Beddoes and his mother made frequent visits to the Edgeworths from 1908 to 1917. As we shall see, Thomas added much of Richard Edgeworth's character to that which had been formed from his own father, and this he came bitterly to regret.

Mrs Anna Beddoes was by 1813 in failing health and the family home at Bristol was given up and they moved to Malvern. From here Thomas was sent to Bath Grammar School. His physical features at that time were strange. With a high forehead and hair cropped very close to the skin, he had large eyes, which seemed fixed in a stare devoid of emotion and accentuated by heavy, highly arched eyebrows. His mouth was large and very flat against his face; his ears protruded. He followed his father's physique in being short and fat. Little wonder that he was not a popular boy. He was, however, an excellent scholar, such that when, in 1817 he transferred to Charterhouse public school in London, he was immediately placed at the top of the fifth year form.

Charles Bevan, who had the misfortune to fag for Beddoes at Charterhouse recalled him well.

> He was shrewd and sarcastic with a stern aspect. He was head boy of his house and ruled it like a tyrant and bully. But for himself he was impatient of control, unable to accept the authorities over him, and full of mischief carrying out many acts of insubordination and rebellion. He had great natural humour and a great knack at composition in prose and verse, generally burlesque, and a great notion of dramatic effect. Beddoes played no games or sport; he neither liked the discipline or the trouble of learning it. His recreation was mischief. He would wander around those parts of the Charterhouse that were out of bounds, tormenting the servants and the old pensioners who had rooms there. One time he sent a boy to steal the fire irons from every room at the chaplain's office. The cook who was responsible for the implements fell into a great rage late that night. Then it was that Beddoes fastened them all around my neck and me to the knocker, so that the least motion made a loud noise, alarmed the household, and answered Beddoes' purpose, though at the expense to me of a licking at the hands of the assembled servants. He was a persevering and ingenious tormentor as I knew to my cost.

At Charterhouse Beddoes found his classical studies easy. In 1818 he won the sixth form Latin prize, and in 1820 he won the school prizes for Greek and Latin. But the bulk of his time at Charterhouse was given over to insatiable reading of poetry and the Elizabethan dramatists. In the shadow of those great dramatists Shakespeare,

130

Ben Jonson, Marlowe, Bacon and John Webster, whom he loved, Beddoes was busy on his own compositions. There still exists today in the library at Charterhouse the manuscript of his first novel *The Mysterious Cave*. The story takes place in a vast Italian forest. The tale includes clouds of poisonous gas, torrents of hot blood, masked assassins who fill a cooking pot with poisonous stings from snakes and use human bones to stir the contents. Here, at the age of 15, we can already see the style that Beddoes is to use, with increasing intensity, throughout his writing. His genre is the macabre and the gruesome and his muse is death.

In July 1819 his first published work, a poem, 'The Comet', appears in the *Morning Post*. He also completes, late in 1819, a series of morbid verses collected under the heading *Alfarabi*, which can be dismissed as of schoolboy quality. In May 1920 he completes his examinations at Charterhouse and is awarded a place at Pembroke College, Oxford University, where he is to study medicine, following in his father's footsteps. At Oxford he finds himself much influenced by the work of his fellow poet Percy Bysshe Shelley who had been expelled from the same college only a few years earlier. Now begins his only period of prolific writing. This lasts for five years.

In early 1820 he produces three ballads. To these he adds a group of sonnets. The whole he produces under the title *The Improvisatore*. The title page bears a line taken from John Webster, 'I have sung with an unskilful but willing voice'. This volume is indicative of what is to come from Beddoes. Pillars of fire bursting from a lake, from which a brave shepherd rescues a beautiful woman, only to suddenly find himself in a graveyard vault embracing a skull and there found gone mad by the caretaker. Star-crossed lovers, the husband struck by lightning and the wife later found dead upon his grave. Murderers uttering wild curses and vanishing into the skies. The overall impact is horrific. When the volume is published in 1821 by J. Vincent of Oxford, it achieves small sales and very little critical acclaim. Beddoes is depressed by the reception given to *The Improvisatore* and reacts by seizing and destroying every copy he can find. However, its publication provokes him and he devotes all his energies in 1821 to writing what is to be the most successful work published in his lifetime.

The Bride's Tragedy is a play in verse, and Beddoes completes it in the early spring of 1822. Particularly notable is one passage in the narrative – 'Albert & Emily' – where Beddoes turns to nature for effect, something that was very rare in his writing.

A sleepy streamlet
Murmured down the hill.
And on its mossy banks the violet blue,
The couch of perfume, in dark beauty grew.
In the mid stream there was a little isle,
Fragrant and cool with liquid odours wet;
Round it the dimpled current seemed to smile;
Twas like a gem in living silver set.

The play opens with a charming love scene in a garden. The titled Hesperus has married the common girl Floribel in secrecy. They gather flowers for each other and express their love. Alongside this is a prison scene where a noble lord, Hesperus's father, is a debtor in chains. The father will only be released upon condition that Hesperus marries the creditor's daughter. No great hardship, for she is beautiful and has loved Hesperus since they were children playing together; but a dilemma for Hesperus for he has no valid excuse. He murders Floribel but does not conceal the act. He weds the creditor's daughter but is arrested at the wedding feast. He is condemned to the gallows and only 'saved' from them by a poisoned bouquet of flowers sent to him by his new mother-in-law.

The play was published by Rivington in 1822 and the first public performances were seen later that year. The reviews are excellent. Barry Cornwall, at that time a respected dramatist and reviewer, wrote for the *Edinburgh Review*, 'A new young poet playwright of outstanding promise', and for *The London Magazine*, 'A verse play in the best Elizabethan traditions brought into the nineteenth century. It contains more promise, without exception, than any first work I ever saw; beyond Keats and everybody else I think.' John Lacy, better known for his condemnation of contemporary writers than their praise, wrote also in *The London Magazine*, 'An interesting, well-constructed play. I have seldom grown so enthusiastic about a new work.' *Blackwood's Magazine*, in a review running to six pages, said, 'Fresh and young and very charming. One so young will be sure to wonder in later years, at some of its naïvety; but it is a play of which the author need never be ashamed.' In a much briefer review, *The Gentleman's Magazine* gave its approval:

'In the *Bride's Tragedy*, T.L. Beddoes displays a fine originality. We hazard nothing in predicting his attainment to a respectable standard of excellence; and we assert, that a brighter promise was never offered by a youthful genius.'

The London Magazine called him 'a scion worthy of the stock from which Shakespeare & Marlowe sprang'. The most incisive review appeared in *Blackwood's Edinburgh Magazine* in 1823:

> A dark and troubled, guilt-like and death-like gloom flung over this first work of a truly poetical mind, sometimes alternating with an air of ethereal tenderness and beauty, sometimes slowly and in a ghastly guise encroaching upon and stifling it.

The notoriety of the horrific *Improvisatore* followed by the acclaim for *The Bride's Tragedy* established Beddoes as an important figure in contemporary literature. But his commitment to writing had caused his studies at Oxford to fall substantially behind target. A period of intensive work away from all distractions was needed. Beddoes chose Southampton as a base and Barry Cornwall provided him with a letter of introduction to Thomas Forbes Kelsall, a lawyer in that city. Ultimately this introduction to Kelsall was to be the most significant of Beddoes' life and was to have a paramount effect upon his reputation after his death.

Throughout the brilliant summer of 1823 they went for long walks together immersed in mutually stimulating conversations. Thomas Beddoes would let nothing restrict him from indulging in these conversations. Under this inspiration the poetry flowed and his output was prolific. He writes his second play, *Love's Arrow Poisoned*. It begins with a beautiful and tender heroine who soon becomes bitterly cynical and, in typical early Beddoes style, the play ends with cryptic curses and death. He starts *The Last Man*, another piece of cynical writing whose theme is the futility of life and whose central characters are skeletons. He is to continue work on *The Last Man* for the rest of his time in England, but it is never finished. Eventually, towards the end of his life, he incorporates it into *Death's Jest-Book*. Nearing the end of summer he starts work on *Torrismond*, another verse play mainly concerned with the profligate young lecher whose name the play takes. Only a few fragments and verses remained at Beddoes' death, but the lyric

'How many times do I love thee dear?' was still being quoted and sung more than a hundred years after he wrote it.

In the autumn of 1823 Beddoes had to face up to the fact that he was seriously behind with his degree work and he returned to Pembroke College. Despite his acclaim as a writer, his reputation there was not good. He had been uncommunicative to his peers and rebellious to his masters. Now he tried to settle to his course work. His efforts were distracted by his publishers who were calling for a new collection of lyrics. He did get together an assortment of lyrics, which he entitled *Outidana*. But any hope of publication was blocked by his professor of poetry, William Millman, who publicly condemned Beddoes' lyrics as degenerate. He soon lost patience with his fellow scholars, his tutors and his own efforts to study.

In January 1824 he left Oxford to live in London. His contact Barry Cornwall had rooms in Francis St, Victoria and found small bedsitting rooms for Beddoes in nearby Wandsworth at No. 6 Devereux Court. From here Thomas threw himself into the literary life of London. He at once attached himself to a group headed by Shelley's widow Mary and including William Godwin, Thomas Jefferson Hogg, Thomas Hood and, for a short period, William Wordsworth. His constant companion, though, was Barry Cornwall. It is clear from Beddoes' letters that they indulged themselves thoroughly in drunken debauchery. Indeed this was probably Beddoes' introduction to that heavy drinking, which was thereafter to play an important role in the rest of his life. Thomas did not spend all of his time in London during this period. He frequently visited his uncle Dr Robert King at Bristol. Here he formed an intimate relationship with his cousin Zoe. On several occasions he neglected his arrangements in London to remain with her in Bristol. In February 1824 he wrote for her a love sonnet. Whether their intimacy was of a sexual nature we do not know. It would not have been unusual in that late Georgian era for a love affair to have continued without consummation. What we can be almost certain of is that it was the only affair with a woman that Beddoes ever had.

In May 1824 Thomas returned to Oxford briefly to prepare for examinations for his degree. Whilst there he received news that his mother, who had been touring Italy, had been taken seriously ill. He at once departed for Florence, unaware that by now his mother was already dead. On arrival, he was told the dreadful news, but, awaiting nothing further, he returned immediately to London. Upon his mother's death, Beddoes had inherited several farm estates in Shropshire, valuable jewellery and some money. The inheritance was not large but it provided basic living expenses and gave him independence. However, he now rapidly became disillusioned with the literary world around him. In fairness to Beddoes it was arguably the most infertile period for poetry and new plays for the past 300 years. Beddoes had begun what was to be his greatest work *Death's Jest-Book*, but now he felt the poetry within him being slowly strangled. He started to believe that life itself was futile and now began his deep and morbid interest in the afterlife. At this time his depression was only lifted by occasional visits to Zoe King at Bristol.

By the close of March 1825 he was writing to Thomas Kelsall to say that he wished to settle his affairs in England and that he had decided to live in Germany where he would study anatomy and pathology. He asked Kelsall to be his agent in England and sent into his safe keeping some drafts of the first act of *Death's Jest-Book* and several poems, lyrics and jottings including 'The Flowery Alchemist', 'Lord Alcohol', 'The Oviparous Tailor' (an ingenious tale of a tailor who stole hen eggs from a witch and was promptly bewitched into laying eggs himself), 'The Snake is Come Out' (a lyric) and 'Song of a Maid Who is Dead'.

In June 1825 Beddoes returned to Oxford and, having completed his examinations, was awarded his BA. But he never received his degree. At the beginning of July, without any further word to his friends, his family, neither Cornwall nor Kelsall, he departed for Germany. In the remaining 24 years of his life he made only two visits of consequence to England.

By 19 July 1825 he was in Hamburg. He stayed briefly at rooms alongside the river Elbe and by September he had arrived in Göttingen near Hanover. Here he enrolled in the university as a medical student specialising in anatomy. Generally this was a very quiet town of about 10,000 inhabitants, and a small military base. There was, of course, no motorised traffic and even horses and carts were little used, most of the day-to-day carrying and delivering being done by women. Of inns there were plenty and these were much used by the students. Often the tranquillity would be broken by student uproars. Excuses were readily found by students to hold 'celebrations'. These invariably ended with tables, benches and windows being smashed up, fights, and large numbers of students becoming hopelessly drunk. Occasionally the military would act to curb these excesses. On these occasions the students would descend upon Norten, a small resort some ten kilometres away, where there was no militia to prevent their riotous behaviour. In all of this, Beddoes enthusiastically took part. Certainly he loved his pipe and his beer and the opportunity to unload his aggressiveness. In fairness it must be said that Thomas also applied himself seriously to his studies, and this was a great change in character to the indolence he had shown at Oxford. Between diligent studies and drunkenness, he found little time for poetry. Apart from some further revisions and additions to *Death's Jest-Book* and the beautiful lyric 'Song on the Water', there is no evidence that he wrote anything else during his four years at Göttingen. Nevertheless, he was certainly happy in the university atmosphere, at least for the first three years.

At the close of his first year he wrote to Kelsall, 'I do not expect to return to England for many years and should be very much annoyed if forced to do so. I was never better employed, never so happy, never so well self-satisfied.' However, by the spring of 1825 his depression had returned and he writes, 'I am now so thoroughly penetrated with the conviction of the absurdity and unsatisfactory nature of human life that I search fanatically for any shadow of a proof of an after existence in the nature of man. I am haunted forever by it.' In the autumn of that year his mind becomes further tormented by thoughts of the afterlife. He forms a close friendship with a failed scholar, a penniless Russian sponger, who had acquired a great deal of knowledge of the Hebrew doctrine of immortality and was only too willing, at Beddoes' expense, to discuss at length 'that undiscovered country from whose borne no traveller returns'. It is from this point in Beddoes' life that we can trace the escalating depression, which eventually overtook him.

By the beginning of 1828 he had shaken off the melancholy Russian. In March Beddoes returns to Oxford for a few days to take his Masters degree. This completed, he goes on to London and Barry Cornwall. In between drinking bouts with Cornwall, he gives a few lectures, some of a radical political nature and some for literary audiences. None are well attended or received. Beddoes quickly grows weary of what he calls 'this dull, pampered island' and on 8 April he writes to Kelsall, telling him that he has been summoned to return to Göttingen by 30 April and that 'urgent necessity calls me to another continental town in the Netherlands where I must consume a day or two on my passage'. It is a reasonable guess that the town was Amsterdam and the necessity was either for drugs or sex. His summons to Göttingen was to account for his financial irresponsibility and gross misconduct. Either he gave his professors an acceptable answer or his excellent work as a student was taken into account. Whatever the reason, he was allowed to continue his studies. Now he attached himself to a group of liberal agitators who opposed the authorities in every sphere. Neither his spirits nor his conduct improved and in the spring of 1829 he was asked to leave the university.

From there he went to Würzburg in Bavaria, where he enrolled at the university to complete his studies for a medical doctorate. He remained there until September of 1832. During this time his behaviour was very erratic. He would alternate periods of diligent and continuous revision of *Death's Jest-Book* with heavy bouts of drinking and reclusive times when he would sit in his room smoking opium. With his Göttingen reputation as a reference he was able to join an anarchist group, which was rapidly spreading throughout the Balkan states. He soon became a close associate of the leading dissident journalist Dr Klaus Wirth. This was to prove disastrous. The Balkan states had combined together to set up a spy system to flush out anarchists across all the central European countries. Many of Beddoes' activist friends from Göttingen were soon arrested and charged in the name of the King of England (who at that time was also King of Hanover). Beddoes was under surveillance because of his Göttingen contacts. He now compounded this by publishing inflammatory pamphlets roundly condemning the King of Bavaria. His association with Dr Wirth was also well known. It was by chance alone that Beddoes was with the journalist on the night the secret service came to arrest Dr Wirth. As the officers pounded on the front door Beddoes exited in great haste through the back door. He fled immediately to Strasburg.

This was unfortunate since he had completed his examinations and been awarded a medical doctorate but he was now unable to have it conferred upon him. Nevertheless, he assumed the title and began to practise medicine. His stay in Strasburg was short. A scientist and political activist Johann Schoelein, a close friend of Thomas, had ran from Würzburg at the same time as Beddoes.

Schoelein settled in Zurich from where he called Thomas to join him. Beddoes had tired of Strasburg within a few weeks and he eagerly accepted. He joined Schoelein in Zurich in January 1833 and the two soon became lovers.

Here Beddoes practised medicine and continued his political activities. There is evidence that he wrote a number of medical pamphlets and essays. He also continued to work on *Death's Jest-Book* and completed his first final revision of it early during this period. There is no trace of any other poetical or dramatic writing. His reputation as a medical practitioner with a high academic background was quickly established. By the summer of 1935 his name was being put forward for a position as Professor of Medicine at the university of Zurich. This application was unanimously supported by the tutors at the university's medical faculty. The administrators, however, knew of Beddoes' political activities and regarded him as an agitator. The application was refused.

It is probably coincidental that Beddoes then decided to make a short trip to England. He had been completely out of touch with his family and friends in England for some seven years. Even Thomas Kelsall had received no correspondence from him since 1831. Although Beddoes had appointed Kelsall his agent and entrusted him with the safe keeping of his manuscripts, it was to another solicitor friend, Revell Phillips, he had given the management of his farm estates in Shropshire. There had been business correspondence with Phillips on a regular basis and it is very likely that business affairs forced Beddoes' return at this time. He landed at Dover in August 1835 and proceeded to London via Canterbury. At Canterbury he recalled that one Smithers lived there, a fellow pupil from his Charterhouse days, and he at once resolved to pay him a visit. Seeking him out, Beddoes was well received and invited to stay for supper. By the time he left his aggressive and outspoken opinions had so upset his host that he was asked never to call again. In London he transacted whatever business he had as quickly as possible. He made no attempt to contact Cornwall or Kelsall but returned to Zurich at once, arriving on 1 September 1835.

There now followed a period of three or four years in which Thomas found more calmness and contentment than at any period of his life. For recreation he hiked his way through many of the Swiss mountains and valleys. He smoked and drank heavily in his leisure periods. He resumed his correspondence with Kelsall and in 1836 wrote that he was very happy and that he would return to his poetry. In March of 1837 he says he has started a new project, 'perhaps half a hundred lyrical Jewsharpings in various styles and humours'. By the summer of that year he tells Kelsall he has about half the lyrics completed and is 'preparing for press'. The title was to be *The Ivory Gate*. Encouraged by this resumption of contact, Kelsall wrote requesting more detailed knowledge of Beddoes' welfare and activities. This was met with a silence that lasted until November 1844. This seven-year period saw Beddoes' mental instability descend further into restlessness and morbid depression, and was to herald his suicide. Beddoes never completed *The Ivory Gate* for publication. At the time of his death Kelsall could only find five of these pieces and they have never been published.

Beddoes had been actively involved in politics ever since his arrival in Switzerland and, by the summer of 1839, he had close friends amongst the liberal political leaders in Zurich. In September of that year a protest rally against the government led by religious leaders gathered outside the city. It was joined by several thousands of peasants whom the religious leaders were quite unable to control. The result was an attack upon the city. Eventually the government fell and those liberal friends of Beddoes who were not killed were forced to flee. Beddoes was well known to the new controllers, The Committee of Faith, as being a close ally of the fallen government. Nevertheless, he managed to remain at large in the city. In January 1840 he wrote to Revell Phillips, 'In consequence of this state of things, in which neither property nor person is secure, I shall find it necessary to give up my present residence entirely. Indeed the dispersal of my friends all of whom belonged to the liberal party renders it nearly impossible for me to remain longer here.' By March 1840 his life was under specific threat and he was forced to flee.

Now he becomes nomadic. First to Berlin where the only matter of note is that he forms an intimate friendship with a young man, Dr Adolph Frey. Then briefly to England to see Revell Phillips, presumably to deal with his financial affairs. Onwards to Baden, Switzerland where he had stored his collection of books, journals and writings when fleeing from Zurich. In 1844 he arrives in Basle, probably to renew his friendship with Dr Frey who is now practising at the Basle Hospital. Now back to Berlin, onwards to Saxony and then by January 1845 to Frankfurt where he dwells for two months. Then to Giessen, Germany, from where he writes to Kelsall with two new lyrics intended for *Death's Jest-Book*.

In August 1946 Beddoes makes his final visit to England. The 20 years that had passed since family and friends had last seen Thomas had resulted in many changes of appearance and manner. Overweight, bearded, eyes sunken, eccentric, with a cynical and abrupt manner of speech, he was almost unrecognisable to those who had been closest to him. When he arrived to visit William Minton Beddoes and his family at Cheney Longville, riding awkwardly on a donkey, he might have been thought to resemble one of the strange characters from his plays. The Beddoes soon found him a troublesome guest. He was at once loud and intolerant in his opinions and frequently drunk. He had planned to stay for a month but when that time was ended he began to complain of severe pains in his nervous system, whereupon he shut himself up in his room and there he remained for a further five months, much to the dismay of the Beddoes family. During this time he smoked heavily and read incessantly, but would admit no visitors.

Suddenly in mid-February 1847 he departed from Cheney Longville to visit Thomas Kelsall in Southampton. Kelsall also found him greatly changed. Kelsall wrote to Zoe King in Bristol telling her Beddoes had become uninterested in poetry, particularly his own: 'The humour has gone from him. The seriousness of his aspect and manner have increased, almost into a sadness. Scientific matters alone appear to fill up the measure of his thoughts.' Beddoes remained there for six weeks. Despite Kelsall's view of his mood, the renewed acquaintance with Kelsall had cheered him up immensely. When he left in early April to go to London he was in much better spirits than when he had arrived. In London he went immediately to the Cornwalls. He was warmly greeted by Barry and Mrs Cornwall, but they soon found his behaviour extraordinary. He would turn up uninvited at the oddest hours but would not come near them if there were any guests he did not know. Those that did know Beddoes thought that he had gone mad. One example may serve to illustrate the behaviour that so shocked Beddoes' friends. He had a dinner engagement with the Cornwalls but failed to arrive; they went searching for him and found him at Drury Lane arrested by the police. It seems he had dined alone and become drunk. He had then gone to the Drury Lane Theatre and, being not pleased with the play, he had sought to burn down the theatre using a five-pound note as a torch. It may be worth reflecting that £5 in 1846 was the equivalent of about £2,000 today. When Beddoes left London to return to Frankfurt in June 1847, he left behind him memories of behaviour so abominable that family and friends were still complaining about it 30 years later when interviewed by Sir Edmund Gosse as he prepared a biography of Beddoes.

In Frankfurt Beddoes soon met up with a 19-year-old unemployed baker's assistant Konrad Degen, of whom he quickly became enamoured. Degen came to live with him and Beddoes devoted a great deal of time to him. Beddoes no longer had any interest in poetry writing but continued with his anatomical studies and produced essays on his findings in German, French and Danish. It was during the dissecting of a corpse that he became infected with a virus caused by some bacteria entering a small cut on his hand. This quickly turned poisonous. With treatment from his old friend Dr Frey, the poison was dispersed and the swelling subsided. But Beddoes was left in low spirits and a lethargy from which it took him six months to emerge. During this time he would see no one but Degen. He taught him English and spent much time persuading Konrad that he had the talent to become an actor. In the spring of 1848, with Beddoes somewhat recovered, the pair left Frankfurt for a touring holiday through Germany and Switzerland. There is little doubt that they were lovers during this period. Arriving at Zurich, Beddoes' enthusiasm for the young baker prompted him to hire the prestigious Zurich Theatre for three performances of Shakespeare's *King Henry IV Part 1* starring Konrad Degen as Harry Hotspur. The opening night thoroughly exposed the young man's inexperience and inability as an actor and only prompt action by the theatre management prevented the audience from rioting. The pair fled to Basle arriving at the beginning of July. Here Beddoes' tempestuous and intemperate behaviour again took hold. With the intolerance of youth Konrad departed, telling Beddoes their relationship had finished.

Thomas booked himself into a room at the Hotel Cicogne. There he sat alone, utterly dejected, and contemplated suicide. He opened his razor. From his studies of anatomy he was aware that slashing the wrists was an uncertain method. Too often the arteries were missed and, even when located, the pumping of blood took long enough to reach the life-threatening stage as to give every chance of the victim being found before death. Beddoes chose an artery in his left leg and deliberately cut it open. The blood pumped out fiercely and Beddoes ought to have died very quickly. But fate took a hand that morning of 18 July. A hotel porter, delivering luggage, noticed blood flowing under the door of Thomas's room, and raised the alarm. Beddoes was quickly removed to Basle Hospital where, by a considerable coincidence, he was attended to by his long-time friend Dr Frey.

The bleeding was quickly stopped and, with good bandaging applied, Dr Frey believed that the wound would heal rapidly. This did not suit Beddoes' plan. He removed the bandages and each time they were re-applied he secretly tore them off, only re-applying them at times of inspection. He must have known that gangrene would set in. During his medical practice in the 1840s he would have encountered several cases where the gangrene infection had spread rapidly resulting in death. Gangrene did take hold in Beddoes' leg and Thomas now set about making his will: £1,000 to Revell Phillips; £400 to Zoe King; £200 to her sister Emmeline; £150 to his own sister; to Dr Frey, his instruments and his library; to Kelsall, his manuscripts with instructions to publish as he felt fit; the remainder of his estate to his brother. The document was brief and to the point with no evidence of an unbalanced mind to be discovered in it. Witness to the will was Dr Ecklin. Another witness was Konrad Degen who, upon hearing of Thomas's admission to hospital, had rushed to his side and had remained there ever since.

Dr Frey, however, was most conscientious in checking his patient and on 1 October he noted the spread of gangrene. Operating immediately, he successfully amputated the infected section of the leg. Once again Beddoes' plan to depart this world had been thwarted. Surprisingly, he seemed to take this quite well. With hindsight it seems probable that he was trying to allay suspicions of his true intentions. On 9 October he wrote to his sister saying that a fall from his horse had badly shattered his leg and had occasioned an amputation 'a month ago' from which he was recovering well. This news was accepted without question in England.

Meanwhile Thomas was quietly making plans for his death. In January 1849 he wrote a carefully prepared suicide note addressed to Revell Phillips, ending with the words: 'I ought to have been among other things a good poet. Now I shall be food for what I am good for, worms.' On 24 January he sent Konrad Degen into town with a prescription to obtain a quantity of curare. This was a resin used in very small doses to relax the muscles, but if introduced directly into the bloodstream in any substantial quantity would cause coma and, in most cases, death. The next day he sent Degen to return some books, which Dr Frey had lent him. Whilst Degen was gone, Beddoes administered all of the curare to himself. It is most probable that he made a small cut upon himself and rubbed it in. When Degen returned he found Thomas in such an alarming state of fever and delirium that he at once rushed back to Dr Frey. The good doctor attended immediately, together with Dr Ecklin, and they found Beddoes dying. Thomas Lovell Beddoes died on 26 January 1849 at the age of 45. He was holding his farewell letter to Revell Phillips, neatly folded, upon his chest. By his side was his bible, in which he had carefully written, 'Bequethed to my dear sister'.

Events concerning Beddoes after his death were even more bizarre than those surrounding his life. To begin with, Dr Adolph Frey's final account of Beddoes' death is highly suspect. Dr Frey wrote to Revell Phillips and William Minton Beddoes informing them that Thomas had died suddenly, but peacefully, of natural causes by a stroke. In the hospital register Dr Frey wrote, 'Cause of death – apoplexy'. At a later date Dr Ecklin stated that death was caused by a self-administered poison. In any event a person dying of sudden stroke is not likely to have a farewell letter neatly clasped to his bosom and a bible first inscribed then carefully placed by his side. It is also curious that on 29 January 1849 Beddoes was buried in the common vault of the hospital at the Church of St Johanntor, but on 15 May 1849 Dr Frey had the body exhumed and buried elsewhere. We may conclude that Dr Frey was simply trying to protect his erstwhile friend and probably lover from the scandal of suicide. If this was the case then the doctor failed. Even from the first receipt of Dr Frey's letters, Beddoes' family and friends were quite unable to reconcile Frey's account of a peaceful, natural, almost happy, death with their recollections of the lunatic behaviour during his visit to England in 1846. Many enquiries were made by Beddoes' relatives and friends in correspondence lasting some five years after his death.

Kelsall went to Germany and Switzerland and saw everyone connected with Thomas's death. He came to the firm conclusion that it was by suicide. In 1857 Zoe King made a lengthy visit to Switzerland to make enquiries. Clearly her love for Thomas had lasted for more than 30 years. She saw Doctors Frey and Ecklin, Konrad Degen, a priest who had regularly visited Thomas at Basle hospital, and the staff of the Cicogne Hotel. She too became convinced of Beddoes' suicide. She wrote up a detailed diary of her interviews and this she gave to Kelsall, obtaining from him an undertaking that it would not be released during her lifetime.

The next mystery concerns what happened to Beddoes' writings. It is true that when Beddoes left England in 1825 he was disillusioned with poetry and drama. Also true that during his early years abroad he had written to his friends telling them that he no longer wished to write for the literary world. But he did say he would concentrate on writing for the medical profession. It is known that he wrote several medical pamphlets in German and French and some were published in continental newspapers. Furthermore, he had sent a completed copy of *Death's Jest-Book* to Kelsall and Barry Cornwall in 1839, and in subsequent letters mentioned many revisions and additions to this play and to the ongoing *Ivory Gate* project, and he mentions 'certain poems and fragments which I have written during this happy time [in Switzerland in the spring of 1848]'. Yet when Beddoes' library boxes were collected from Baden and sent to Kelsall they contained only some revisions and additions to *Death's Jest-Book* and some fragments of poems. Of his medical essays and pamphlets there was nothing to be found.

Degen told Zoe King in 1857 that on one occasion Beddoes flew into a rage and tore up pencilled drafts of poems and stories, and that on another occasion he had set fire to 'some drafts of a play'. That may in part explain the paucity of literary work but it does not explain what happened to the 'perhaps a half hundred' lyrics for *The Ivory Gate* project of which Beddoes wrote to Kelsall. Relating this to the fact that only about 70 in total of Beddoes' poems ever came to light, it does seem that a great number were missing. So far as his written works on medical subjects are concerned, it seems inconceivable that he would have destroyed them so we must assume that they were stolen.

We now come to the unusual events surrounding publication of Beddoes' work after his death. Thomas Kelsall had come into possession of Beddoes' box of literary effects about three months after his death. He first set about gathering together and editing the drafts, revisions and additions to *Death's Jest-Book*. Kelsall arranged in 1850 for this play to be published by William Pickering. They were, for some unknown reason, unwilling to put Beddoes' name to the play, and it was published with the playwright stated as 'anonymous'. It took only a year before it became open knowledge within literary circles that *Death's Jest-Book* was Beddoes' work. Pickering then published it together with *The Bride's Tragedy* and other poems edited by Kelsall and in Beddoes' name in 1851.

Kelsall found during the 1850s and 60s that there was considerable interest in Beddoes' work but realised that to achieve publication of all his work would need support from a leading name in the literary world. Amongst those who expressed admiration for his work were Alfred Lord Tennyson, Walter Landor and Robert Browning. Kelsall decided to place his hopes upon Robert Browning and opened correspondence with him about Beddoes' work in 1867. This correspondence continued for five years with Kelsall seeking to persuade Browning to edit a Complete Works edition with the Browning name to support it. Certainly Browning was considerably interested in Beddoes' work. Browning at that time wished to be elected Professor of Poetry at Oxford University (which he never was) and declared that if appointed his first lecture would be upon 'that extravagant and macabre poet Beddoes'. Eventually, in 1873, Browning wrote agreeing to receive everything that Kelsall had concerning Beddoes. Whereupon Thomas Kelsall passed away. The widowed Mrs Kelsall gathered up everything; manuscripts, publications, fragments, letters, Zoe King's journals, notes and hospital entries from Basle, Beddoes' suicide note, etc. These she sent to Browning in one box, later known in literary circles as the Browning Box, together with a letter asking him to open it in private. However, Browning paid little attention to the contents of the box and never edited or published the edition of Beddoes' work that Kelsall had hoped for.

Ten years were to pass before any further progress was made. In 1883 literary scholar Sir Edmund Gosse commenced work on a major essay of Beddoes' life and works. He was given permission by Browning to make a transcription of the papers in the Browning Box and this task Gosse entrusted to his pupil James Campbell. This proved to be most fortuitous. In 1889 Browning died in Venice; his house was immediately ransacked and the Browning Box has never been seen again. The transcripts led to Gosse editing *The*

Poetical Works of Thomas Lovell Beddoes, which he caused to be published by J.M. Dent & Co. in 1890. Gosse then edited *The Letters of Thomas Lovell Beddoes*, which was published by Elkin Matthews in 1894. Thus, finally, more than 40 years after his death, were Beddoes' works brought to the widest possible public attention.

Undoubtedly *Death's Jest-Book*, 25 years in preparation, was Beddoes' greatest work. He began it aged 22 in Southampton with Kelsall as his sounding board. Kelsall reported that he wrote it at breakneck speed and with great enthusiasm. Later, although he lost his interest in literary work, he persevered with *Death's Jest-Book*, continuously revising it until his death. It is mainly upon this play that his fame must rest.

In *Death's Jest-Book* Beddoes' spectacular and morbid genius comes to its fruition. In it he creates a central character, Isbrand, a court jester, who sings wild songs and shakes his cap and bells to music, which is in tune with the laughter of devils. Isbrand's one desire is to hate. Probably Beddoes wrote some aspects of his own character into this part. This, from Act 2 Scene 3:

A sceptre is smooth handling, it is true. And one grows fat and jolly in a chair. That has a kingdom crouching under it, with one's name on its collar, like a dog, to fetch and carry. But the heart I have is a strange little snake. He drinks not wine, when he'd be drunk; But poison: he doth fatten on bitter hate.

Skeleton figures, seemingly painted on the wall of a ruined church, step down to feast and to dance a gavotte. The decayed flesh of a dead knight is made whole and rises to haunt his murderer. A duke, at war with his enemies in Africa, is saved by a devoted friend from capture, and repays the act by murdering him during a quarrel over a woman. The ghost of his friend comes back to haunt the duke.

This, from Act 2, Scene 2:

The days come when scarce a lover, for his maiden's hair, can pluck a stalk whose rose draws not its hue out of a hate-killed heart. Nature's polluted, there's man in every secret corner of her, doing damned wicked deeds. Thou art old world, a hoary atheistic murderous star; I wish you would die, or could be slain.

A lover, Wolfram, lies dying beneath the window of his mistress Sibylla. She sings a bridal serenade to him as he writhes to death. Later, whilst she sleeps, the ghost of Wolfram visits her. He angrily accuses her of letting him die alone and calls her to come to him. She answers:

O death! I am thy friend, I struggle not with thee, I love thy state: you can be sweet and gentle, be so now; and let me pass praying away, into thee as twilight still does into starry night.

The action is erratic and confused. A conventional murder play becomes chaotic. Thus to some degree the play is ineffectual. Such is the flavour of Beddoes at his best and worst.

After 1851 *Death's Jest-Book* becomes more widely known and attracts extensive criticism, mostly highly favourable. Tennyson wrote to Zoe King and Sir Henry Warren stating he rated the play 'highly' and much admired the enthusiasm of the work. Browning said he admired it and that 'the author interests me greatly'. Walter Landor said, 'No work of the same wealth of genius as *Death's Jest-Book* has been given to the world since Elizabethan times.' *Blackwood's Magazine* spoke of the anonymous 1850 edition: 'Wait a little before you throw this book out of the window. In this mad and plotless play there are finer passages than any living dramatist has composed.' Bryan Waller Proctor (a.k.a. Barry Cornwall), whose criticism of the play Beddoes had invoked since its first inception, called it 'the finest dramatic work seen in my lifetime'. The *Athenaeum Magazine* reviewed the play on several occasions from October of 1850 through to December 1890. Its appraisals varied. Of the 1850 edition it said, 'There are many things too bad for blessing and many things too good for banning', and 'an empty tragic mask with no face behind it'. The 1851 edition produced a two-page review, mainly favourable, and notable for a description of the lyrics 'delicious in their wild singing though they be grave flowers'. Their review of Sir Edmund Gosse's edition of 1890 was shorter and uncomplimentary, referring to Beddoes as an 'egregious failure'.

What then are we to make of Beddoes? A gifted young poet and dramatist certainly. In 1832 the *Athenaeum* described him as 'one of the most imaginative poets which our age has seen'. His education was of the highest level. The gift of tongues was his; he spoke and wrote fluently in English, including ancient Anglo-Saxon, Greek, Latin, German, French, Danish and Arabic. An excellent letter writer when he chose, Swinburne said of him, 'A brilliant correspondent. On poetical questions he gives to me a higher view of his fine and vigorous intelligence than in any other of his written works.'

He was a man with a great store of general knowledge, much gathered from his wide spectrum of reading and from his travels, which were extensive by the standards of his era. He became a professionally qualified man of medicine and science, yet retained all of his artistic flair. He was an outspoken radical political activist. Beddoes led a bohemian lifestyle to the extreme. Somewhere quite early in his life he became deeply disillusioned. At first with poetry and drama. Who could blame him for that in an era almost devoid of any new work of quality? An era when such a modest reviewer and dramatist as Barry Cornwall was reckoned to be a great name. In his last days at Basle he continued to lament the lack of contemporary exciting poetry. Where now, he asked, are the great poets such as Keats, Shelley and the latter-day Wordsworth, who had preceded the current void? It is surprising that he omits from that list Samuel Taylor Coleridge whom he had met as a young boy. Then came disenchantment with politics. He had believed that revolution could sweep away the aristocrat rule which presided in many continental countries; but it was not to happen in his time. On England, he had quite given up hope: he thought that the stagnant minds of the English middle classes were incapable of creating radical change. At the end of his life he continued to attack them: 'It is typical of the English middle classes that they are even proud of Liverpool and Manchester, the poorest of places.'

Disillusionment over the futility of life itself led to an unnatural interest in the power of death, the afterlife and the abnormal; they are ever present in his mind and work. That there was madness in his mind, there can be little doubt. Without it he could not have created the best of his drama and poetry. His mind had long been unstable. Part of the interest in his writing centres upon the ability of his mind to dart off in different directions and fix quickly upon wild and unexpected ideas. He expressed contempt for sentimentality yet this emotion was often felt in his poems. Never was his

148

instability clearer to his friends than when he suddenly would swing from a mood of dark despair into a state of excessive high spirits.

Yet his suicide was no sudden act of madness. Frustrated by his own choice of subjecting his latent literary talents to the logic and disciplines of medicine and science; disillusioned by the defeat of his political ideals, his mind became bitter and humourless. Lonely in a foreign country. Uncertain of his gender preferences. Weakened by a virus. Is it any wonder that a depression fell upon him so deep that he could not overcome it? Once that logical part of his mind had decided to depart this life and investigate the next world then he allowed nothing to prevent him from carrying out his objective.

The suicide of Thomas Lovell Beddoes was carefully calculated and carried out with determination. What he found on the other side of this earthly world we shall never know in our lifetime. There, with his underachievement and his penchant for the macabre, we must leave him.

Cesare Pavese

The Vice of Genius

Tall and dark Cesare Pavese may have been, but handsome he was not. His large hooked nose, thick glasses, unstyled mop of greasy black hair and emaciated frame made him physically unattractive. Yet many women were attracted to him because of his intelligence and wit and his ability to think and converse profoundly. But his predilection for prostitutes made him a poor lover and despite many brief affairs with women he was quite unable to create what he most desired, a stable long-term relationship. Thus women and Pavese's attitude towards them became one of the most important factors in his life and his death by suicide.

Photo: Leemage/Lebrecht Music and Arts

151

Cesare Pavese was a great intellectual. He was considered the best Italian poet and novelist of his time. He was also the most important translator of his era. His translations of American authors, courageous at a time when Italy was under Fascist dictatorship, made American culture known in Italy and Italian literature known in the USA. Americans today read his works and through him understand the Italy of that era.

Why then does he commit suicide when 42 at the height of his literary powers? To understand Pavese we must recall the difficult political and social times of his generation. The Fascist dictatorship and the poverty of his people. If we are to draw any conclusions from his actions we should also be mindful that he was schizophrenic. Only then shall we gather any understanding of his obsession with the act of suicide.

Cesare Pavese was born 9 September 1908, weighing an extraordinary eleven pounds. His mother came from a rich family of traders at Casale near Turin. His father's family had been established in the Piedmont region for many centuries. His father Eugenio was employed as a clerk to the magistrates at the Court of Justice in Turin. At this time the family lived in Turin but spent the summer vacation at their farm in Santo Stefano Belbo in Piedmont. It was here, in the Langhe countryside that Cesare was born during the summer holiday. The land here is hilly and lends itself naturally to vineyards and winemaking. It is famous for its Asti Spumante.

The open level road between the hills on the Asti side of the province leads to Canelli and onwards to Genoa. At Genoa is the sea; beyond the sea is the America and 'South Seas' of Pavese's poetry in *Work Wearies*. In his final novel, *The Moon and Bonfires* Pavese tells us that as a boy it is upon this road that he set out when he wanted to go towards life, the city and women. He spends every vacation of his first six years happily in the hills of Santo Stefano.

In 1914 his boyhood happiness is shattered by the death of his father. Eugenio dies of a brain tumour, which has been developing since before Cesare's birth. His mother, already a grieving woman who had lost three children at early ages, now finds all the family responsibilities falling upon her shoulders. She becomes very hard of heart and makes the children feel the weight of her authority. Cesare is regularly beaten as punishment for small misdemeanours.

At the end of the summer vacation his sister falls ill with

diphtheria so the entire family must stay at Santo Stefano until the end of the year. It was during this long stay in the Piedmont country that Cesare first developed the intense love of country scenery and the ways of country people that had such a profound impact on his personality for the rest of his life.

Cesare returns to school in Turin. It is a fee paying private school, the Trombetta situated on the Via Garibaldi. His yearly reports are very average. On several occasions the head teacher writes 'could do better, he is intelligent but too lazy'. From age eleven he transfers to the Jesuit school. This private school is mainly attended by sons of the aristocracy or wealthy traders. As a farm boy he felt out of place and could not concentrate. He developed a nervous habit of pulling his hair into tangled knots, a habit that continued throughout his life. His progress was poor, so he was taken out of the Jesuits and sent to a state school, the Moderno. He continued to be silent and introspective at school and at home.

His appearance made him appear odd to other boys. His huge weight as a baby was gone, he was now thin and tall causing him to walk crouched over. He continued to wear short trousers until he was 15. His hair was unkempt and he wore a cap pressed firmly down upon it. He wore thick-lensed glasses, giving his eyes a bulging appearance. All of this was compounded by asthma, which caused him to cough violently throughout the winter months. Little wonder that he lacked friends and confined himself to reading, gradually retreating further inside himself.

In much of his writing towards the end of his life, Pavese makes it clear that he was always sad when he lived in the city and that by contrast the countryside seemed to him a place of great joy. Nevertheless, from his early teens he slowly started to relate to city life. Its hustle and bustle, its wealth and well-dressed people, the music and gaiety on the one hand, and on the other, its squalid areas with lonely people, drunks, thieves, whores and queers began to fascinate him. But he always remained the introspective country boy on the periphery of all the activity, always suspicious, ever nervous. His defence always was silence. Describing his country boy attitude to the city he wrote:

> We of the countryside are like this; we like to look at the other side of the hedge, but never jump over it.

At the age of 15 he transfers to the Lyceum, a senior high school. He makes several new friends, one in particular being Mario Sturani who remains a friend for life. He also comes under the influence of Monti, one of the tutors, who will be a guiding influence and friend long after both are gone from the Lyceum. Pavese makes great progress in his first year. He also develops an interest in women, which soon becomes an obsession.

Typical of his dramatic involvement with women was an encounter in 1924 with a cabaret singer who was performing at the Meridiana nightclub in Turin. Pavese had seen her act several times and became besotted with her. He managed to speak briefly with her on two or three occasions. Eventually he gathered up enough courage to ask her out and she agreed to meet him outside the front entrance to the club one evening at 6 p.m. Cesare was there promptly, but she was not. Cesare waited despite being lashed by heavy rain. The hours passed by and still he waited. He left at midnight soaked to the skin and freezing cold. Next day he was told she had left at 6 p.m. through the back door to meet another admirer. This news devastated him. The rain and bitter cold struck him down with pleurisy, which kept him off college for 14 weeks. During this time he lost weight from his already thin frame and he became very weak physically. His confidence in himself was also greatly weakened. When he returned to college his friends rallied round him; some of his depression left him and his physical strength began to return.

By 1925, aged 17, he is already writing to his friends that his mind is stagnating and that he is in a depressive state about which he can do nothing. At the same time he writes to Mario Sturani saying that he is fairly satisfied with himself and the progress he has made that year and that he is changing from his usual depression into a 'kind of pain, which is of itself constructive'. His schizophrenia has already begun. He writes many letters and is torn between the urge to communicate constantly with his friends and a desire (in his own words) 'for that splendid isolation which men of genius know'. Death is an 'absurd vice', which enters and leaves his blood, ever returning as an incurable disease, 'a syphilis'. The only balms for this disease were poetry and women, nothing else really existed.

Cesare passes the extremely difficult university entrance examination. He has to say goodbye to his old professor, Monti. They talk at length. Pavese tells Monti that he feels sexually

154

inadequate and desires, when with women, to be as virile as any other man. He admits to Monti that he frequently visits prostitutes to act out his desires for virility. He also tells Monti of his ambition to write works that will establish him as a hater of all tyranny. At this time Pavese saw himself as a Liberal and believed that through his non-conformist writing he could rally anti-Fascist opinion. He carried these thoughts with him for some 20 years, but refused to participate in the resistance movement against the Fascists.

The two matters discussed with Monti are also the subject of several letters at this time to his friend Mario Sturani. In December 1925 he writes:

My soul is hopelessly consumed by the desire for a living woman, soul and flesh, to be able to hold her without restraint and excite her, pressing her trembling body close to mine; but on calmer days to lie serenely beside her, with no carnal thought, and to gaze upon her sweet face and listen to her sweet voice.

Again in May 1926 he writes to Sturani:

I am without a woman to clasp to my heart. I have never had one and I shall never have one. I am alone, exhausted by immense passionate desires and unceasing, aimless thoughts.

In February 1926 he writes:

Dear Mario, my sister is writing for me because I am in bed. Let us hope I stay there for I do not feel like working. That famous work I told you about two years ago is coming along [*Work Wearies* – a collection of poems, many of which express his anti-Fascist sentiments]. But it proceeds with great difficulty. My will to work gets feebler every day, but if I lose it altogether I shall kill myself and you shall deliver my eulogy.

It is now that his thoughts of suicide begin to crystallise.

In December 1926 he goes to a desolate place in the Piedmont countryside with a gun, probably with the thought of shooting himself. He cannot do it and fires the gun into the ground. But the intention is there and he writes (to Sturani):

155

I imagined the tremendous jolt it will give me on the night when the last illusions and fears will have left me, and I will place the gun against my head and fire it to shatter my brain.

In April 1927 he writes again to Mario Sturani to say:

I shall write no more. I no longer have the strength, I live in an agony of uncertainty, shall I kill myself or shall I not? I would like to stupify myself with drink and do the deed. But I cannot. I am just a fool. As for cocaine or morphine, heaven knows what they would cost. That way I should at least have a grandiose ending. But I haven't the courage. I am childish, a cretin and a poser. Most probably I shall masturbate myself to death. I behave like a man in desperation. I am lucky that no woman has ever accepted me; with the fine personality I have now, we would both be in trouble. Pavese is dead.

We must remind ourselves that this was Pavese at the age of 19.

But he does continue to write and only three months later produces one of his most imaginative poems 'Gardens'. Still he cannot avoid his obsession with death; one of the final lines of 'Gardens' reads: *I await death, the last song and the most beautiful.* For Pavese no joy surpassed the joy of suffering, as he was to say many times to his friends.

Around this time his friend Baraldi committed suicide. He had a suicide pact with his girlfriend. He shot himself but she did not. This event shook Pavese badly. Once again he went to the woods, this time at the Parco Naturale in the Bardonecchia area, to shoot himself. Again he failed. He suddenly found a desire to live and he fired his shot into a tree.

Cesare writes his first short stories shortly after joining university. He shows them to his old professor, Monti. Monti criticises the endings, in all of which the characters commit suicide. Pavese stands his ground, insisting that every day one hears of suicides. But Monti wins the argument mainly because Pavese sees himself in the characters and whilst, on the one hand, he is obsessed with thoughts of suicide, on the other, he is frightened of the act.

Now Cesare enters a period of regular meetings with new friends from university and old friends from the Lyceum. It is one of the very few times in his life when he is not a loner. He begins to go to the cinema frequently and he enjoys very much American films. This leads to a great interest in American literature. For his degree thesis he writes an analysis of the poetry of Walt Whitman. Although Whitman was almost unknown in Italy at that time, the examining professor attributed an anti-Fascist political theme to the thesis and Cesare's work was rejected. Pavese appealed against this and was successful. He was awarded a First-Class degree.

He leaves university in 1930 and now begins a long period of translations of American literature. In Florence in 1931 his first translation, *Our Mr Wrenn* (Sinclair Lewis) is published. It is the first translation into Italian of any contemporary American literature, and introduces to Italians the American colloquial language of the era.

His mother had sold their farm and had bought a small house in Reaglie. It was here that Pavese would spend his long vacations, often bringing several of his new friends. They eat and drink heavily and discuss their own poetry. Cesare's only other recreation was to swim or row on his beloved river Po. As he rows along the Po his vivid imagination allows him to picture himself as Captain Ahab from *Moby Dick*. Thus begins his most important translation from American literature. The regular exercise on the river Po strengthens him physically and his asthma and migraines cease.

Early in 1932 his translation of *Moby Dick* (Herman Melville) is published in Turin by Einaudi Publishing House. It is at a literary gathering shortly afterwards that he meets Tanya, the only woman he ever really loves. He writes much about her, but never writes her name, referring always to her as 'the woman with the hoarse voice'. She was not beautiful, but she was athletic and had a strong personality. At university she studied mathematics and seemed the antithesis to the poet Pavese. But for Pavese this woman was different from all others. He is fascinated by her robustness, her self-assurance, her firm, almost hard features. His weakness of character found strength in her.

Almost every poem in *Work Wearies* (his first published work) carries some allusion to her. Here are two extracts:

...

These hard hills that have made my body
Opened to me the wonder

157

Of this woman, who does not know I live her and cannot
understand her

. . .

I have never been able to grasp her: her reality eludes me
every time.
I don't know if she is beautiful. Among women she is very
young:
. . .
She is like the morning. Her eyes suggest
All the distant skies of those faraway mornings.
And she has in her eyes a firm purpose: a light clearer
Than the dawn has ever had on these hills.

(From 'Encounter')

. . .

There is no man who can leave a trace on her. What has been
Dissolves like a dream in the morning, and only she lasts.

. . .

She is firm in all that she does.

. . .

But her hard body and her unforthcoming eyes
Unfold in a voice that is low and a little hoarse:
The voice of a tired man. And no tiredness can touch her.

If one stares at her lips, she cautiously offers
A waiting glance: no one dares a bold act.
Many men know her ambiguous smile,
The sudden shadow on her brow. If there is a man
Who knew her moaning from passion,
Now he suffers for it day after day, not knowing for whom
She is living today.

She smiles to herself
The most ambiguous smile as she walks

(From 'A Memory')

158

Tanya was a member of the Communist Party, which was in effect the underground movement against the Fascists. She was active at a high level locally. She had already been convicted, in 1926, of subversive activities along with her lover of that time, Alto Spinelli. She had avoided a prison sentence, but was under surveillance by the Fascists. Though not an active dissident, Pavese was known to be a sympathiser and was therefore also under casual surveillance. This all created difficulties in Cesare and Tanya meeting alone together. Nevertheless, during this period from 1932 to 1935 Tanya reciprocated Cesare's love.

In 1935 Alto Spinelli was still in prison in Rome. But Tanya continued to correspond with him. To avoid the risks involved in receiving his letters Tanya asked Pavese to use his address. In his weakness and obsession for her he agreed. In May 1935 the police raided Pavese's house and found a letter from Spinelli. Cesare and Tanya were arrested. At the trial Pavese refused to give any explanation of the letters; this resulted in Tanya being released. Pavese was charged with subversion and sentenced to three years detention at Brancaleone open prison 700 miles away at Italy's southern most point on the Ionian Sea.

During his imprisonment at Brancaleone, Pavese exchanges a few postcards with Tanya but writes only one letter. It is short and simple. It ends: 'I thank you for all the thoughts you have for me. For you I have only one and it never ends.' However, he corresponds extensively with his friends and relatives. He retains his sense of humour and this comes across particularly in his letters to his friend Sturani. In one he tells him how hilarious it was when the police officer searching his flat found his pornographic writing: 'Reading some of them he forgot everything else including his duties.' In another letter to Sturani he says he has written a very funny short comedy piece entitled *He-Goat God*, but which is so sexually filthy it cannot be printed.

Sturani it is who is also told that being in detention in the fishing village at Calabro has turned his love of the sea to hatred.

His thoughts are never far away from suicide and on 11 September 1935 he writes to Monti: 'We shall see one another on my return to Turin which will be in 3 years, unless my hand slips while making the knot in my tie, in which case I say goodbye to you now.'

Pavese's asthma now returns with force. He is having four attacks

159

a day and cannot walk 200 metres without collapsing. His schizophrenia now becomes more overt. If his family write encouraging letters he answers with abuse; if they write without sympathy he curses their lack of encouragement. Einaudi writes to tell him that he has published *Work Wearies* in Turin. Yet this does not lift his spirits. The poems find few readers at this time. Pavese's boredom with life intensifies and he suffers from bouts of anxiety and morbid thoughts. He tries to overcome this crisis and turns now from writing poetry to short stories.

In fact his confinement at Brancaleone lasts only one year. His friends had arranged an appeal and the remaining two years were suspended. When given the news, Pavese expresses no joy. His first words after receiving the news are, 'I must return to Turin for her immediately.' The woman 'with the hoarse voice' has continued to dominate his thoughts. Throughout the long train journey to Turin his thoughts of her, and his emotions, build up.

At the station he is met by his old friend Sturani. He does not greet Sturani but asks him immediately, 'Where is she?' Sturani does not want to answer. He begins to talk to Cesare of recent events in Turin. Pavese shouts at him, 'Where is she; where is Tanya?' Now Sturani must answer. 'Forget about her; she got married yesterday.' Cesare faints and falls crashing to the ground. He is helped home and soon recovers physically. But the news has hit him hard. He shuts himself away and will speak to no one, nor will he eat. In April 1936 he writes in his diary:

Having reached a moral state where I am lacking in any self-respect I feel there should be material abjection as well. For example, how fitting it would be if my shoes were full of holes. Only this way can I explain my present suicidal state. I know I am forever condemned to think of suicide when faced with any embarrassment or grief. This is what terrifies me; my basic principle is suicide, never committed ... but the thought of it embraces my sensibility. This is what she has done. I've had an affair during which she judged and found me unworthy to continue. Compared to this disaster, the regret of my having lost a lover, even with all its terrible emotions, is as of nothing. The awareness of this defeat becomes confused in my mind with the heavy set backs which I have not known since 1934. Away with aesthetics and poses! away with genius!

160

away with the lot! Have I ever done anything in my life that was not the action of a crack-brained fool? A fool who does not know how to live, who has not developed morally, who is frivolous, who sustains himself with thoughts of suicide but not committing it.

When at last he his able to contact her, Tanya tells him, 'I could not marry you because although you are a good writer you are not a good man for a woman.'

Pavese remains under police surveillance. Most of his friends, including professor Monti and Leone Ginzburg from his university days are still in jail. Now he enters the most intense period of his literary life, reading to the point of exhaustion and seeking new material for his writing. He also takes work at Einaudi's publishing office in Turin. At the same time he is working diligently during his most productive and important period of translations. These include: John Dos Passos – *The Big Money*; John Steinbeck– *Of Mice and Men*; and Gertrude Stein – *The Autobiography of Alice. B. Toklas.*

In 1938 he completes a volume of short stories, *Festival Nights*. His mood at this time may be judged from this extract from one of the stories, 'Suicides':

For some years now I have suffered from delusions and bitter remorse. I am not made for storms or struggles. Even if on some days I go into the streets full of daring and stride around with a challenging pace, I repeat that I ask nothing more of life than to be allowed to watch it.

Einaudi refuses to publish the volume at this time and in fact it is not published until 1953 in the wake of his death.

In the summer of 1939 he determines to write a book of opposition and revolt against the poor conditions being experienced by the peasants of the countryside under Fascist rule. In only three months, from June to August, he writes *The Harvesters*. In this book Pavese diverts from contemporary Italian literature, which is often based on conventional plots of an idyllic nature. This novel is set against the background of the Piedmont countryside and throughout it we find sex, violence, brutality towards women, illiteracy and the hard-working life of the peasants. The language is more incisive and immediate than had been seen before in Italian contemporary literature. Perhaps Pavese cannot be as bold as he wants in this book, because Fascism is at the height of its powers. Some 18 months elapse before Einaudi will publish it; and even then it receives mixed reviews.

In 1939 Pavese completes his translations of *Moll Flanders* (Daniel Defoe) and *David Copperfield* (Charles Dickens), and these are immediately published and receive wide acclaim. He is also working on his translation of *Three Lives* (Gertrude Stein), which is published early in 1940.

Throughout 1939 he attends many discussions, meeting with his communist friends although he still does not become a member of the party. He is now attempting to replace women and the unrequited love of Tanya with written work and political involvement. Although only 31, his name is known throughout Italy and his literary, cultural and political contacts are widespread.

Towards the end of July 1940 Cesare meets, by chance, Nando Pivano, a former student from his days as a temporary teacher at the Lyceum. She is young, beautiful and articulate. He immediately forms a serious attachment to Nando. They see each other almost every day for the next three years, whenever Cesare is in Turin. Pavese is always waiting for her on the Stupingi Boulevard and they sit drinking coffee together whilst Cesare reads to her. He writes many letters to her. In one letter during the first months of their relationship he enters into a long self-analysis. Here are a few brief but significant extracts from that letter:

His basic inclination is to give his actions a significance that is beyond their actual worth, in anything he says or does Pavese reveals his split personality; he can only regard his life as a great drama in which he performs. He is controlled by contrasting needs; he wants to be alone but at the same time is desperate to be at the centre of a group which understands Pavese's solitude. Pavese takes things too seriously and gets worked up in the manner of an actor from the old school of Greek Tragedy.

This craving for a home and life he will never know was summed up by Pavese when he said, 'The only women worth marrying are those you cannot trust to marry.' Perhaps I am summed up by another of my frequent sayings, 'all or nothing'. Pavese never stops halfway.

162

In another letter to Nando in March 1941 Pavese refers to her as a virgin and claims that she has said many times that she is a masculinised woman. In this letter he also infers that Nando is a lesbian. There is little doubt that some aspects of Nando's character remind Pavese again of Tanya, and at times Pavese fantasises that she is Tanya.

In 1940, at the time when he first meets Nando, he writes *The Beautiful Summer*. It explores the corruption caused to the working classes, particularly women, by Fascism. In this volume Pavese enters into a new style of writing. The novel is entirely dominated by conversation between the characters. However, the book is widely regarded as decadent and is not published. Pavese must wait until 1949 to see it in print. From 1940 through to 1942 Cesare is immersed in his writing and his love for Nando. He is also heavily engaged in work for the Einaudi publishing house.

Thoughts of suicide recede. But some frustration builds and, relenting on his hatred of the sea expressed at Brancaleone, he takes a vacation for several weeks at Varigatti, a seaside town. This inspires Pavese to write *The Beach*. In this novel he stretches his abilities by examining characters of whom he knows little. They are the new social order, the bored bourgeoisie.

The publication in 1941 of *The Harvesters* initially receives a cautious reaction for it was, of course, unpopular with the Fascists. But critical and public acclaim gathers pace and it becomes widely regarded as a work of great interest. Cesare now enters a period of relative calm emotionally, indeed letters to his long-time friend Einaudi in the spring and summer of 1941 show that he is in very humorous mood.

This is from May 1941:

Most esteemed publisher Einaudi. I accept the terms you offer me for the publication of *The Harvesters*. I would appreciate receiving, as a symbolic advance, a pipe, so that I could smoke it and calmly prepare other even more seductive stories. Most devotedly yours, Cesare Pavese.

In 1942 Pavese is commuting between Turin and Rome. He spends many weeks at a time in Rome preparing for the opening of the new Einaudi offices. He misses his Turin friends, especially Fernanda (Nando) and, by the beginning of 1943, he feels isolated again and enters into another of his periods of melancholia. He now threatens to leave the job with Einaudi. He writes: 'I have a life to lead, a bicycle to ride, sunsets to enjoy ... life beckons us and we must follow.' Before he could make good the threat he is drafted into the army and posted to Rivoli with the Italian Infantry Regiment.

Immediately his asthma worsens and he is put into hospital. After some observation he is sent to convalesce in a remote part of the countryside for several months. He again isolates himself, even from the few social activities of the area. He begins a series of fantasies in his mind, dominated, again, by thoughts of suicide. But his physical health improves a little and he is released from the army.

Now, in July 1943, he visits Rome and informs Einaudi by letter that the Rome offices must be closed due to the risks from bombing by the Allied forces. Enclosed with the letter are some small drawings; a paratrooper is seen descending into gunfire, a house is burnt and a man is hanging from a tree. The last drawing depicts a man lying on the ground holding a gun pointed at his head.

His health continues to improve and he returns to Turin in September 1943. He finds the city under constant Allied bombing. His sister Maria and her family have fled to the house of her husband's sister in Serralunga. His feeling of isolation deepens and his mood darkens when he receives news that his long-term friend and fellow writer Leone Ginzburg has been tortured to death in a Fascist prison in Rome. Throughout the year of 1944 he goes for long walks alone, and there are few entries in his diary. He often spends long hours in the monastery at Crea, meditating upon religion. Now he believes he has found God.

Early in 1945 he asks Nando to marry him. She does not respond and their relationship ends. He now denounces his new found faith as superstition. But again his work comes to give him the strength to come out of this isolation period. He completes *Festival Nights* and works on the creation of future novels *The House on the Hill* and *The Comrade* and again returns to his poetry. Women are again in the forefront of his mind: in 'Death will come and it will have your eyes' (written in the summer of 1945 but not published until after his death), we read:

We all fled
We all abandoned

Our rifles and our names. A woman watched us flee

...

A woman waits for us in the hills

...

Women, always women.

At the end of the Second World War, after liberation of Italy from the Fascists, Einaudi calls Pavese to Rome to reorganise the publishing house. He goes but once there he is consumed by guilt that he has not been able to take any direct part in the liberation struggle. His mood deteriorates further when he discovers that several of his friends have been shot or hanged by the Fascists. He cannot share the joy and happiness of everyone around him and thus begins another period of feeling isolated and depressed. He now joins the Communist Party, which he had been afraid to do while the Fascists were in power.

He continues to write prolifically. Translations, working on a series of novels, articles for magazines. In 'Return to Man', an article for *L'Unità*, the official newspaper of the Italian Communist Party, in May 1945, he expresses his opinions on the value of writing:

To speak. Words are our business, we say it boldly. Words are delicate things, intractable and alive, but made for man rather than man for them. We all feel that we live in a time in which words must be brought back, to the solid and bare clarity they had when man created them to serve him. Just because they are useful to man, it happens that the new words move and grab us as no other voice does, not even the solemn words of a prayer or a war bulletin. Our task is difficult but alive with sense and hope. Those who await our words are men, poor men, as we are when we forget that life is a communion. They will listen to us with faith and strength, ready to incarnate the words we say. To disappoint them would be to betray them; it would be to betray our past as well.

He develops his series of articles for *L'Unità*. He begins to express his opinions not only about writing but also about the value of books. This extract is from 'Dialogues with a Comrade', written in early 1945, published in May 1946:

> The more time you spend with a friend the more you know him. So it is with books. Is it not beautiful to understand a friend who for many years, for his whole life, has tried to speak with you? And is it not a joy to read again that book which you had not understood many years before, but which now reveals to you all of its wisdom?

Whilst working for Einaudi in Rome, Cesare started up a free newsletter, which was widely circulated. In some of the articles for this newsletter he expresses his concern about his low salary and the late payment of wages due to him. It is clear that he is going through a period of financial difficulty. In one letter to his friend and colleague Mila, sent through the circular system, he addresses Mila's concerns that Pavese himself might be fired:

> It is obvious that I am supporting our boss. I am aware of your fear of our being fired; but really it is like the misadventures of love: one is always dismissed when, through clear signs, he has proved himself dismissible. But we are indispensable to the publishing house.

That, I think, tells us a great deal about Pavese's experiences with women.

Rome at that time was in a post war mood of euphoria. This did not suit Pavese's taste for solitude. He lived in a small hotel and really did not want to be in Rome. He was only able to carry on because he was successful in his work as editor for Einaudi. Bianca Garufi worked with Pavese at Einaudi's publishing house. She tried to collaborate with Cesare to write a novel, *A Great Fire*. Bianca arouses a great passion in him but he is unable to find sexual satisfaction with her and the relationship ends in disaster. The novel lies unfinished but is eventually published some ten years after Pavese's death.

As 1945 draws to a close Pavese's thoughts are very much dominated by the three failed love affairs in his life so far. In his diary on 27 November 1945 he writes the dates upon which he was 'dismissed' by these three women, whom he describes as 'the woman with the hoarse voice', 'another woman from Turin' and 'the one here in Rome'.

This extract is from his diary of December 1945:

Several times in the past few days you have written of T, F and B alongside each other. It seems you fantasise about a return to what might have been. What has been will be. There is no reprieve. You are thirty seven and conditions have been favourable. But you have looked for defeat.

The women are of course, Tanya, Fernanda (Nando) and Bianca.

At Christmas 1945 he returns to Turin. He does not contact his old friends or his new ones in the Communist Party. He enters into another mood of withdrawal, spending almost all his time at the Einaudi offices or in solitary walks. This from his diary in February 1946: 'Alone again. You make the office your home and your mouth is always shut tight.'

Well into 1946 and Pavese is writing two short novels, *The Political Prisoner* (published in 1948 within the volume entitled *Before the Cock Crows*) and *The House on the Hill*. In *The House on the Hill* we see revealed his longing for a child of his own. Contained there are also the usual fragments of Pavese's emotional experience: childhood, women who refuse to marry him, women he rejects although they love him, and of course the regular intruder, suicide.

In February 1947 Cesare begins a relationship with Maria Serini, a 20-year-old girl whom he had taken on to work with him at the Einaudi offices in Turin. Throughout 1947 and early 1948 he wines and dines her at good restaurants and they go for long walks together in the hills. He takes her to visit cafes along the river Dora where much of his poetry had been written in previous years. He begins to dictate to her his new novels, *The Comrade, Dialogues with Leuco* and *The House on the Hill* for typing.

As 1947 ends his novel *The Comrade* is published. This novel uses characters he had known in his years in Turin. One senses his feeling towards those people and, unusually for him, Pavese comes across as lively and outgoing. It wins the Salerno Prize. For a time he is happy and contented. In 1948 he completes the last of his new novels, *The House on the Hill* and delivers it up for publication.

Now comes yet another anticlimax. He has exhausted himself. He is physically weakened and asthma returns after a long period of relief. A bitter mood sets in. This is heavily compounded when he loses Maria. Einaudi transfers her to the Rome offices. One suspects that Einaudi disapproved of the time and energy Pavese was spending on his young assistant. Enter another period of withdrawal and feeling of inadequacy. The old obsession with thoughts of suicide returns and, with it, new doubts even about his own gender.

In April 1948 he writes in his diary:

You are alone and you know it. You are a woman, with a woman's feelings, and like a woman you are stubborn. But alone you are not enough and you know it. Now everything in the future looks disastrous.

Despairing of his own solitude, Pavese leaves Turin to spend Christmas 1948 in San Stefano. He returns to Turin in a calmer mood, but cannot rest. He goes to Rome for a few days but hurries back to Turin. Most days he sits alone at one of the cafes near Corso Umberto. Most evenings he sits in the Cinema Verona until it closes. Occasionally to break his solitude he picks up prostitutes in the Corso Umberto area and takes them to the Einaudi offices. Confronted about this by his secretary, Rosita Vialli, he swears that they only drink and chat together. This is probably true given his paranoia at that time about his sexual inadequacy.

He now begins to write again. He completes *The Beautiful Summer* and writes *Among Women Only*, a new novella, which is not, as you might think, about women, but rather has suicide as its central theme. This short quotation encapsulates his thinking at that time: 'I understand killing oneself; everybody thinks about it. But one must do it well; do it without causing controversy, do it realistically.'

Among Women Only concludes with the noise of a cat inside the room of the 'heroine' leading to her discovery dead from an overdose of sleeping pills. In this novel Pavese rehearses his own death, as we shall see later.

Paradoxically Cesare now meets two American actresses, Constance and Doris Dowling and enthusiastically joins their group of friends who are mainly theatre types from France and USA. He immediately

168

falls for Constance. He takes her to Rome and then to an expensive ski resort at Cortina d'Ampezzo. He gives up his modest and austere ways. They stay at the best hotels, dine expansively, drink heavily. Cesare discovers bourbon! He is happy again, and becomes almost extrovert, seeing himself as an actor upon the stage of life.

He writes a short novel *Devil in the Hills*, which he combines with *The Beautiful Summer* and *Among Women Only* for publication as one book, *The Beautiful Summer.* However, after a few months of happiness with Constance, he awakes one morning in a hotel in Rome to find that she has fled in the middle of the night. She has gone straightaway to live with one of her French actor friends. Later she is to tell Pavese, 'You could not give me the warmth a woman wants.'

Cesare immediately runs back to his old roots at San Stefano and to his oldest and truest friend Pinolo (Scaglione). Back in Piedmont country his thoughts turn to writing again and he discusses at length with Pinolo the writing of a new novel centred around the families of San Stefano. At this time he becomes 'extremely fond' of a young student girl called Frederica, who is the daughter of one of his cousins. He cannot consummate his relationship with her, and he returns to Turin, but he starts correspondence with her and they continue to write to each other until shortly before Pavese's death.

Back in Turin his mood swings again to depression. He seeks out his old professor Monti, to unburden himself. Monti accuses him of swinging wildly between a superman complex and feelings of inadequacy, and of loving all the people of the Piedmont countryside whilst simultaneously harbouring a general hatred of his fellow man. Monti tells him to get back to writing.

As 1949 closes Pavese reaches his writing peak. Closeted every day in his single room on the Via Lamarara, he completes in only 87 days his most complex yet most complete novel, *The Moon and Bonfires*. Throughout these days his asthma attacks have become very frequent. He also develops severe headaches. He tells his friends, 'It feels like a drummer beating in my head, I think I am suffering from the brain cancer which killed my father.' Is it despite these problems or because of them that he completes his major work in record time?

The Moon and Bonfires is almost autobiographical. Set in the San Stefano valley, it looks at his own childhood and diverse events that have regularly occurred in the surrounding countryside villages, the character 'Nuto' is based upon his faithful friend Pinolo Scaglione. It develops into a novel of the resistance against the Fascists. Once again he writes of human desperation, suicide and violent death. *The Moon and Bonfires* reveals again, and for the last time, Pavese's schizophrenia. The strongest of the variants in his mind is probably his ideological commitment to living his life as a man of strength and his despairing conviction that he is incapable of doing so. He dedicates the book to his erstwhile lover Constance Dowling.

After *The Moon and Bonfires* Pavese is exhausted and strangely disillusioned. He is not the same Pavese who only six months earlier had expressed long-term literary ambitions. Once again the pendulum of his mind has swung. In his diary early in 1950 Pavese begins to record his physical deterioration. He notes palpitations, extreme agitation of the mind and chronic insomnia. However, it is surprising that he does not speak of it to his medical friend Dr Fabrio Rubino and seems not to have discussed it with any of his friends.

Constance and Doris Dowling are again in Italy. Cesare persuades Constance to return to him. For a few weeks, and despite his poor physical condition, he is happy with this intelligent and inspirational woman. But in April 1950 she leaves him and returns to America with another man. Probably Pavese had anticipated this because he wrote in his diary on 26 March: 'It is a fact that there is in her not only herself, but all my past life.'

The women Pavese loved always left him.

Now the drum-like beat of the headaches increases. With this final defeat in love he feels a general sense of failure in everything. Suicidal feelings increase. In April he writes in his diary:

One does not kill oneself for love of a woman. One kills oneself because love, any love, reveals in us our nakedness, misery, vulnerability, our worthlessness.

In May at various dates his diary reads:

The act (of suicide) must not be an act of revenge... It must be a calm and weary renunciation, a closing of accounts, a private deed... Now even the morning is filled with pain... I contemplate my impotence. There is only one answer: suicide.

170

The Moon and Bonfires is published in May 1950. On 30 May he writes to Aldo Camerino, a literary critic and friend:

> *The Moon and Bonfires* is the book I have carried the longest in my thoughts and which I enjoyed writing the most. So much so that I think I shall do nothing else. One ought not tempt the Gods too much.

In June 1950 he is awarded the prestigious Strega Prize for *The Beautiful Summer.* At once his mood changes completely. When he arrives in Rome for the prize-giving ceremony his whole appearance and manner have changed. He is wearing a stylish new suit and on his arm is Doris Dowling. As he accepts the prize he smiles expansively. He spends the evening chatting and drinking wine with several acquaintances. The next two weeks are spent visiting friends and drinking heavily. He seems in very good humour. But at the end of the month he writes to Frederica, in what is to be his last letter to her, and begins by apologising for not having written for a few weeks: 'Because I have been in Rome and travelling around, cavorting, drinking, and I am half dead with exhaustion', and he ends by again pouring out his inadequacies. 'Your father was the only Pavese who amounted to anything, the only one who has been a man.'

Now in July physical exhaustion overcomes Cesare. He remains alone in his room, his only outlet being the writing of letters to friends and acquaintances. At the close of July 1950 he writes to 'Dearest Calzecchi', a woman employed by Einaudi publishing as a translator: 'Once I would have liked the fact that you find me a tormented writer; now I like it less. Now I would like to have peace and that is all.'

In August several friends invite him to dinner at The Bagutta in Milan. He arrives in Milan but he has no appetite for eating and decides he does not have the strength to go to the dinner. However, his friends introduce him to a young blonde woman and she persuades him to attend. They talk animatedly about his books and he is reinvigorated. He walks with her through the moonlit streets of Milan until dawn. We do not know what happens between them but the next day he leaves for Genoa.

He tells his friends that he will return to Piedmont at the end of August, and that they will meet together in San Stefano and together will visit Nuto. As soon as he is in Genoa his mental and physical condition deteriorates again. He stays until the beginning of September and then returns to San Stefano, but without telling anyone. He visits Nuto but is in a very disturbed state of mind. He tells Nuto he will return immediately to Rome:

> I am expecting a call from Doris; I have discussed everything with her. We have agreed it will be best for me to marry Constance if she will have me. Doris is expecting her call from USA. If the answer is yes, we will marry. I know it will not last, maybe only two years, but that will be two more years to live.

The next day Cesare goes to Rome. There is no answer from Constance. Within a few days he returns to Turin.

It is the final rejection. It brings back all the memories of his persistent failures with women. He feels he has no more to write. He is convinced he is useless. Suicide is peace and should be accepted stoically.

On 15 August 1950 he decides to go alone to the Gai dancehall. There he meets a young attractive student girl. They leave together. He telephones her frequently from that day until the day of his death. The entry in his diary the next day says: 'Why die? I have never been so alive as now, I feel like a teenager,' but the very next day he writes: 'This is the account of a year which is not yet finished, but I shall not finish it.'

His mind is now totally unstable. The same day he writes to his sister Maria in Serralunga. She is so disturbed by the tone of his letter that she comes immediately to Turin. Here she finds Cesare emaciated and with hollow, sleepless eyes.

He does not respond to her questions in which she worries about his health. Now he begins to burn, in his room, many of his writings, letters and photographs. On 18 August he writes: 'All this is sickening. Not words. An act. I shall write no more.' This is the last recorded entry in his diary.

When he leaves his room on 26 August he has with him a carefully packed overnight suitcase. He goes to the offices of *L'Unità*. Once there he goes to the archives and, with the help of the clerk Spriano, he seeks out photographs of himself. He selects one in which he is looking particularly depressed and tells Spriano, 'This one is fine'. He leaves, smiling. He takes the bus to Porta Nuova and walks to the Hotel Roma in Carlo Felice Square. He takes a room on the third floor. Immediately he makes four telephone calls. Each call is to a woman, whom he invites to dinner. One is Fernanda, another is the girl from the Gai dancehall. All refuse him.

The next day, 27 August 1950 at 8.30 p.m. a hotel employee, concerned that Pavese had not been seen since the previous day, knocked upon his room door. Receiving no answer and believing he detected a strange smell, the employee forced the door open. Coincidentally (see *Among Women Only*), a cat rushed past him to be first on the scene. Pavese lay upon the bed dead, fully dressed except for his shoes. On the dressing table lay several empty packets of sleeping pills which he had taken. Beside him was a copy of his book *Dialogues with Leucò*; on the first page is his photograph. He has written: 'I forgive everyone and ask forgiveness of everyone. Not too much gossip about me please...'

Here then is Cesare Pavese, a man of originality; an intellectual, an inspired translator, a creative mind that constructs imaginative poetry and writes thought-provoking short stories and novels. A man who wanted a dramatic termination to his life. Why then does he choose such a mundane method for the ending that has preoccupied his thoughts for 25 years?

Certainly Pavese suffered for many years from depression, a symptom of his schizophrenia. He tried to combat this depression with intermittent bouts of heavy drinking. Clearly he had serious sexual problems. What might be seen today as promiscuity might have been viewed in the 1930s and 1940s as sexual addiction. Although he had affairs of varying durations with many women, it appears that he was unable to give them physical satisfaction. We know that in his final days he felt he had reached his writing zenith and that he had nothing more to contribute. We know too that for many years his mind had been obsessed with thoughts of suicide: indeed this precludes any inference that he suddenly committed suicide whilst the balance of his mind was disturbed.

But surely these facts and conclusions do not answer fully the question of his choice of method of suicide. Is his low-key choice of ending his life due to a desire not to have the act sensationalised and scandalised? Does he wish only to retain some dignity in death? Is he simply scared of the physical act? Perhaps we shall find the answer to Pavese as we consider the other brilliant writers who chose to end their lives in suicide.

Virginia Woolf

Myth and Mystery

Adeline Virginia Woolf (née Stephen). It is arguable that more has been written, lectured, broadcast and filmed about her than any other twentieth-century writer. Scarcely a reader in Britain or the United States of America does not know of her.

Many are the myths that have been created about Virginia Woolf. She was a wonderful novelist and diarist. She fought for the liberation of women and was a champion of equal rights for the working classes. She was a lesbian. She was a lifelong manic depressive and committed suicide.

In varying degrees every one of these myths can be disputed.

Photo: Lebrecht Authors

175

I agree with the many critics who say that her essays are excellent and her letters humorous. But I share the opinion of William Empson, Max Beerbohm, David Sexton, Wyndham Lewis and others in finding her novels insufferable. They tell no stories. As a substitute, Woolf tries to link together single events or feelings into a collection of sensations they suggest to her. She peeps out at the dangerous outside world from the security of her private mind. To some this suggests an immoderate vanity. This vanity, together with snobbery and spite, sometimes comes through in her diaries.

Certainly Virginia Woolf made a substantial contribution to the liberation of women writers. In the early 1900s women were generally discouraged from writing. Those women that did write were inhibited and seemed almost to censor their own work. In 1907 in an article 'The Feminine Note in Fiction', for the *Times Literary Supplement*, Woolf writes: 'Women, we gather, are seldom writers because they have a passion for detail, which conflicts with the proper artistic proportion of their work.' When women did write novels, it was almost mandatory that they adhered to the old Victorian style of romance and happy ending tales. Virginia was absorbed in her writing with how women might write their own life stories when there was so little encouragement, so few precedents. Woolf established that precedent. Much of her fiction, from her first novel, *The Voyage Out*, through *Mrs Dalloway* and *Orlando*, to her final novel *Between the Acts*, focuses upon the telling of a woman's life story. Her feminist essays, 'Three Guineas' and 'A Room of One's Own', are almost painfully thoughtful about the symbolising of women's lives. Certainly she was the catalyst for the dramatic change in women's writing from the Edwardian era onwards.

That Woolf was an activist, or stood up to fight for the rights of women or the working classes, is debatable. I find little evidence of it after reading more than two million words about her life. 'A Room of One's Own' does examine the difficulties facing women, but read 'Kew Gardens' to observe her poking fun at lower middle-class women. Woolf, who came from an upper-class household attended by servants, and never worked in her life, had no affinity with the working classes. She did believe in decent wages for 'the workers' and did give many lectures to working-class audiences. However, note her letter to Vita Sackville-West in May of 1940:

'April 27 gave a lecture on "The classless society" to the Brighton working classes. 200 betwixt and betweens – you know the type. How they stare and stick and won't argue.' In her animated conversations with members of the 'Bloomsbury Group' she frequently discussed the structure of class in society and was a supporter of meritocracy. That Group, of which Virginia was a leading light, has been described by several writers as precious, remote and upper class.

As to her lesbianism, it is upon Virginia's own admission that she much preferred the intimate company of women to that of men. She makes this clear in letters to several different female friends throughout her life. One example will serve. In the autumn of 1905, then only 23 years old, when writing about the men in the early Bloomsbury Group to her first intimate female friend Violet Dickinson, she said, 'Oh, women are my line and not these inanimate sexless creatures.' The conflict with that statement lies in the fact that Virginia had five proposals of marriage during her twenties and it would be foolish to suppose that her relationships with those young men did not encourage their advances. She did have several close relationships with women, always much older than herself, from her late teens through to her forties. These were almost certainly substitutes for a mother's love, which she never had. Virginia was 43 before she had her first full-blown sexual affair with a woman. By that time Woolf had matured enough to realise that she needed physical love in her life. Entrenched in a sexless marriage to a control freak, Woolf knew her husband would not tolerate an affair with another man, but thought that he might just accept a discreet liaison with a woman. Enter Vita Sackville-West. However, for most of her life, Virginia Woolf was not a lesbian in the sense we understand it today. We must bear in mind that in those Edwardian times, when discretion in affairs was the order of the day, any proclivity towards same-sex affection would be liable to the stigma of lesbianism or homosexuality.

Virginia's family history is filled with relatives who suffered depression. Her grandfather, Sir James Stephen, had three serious bouts of depression, which effectively ruined his career as a colonial administrator. Her father, a nervous child subject to fits of uncontrollable rage, was a melancholy man who twice suffered episodes of depression. Her mother had two severe bouts of depression following deaths of loved ones. One brother, Thoby, was an emotionally disturbed child, another brother Adrian underwent periods of nervousness and depression. Her sister, Vanessa, had a period of depression, which lasted two years. Laura, her stepsister, was sent to a mental institution when 17 and eventually died there. There can be no doubt that Woolf inherited a tendency towards breakdown of the nervous system.

Virginia's own childhood was deeply disturbed. Her grandfather died when she was five. At six she was sexually interfered with by her step-brother Gerald. Her mother, a strict disciplinarian, was such a controlling, busy person that she was never able to give Virginia the mother love she craved. Her death, when Virginia was 13, led to her father spending the rest of his years in inconsolable grief and he became unbearably demanding. Virginia's other stepbrother, George, sexually abused her throughout her teenage years. Coming from this background, Woolf was susceptible to mental disturbance from her early adulthood onwards. But was she a manic depressive? Leonard Woolf made this diagnosis and insisted on repeating it continuously in writing and conversations for 50 years. Yet he had no medical or psychiatric knowledge and none of the many doctors whom Leonard forced Virginia to see ever made that diagnosis. Virginia's alternating periods of depression and elation were cyclical. With hindsight we can now hypothesise that she suffered all her adult life from a severe form of SAD syndrome. This illness was not known in the early 1900s, therefore effective treatments, such as melatonin and a light, airy environment, were never suggested. Leonard Woolf took her to at least a dozen doctors over a period of 30 years, always changing them when they did not agree with his assessment. In general, medical advice was for complete rest, sedatives and a milk diet. Leonard, being a control freak, took this advice to extremes. At the first signs of excitement, headaches, fever, flu, he would confine her to bed in a darkened room for periods of several weeks at a time. During these spells she would be allowed no visitors. Naturally, this exacerbated Virginia's condition. She needed light, air and social contact. Virginia did suffer from illnesses other than suspected SAD syndrome. Frequently she had headaches, fever and persistent influenza. However, these illnesses are not symptoms of manic depression.

Did she commit suicide? Certainly the two 'suicide' notes, which Leonard Woolf says Virginia left for him, are strong circumstantial evidence, if they are genuine. They are not proof. No one saw her commit that act. It was entirely upon Leonard Woolf's evidence that the police and the coroner accepted that Virginia committed suicide. Leonard spent 25 years after Virginia's death telling everyone that manic depression had got the better of her and she had taken her own life. No doubt that has contributed greatly to the acceptance by most reviewers of Virginia's madness and death by suicide.

I should say that I have read very little of the vast amount her husband wrote about her. This is because I believe it is compromised by the events surrounding Virginia's death and Leonard Woolf's actions afterwards. My reasons will become apparent when we come to look at those events and Leonard Woolf's performance.

First, we must briefly examine her life and her writing. We will pay particular attention to the early causes of her mental illness: her family background and her childhood. Her husband's role in her life and death we shall also consider.

Adeline Virginia Stephen was born at 22 Hyde Park Gate, South-West London on 25 January 1882, the seventh child of eight for Julia and Sir Leslie Stephen. Both her parents had been married previously. Four of the children came from the previous marriages. Stella, George and Gerald were from Julia's marriage to Herbert Duckworth. Laura, an autistic child was born to Minnie (daughter of William Makepeace Thackery), the first wife of Leslie. Vanessa, Thoby, Adeline and Adrian were born to Julia and Leslie Stephen.

Virginia's mother, Julia, was born in India in 1846. She came from a family more renowned for looks than for intellect. She was often cold and remote and many saw her as stern and judgemental. Yet she could be warm and gay and had the ability to put others at their ease, especially at social gatherings. In 1867, when 21, she married Herbert Duckworth, 34, a barrister. He was handsome and athletic and Julia was very much in love with him. She bore him two children and was pregnant with a third, all within four years of their marriage. At that time Herbert died of a brain haemorrhage. Julia was devastated and fell into deep despair. Now she busied herself with humanitarian activities, her children and her friends. One close friend, who lived next door in Hyde Park Gate, was Minnie Thackery (now Stephen), and Julia was a regular visitor.

Leslie Stephen was born 1832. He had a fragile nervous system as a child and received so much attention that he became thoroughly spoilt. He became very dependent upon his mother and, when ever not receiving sufficient attention, would fall into a rage. Educated at Cambridge University, he was elected a Fellow of Trinity Hall in 1854. This required him to take holy orders and he was ordained in 1855. Inexplicably, he does not enter the priesthood until 1859 and then only resulting from his dying father's last wishes. Thereafter he soon loses faith and, in 1861, gives up the priesthood and the Fellowship. He becomes a militant agnostic writer. Leslie Stephen married Minnie Thackery in 1867 when he was 35. Minnie was a bit of a dreamer, but excellent at running the Stephen household. They had one child, Laura, born autistic in 1870. In 1876 Minnie was again pregnant, but this time complications arose and Minnie fell into a series of fits ending in her death.

Julia Duckworth continues to be a regular visitor to the Stephen household. She has always respected Leslie as an intelligent man and shared many of his views; both were atheists. Now she becomes his listener, as he pours out his complaints about the unfairness of his situation and his need for a partner. Leslie soon asks Julia to marry him. Though not physically attracted to him, Leslie represents security and a father for her children. Eventually Julia agrees to marry him, but makes her feelings known to Leslie and tells him that all she can offer is to do her best to be a good wife. Leslie is 46, Julia 32 when they marry on March 26 1878.

Julia certainly intended to honour her undertaking to Leslie. Julia soon gave Leslie two more children, Vanessa in 1879 and Thoby in 1880. However, the marriage soon fell into difficulties, mainly due to Leslie's selfishness, demanding nature and ill-temper. Julia did her best to cope, but now found there were many other demands upon her time. In January 1881 her sister Adeline fell ill. Julia spent three months away from home nursing her day and night. Throughout that time Leslie complained bitterly about Julia's absences. Adeline died in March 1881. Julia returned to Leslie in a very depressed state. He found he was now quite unable to deal with Laura's inability to communicate and he now handed over sole responsibility for Laura to Julia. Being a firm disciplinarian of the old school, Julia tried to remedy Laura's problems with strict training. This failed and she soon banished Laura to the attic rooms and into the care of a governess.

Julia immediately became pregnant with Virginia and was ill for some months following her birth. When she recovered, Julia spent long spells away from home caring for her mother.

Into this stressful parental background, Virginia was born. Julia had yearned for a boy and had chosen the name 'Chad'. She was deeply disappointed when a girl was born. Virginia was a most attractive child and soon earned the nickname 'Beauty'. The happiest times of Virginia Woolf's early childhood were the three months holiday they spent every summer at St Ives, Cornwall. Here her mother was ever present, ever available and could give Virginia a little of that mother love that every young child craves. In London, Julia worked to a rigid timetable, being very busy attending to Leslie's constant demands and giving care and attention to many. At those times Virginia hardly ever saw Julia. Vanessa took Julia's place, bathing 'Beauty', rubbing scents into her body, sleeping with her and taking long conversational walks with Virginia. This was the background to what later happened between them, which many have called the love affair of two sisters.

The first traumatic experiences of Woolf's life occurred when she was six. Several blows hit her within a short period, as was to be the pattern throughout her life. Virginia disliked Laura because she was unable to communicate properly and, when unable to express her feelings, would break things in rage. However, when Julia washed her hands of Laura and committed her to the lunatic asylum, Virginia was deeply disturbed. She could not relate to her mother's cold harshness and rejection of Laura, when it was obvious that she simply was unable to conform. It was to have a profound effect on Virginia, and all her life she would shrink away from anyone mentally handicapped or even acting oddly. On one occasion she went so far as to tell Leonard, 'Imbeciles should certainly be killed off.' At that time she could not have guessed that her husband would on two occasions send her to 'rest homes' (which Virginia's nephew Quentin Bell called madhouses) and that, long before her death, Leonard considered her mad. The shock of Laura's removal was immediately followed by a severe attack of whooping cough. Virginia was sent to Bath to recuperate at the spas. There she spent several weeks, returning thinner, more withdrawn and anxious at night times.

One further trauma awaited her return. Her 16-year-old stepbrother, Gerald, insisted upon her standing upon a table and lifting and removing some of her clothes. He told her he was carrying out an examination of her private parts. He then proceeded to sexually explore her. It is difficult to assess the effects of this sexual abuse on Virginia's later life. Later she was to say, 'I can still remember how I stiffened and wriggled as his hand explored my private parts.' It may very well have been the cause of her sexual frigidity within her marriage.

Later came the worry for Virginia of her father's rapidly deteriorating mental health. The problems had begun shortly after Virginia's birth. With Julia absent caring for her mother, Leslie was without the constant attention he demanded and fell into depression. At that time *The Science of Ethics*, which had taken him five years to write, was published; but to a lack of critical and public enthusiasm. Obviously this increased his depression. It was immediately followed by the news that *The Cornhill Magazine*, which he had edited for the past ten years, had been losing readers, and money, for some time. He resigned and soon thereafter became editor of *The Dictionary of National Biography*. The work and pressure of this publication upon Leslie was unremitting. Gradually his mental breakdown began.

All this surrounded Virginia and had a deep impact upon her. Now Julia was again called away, this time to nurse her dying father and, when she stayed on after her father's death to nurse her grieving mother, Leslie was beside himself with fury and demanded her immediate return. Julia's patience gave way and she told him bluntly that she was exhausted and needed time away from him and the family. Leslie responded by commencing a series of panic attacks. In 1891 he relinquished his editorship of *The Dictionary of National Biography*. Julia returned but there were constant violent quarrels as her exhaustion and Leslie's mental distress both increased. In 1892 Julia's mother died and Julia was inconsolable. In the bitterly cold March of 1895 she contracted severe flu. She deteriorated and, by May, she was dead.

Virginia was now 13. Reviewing the background and events of her life until this point, can the reader wonder that she was now to have the first of her mental breakdowns?

Following the death of her mother, Virginia's father took to unceasing, voluble despair, soliciting and receiving a constant stream of visitors. It was impossible for Virginia to grieve properly. Anxiety and depression created a near paralysis in Virginia. She retreated to her room and would see no one other than family members. Sleep came only with medication. Let us be clear that Virginia had not gone out of her mind. Moreover, this illness bore no relationship to the severe form of SAD syndrome from which she almost certainly suffered later in life. But certainly this was a breakdown from which it took her many months to recover. It was 1897 before she was well enough to start writing again and began keeping a diary for the first time.

Following Julia's death, Leslie Stephen demanded that her daughter Stella take over the running of the household. After two years of being worn down by Leslie's demands, she sought sanctuary in marriage. In April 1897 she married long-time suitor John Hills. Virginia was bridesmaid and was overjoyed at her stepsister's happiness. However, Stella became ill on her honeymoon and was bedridden thereafter. Virginia mimicked Stella's illness and took to her own bed. Leslie Stephen took to raging around the house at Hyde Park Gate, complaining of the inconsideration of Stella and Virginia. The doctors at first thought Stella was pregnant. Later they changed their diagnosis to appendicitis. The operation was botched and Stella died in July 1897. It was surely this event that created Virginia's lifelong distrust of doctors.

Now the onus of organising the household and dealing with their father fell upon Vanessa and Virginia. An onerous task it was too, for they were now fully exposed, without protection, to the violent, uncontrollable rages that Leslie Stephen would work himself into. These were brought on usually after bouts of depression during which his frustrated desire to be a man of genius left him bereft of any control over himself. Vanessa consoled herself by having an affair with Jack Hills (Stella's ex-husband); but Virginia's nature would not encourage such an outlet; indeed she was deeply distressed by Vanessa's actions. Leslie lingered on for seven more years until his death in 1904. They must have seemed like 70 years to Virginia.

It was during this period that Virginia was persistently sexually abused by her stepbrother George. In Virginia's own words, taken from autobiographical accounts of her life *22 Hyde Park Gate* and *Moments of Being*: 'After our outings George would come to my room in the dark at night; "Don't be frightened," he would whisper, "and don't turn on the light, oh beloved. Beloved." And fling himself on my bed, cuddling, kissing and otherwise embracing me.' Nowhere do we discover what 'otherwise embracing me' means. It is not therefore possible to determine the contribution this made to Virginia's later mental breakdowns. Virginia Woolf herself thought that what had been done to her was very damaging. Following this period, in 1904, Virginia had her first major breakdown.

In the final years of her father's life, Virginia had become increasingly hateful of him, due to his lack of interest in anything but his own well-being. At the same time she felt guilty about her feelings towards him. Increasingly she turned for consolation towards Violet Dickinson, a long-time family friend. Violet, a tall, thin, angular woman almost twice Virginia's age, gave Virginia the physical affection she craved and encouragement to develop herself as a writer. At the same time, Violet aroused passion in Virginia. Some of their correspondence reads much like love letters.

Upon Leslie Stephen's death the children inherited an estate worth, at today's values, about £750,000, plus the freehold of 22 Hyde Park Gate. The Stephen children were now financially independent. Vanessa now took charge. She decided that Hyde Park Gate would be sold. She felt happy to be free of her father, but also had regard for Virginia's low spirits. They would travel and enjoy themselves, she decided. They went to Venice and onwards to Florence. Initially Virginia's spirits improved greatly. But depression quickly returned. This was exacerbated by a resentment of Vanessa going over the top in pursuit of a good time. Virginia became unstable, her moods swinging from bursts of ill-temper to sulky, non-communicative periods. To try to deal with this, Vanessa invited Violet Dickinson to join them in Florence. They moved on to Paris, but Virginia did not improve. They fell in with a boisterous set from the Left Bank and Virginia now became hyperactive. By the time they returned to England, she had become uncontrollable, giving vent to wild bursts of verbal and physical violence, mainly directed at Vanessa. Violet Dickinson came to the rescue, inviting Virginia to her country home at Burnham Wood in Hertfordshire for a 'long rest'. Virginia remained unstable for several months, she suffered delusions and heard voices commanding her to commit wild acts. She had to be confined to her room. At one point she leapt from a first-floor window, whether to escape, or in a half-hearted suicide attempt, is not known. In any event, she landed in a bush. She was unhurt but the bush never flourished again. Her manic behaviour gradually subsided, but it was not until January 1905 that doctors agreed that she was sufficiently in control of herself to return to her family. Hyde Park Gate had been disposed of and Vanessa had moved to 46 Gordon Square, Bloomsbury. It was to here Virginia returned. Her stepbrothers had moved on and Virginia had Vanessa to herself.

Virginia returned from her illness with a desire to write and a need to work. Despite their inheritance, the Stephen family were running out of money. The move to Gordon Square, and Virginia's illness, had been costly. The inheritance had been invested in stocks and shares to produce annual income; but this was not enough to meet their outgoings. They now had rent to pay and servants to keep and none of them were working. Virginia said, 'Our bank passbooks were greatly overdrawn.' It was not difficult for Sir Leslie Stephen's daughter to find work in literary journals. Soon she was writing for the *Guardian*, the *National Review*, *The Times*, and had regular commissions from her father's old magazine *The Cornhill*. She soon disciplined herself to do nothing other than read and write each morning. One evening each week she taught English Literature at Morley College, to what she called 'lower-class women'.

In the summer of 1905 the four Stephen children rented a house at St Ives. They had not returned to Cornwall since their mother died ten years previously. Much bonding took place that summer.

When they returned, Thoby initiated the Thursday evening weekly discussion groups at Gordon Square. These meetings simply consolidated contacts that had continued between Cambridge students who had graduated together at the turn of the century. They became known as 'Old Bloomsbury'. Made up mainly of intellectual young men, the group would gather to discuss literature, religion, current affairs and the structure of society until the early hours. Leaders among them were Saxon Sydney-Turner, economist Maynard Keynes, writer and critic Lytton Strachey, writer David Garnett, and critics Clive Bell and Desmond McCarthy. The group flourished initially but began to wane after Thoby's death from typhoid fever in November 1906. Although Virginia complained of 'the dullness of these young men', she in fact delighted in their conversation and made enthusiastic efforts to join in. Virginia was to receive five proposals of marriage during her twenties and they all came from this set. She turned them all down; but her sister Vanessa did not. Clive Bell had a crush on Vanessa and persuaded her to marry him in April 1907. This was to herald the closure of 'Old Bloomsbury' and the beginning of the infamous 'Bloomsbury Group'.

After their honeymoon, Vanessa and Clive Bell wanted to live alone together and Virginia and her brother Adrian were asked to move. Virginia found a house to rent nearby at 29 Fitzroy Square. Here Virginia had time and space to develop her novel writing seriously for the first time. Now too the 'Bloomsbury Group' began to flourish. The gatherings continued to take place at 46 Gordon Square hosted by Clive and Vanessa Bell and, occasionally, at Fitzroy Square, hosted by Virginia. New participants included artists Duncan Grant and Roger Fry, Jean Thomas, Ka Cox, Lady Ottoline Morrell and Leonard Woolf. The respected American writer Dorothy Parker described the group as '...comprising pairs who had affairs in squares'. Rupert Brooke called it 'a treacherous and wicked circle'. Certainly there were homosexual and lesbian relationships within the set. Rumours were rife, never denied by Virginia or Vanessa, that there were wild parties at which women ran around the house naked, various combinations of sexes copulated openly, and wildly animated conversations of a scandalous nature continually took place.

In February 1908 Vanessa gave birth to the Bells' first child, Julian. She suffered postnatal depression and now relied heavily on Virginia for support. At the same time, the Bells' marriage began to break down and suddenly Clive began to pursue Virginia. Their affair lasted through 1908 and 1909, and although intercourse did not take place, the affair was certainly serious. By March of 1910 Virginia had developed a guilt complex and the liaison ended. Virginia was also suffering stress for a number of other reasons. Vanessa was now expecting the Bells' second child, at the same time as having an affair with Roger Fry; the pendulum had swung again and Vanessa now had no time for Virginia.

Since 1908 Virginia had been struggling, unsuccessfully, to complete her first novel. She was also concerned since the lease of Fitzroy Square was soon to expire. Now she began to suffer headaches, extreme irritability and lack of appetite. Dr Savage was consulted and advised a quiet holiday. Virginia went to Studland Bay, Dorset, but there was no improvement. Dr Savage was again called in. He advised a rest cure at Miss Thomas's nursing home at Burley Park, Twickenham. Although this was Dr Savage's usual treatment for the mentally unstable, nevertheless he did not believe that Virginia was mad. His prescription was four hearty meals a day and long periods of rest in a darkened bedroom. Virginia spent six weeks there before recovering enough to return to normal life. Through the winter of 1910 and 1911 Virginia kept depression at bay. She worked diligently on *The Voyage Out*, her first novel. By the summer of 1911 her hyper mood had returned and remained with her until the end of August. Typical examples of her behaviour at that time were performing ritual dances with a pagan sect and swimming naked with Rupert Brooke in the river Cam.

By September 1911 she had a major problem to occupy her mind and calm her down. The lease of Fitzroy Square had entered its final quarter. Virginia and Adrian no longer wished to live as a partnership of two. Virginia, driven by her ambition to write novels, desperately felt the need for more space. She had already taken a lease, jointly with Vanessa, on Asheham House at Firle, Sussex; but she could not give up her Bloomsbury connections. With Adrian, she sought and found a four-storey house at 38 Brunswick Square, Bloomsbury. Maynard Keynes and Duncan Grant, who were lovers, rented rooms from them. This still left the attic rooms vacant.

Leonard Woolf had returned to England in June 1911, on one year's leave, having spent six and a half years with the Colonial Office in Ceylon. Part of the 'Old Bloomsbury' set, he had met the Stephen sisters only a few times previously. At first he had fallen for Vanessa, but soon transferred his affections to Virginia. Lytton Strachey encouraged Leonard to believe that Virginia might respond to him and told him there were rooms vacant at Brunswick Square. Leonard moved in, strictly as a lodger, in December 1911. He courted Virginia, but with some difficulty. He was a thin, slight man with hollow cheeks and a pronounced nervous tremor in his hands; he was Jewish and the lengthy period in Ceylon had darkened his skin, giving him a foreign look. In the climate of prejudice which prevailed, his appearance was a major obstacle. Virginia found him physically unattractive and referred to him as 'my misanthropic little Jew'. However, they shared a love of literature and conversation and enjoyed each other's company. Leonard was determined and he made sufficient progress by the end of January 1912 to propose to Virginia and to give up his post in Ceylon.

Virginia felt pressurised and this was compounded by wanting to complete her first novel but being unable to draw it to a conclusion. The winter depression, by now a recurring ailment, hit her, and in February she went to Burley Park, Twickenham for a rest cure. She was looked after, as before, by Jean Thomas, who communicated regularly with Leonard Woolf and made it clear to him that, in her view, Virginia was affected mentally by far more than exhaustion. Virginia improved quickly as winter turned to spring and by April she was in Asheham convalescing. Her attitude to Leonard's proposal may be best understood by her letter to him, written from Asheham.

Dearest Leonard

To deal with the facts first (my fingers are so cold I can hardly write) I shall be back [at Brunswick Square] about 7 tomorrow, so there will be time to discuss – but what does it mean? You can't take the leave, I suppose, if you are going to resign certainly at the end of it. Anyhow, it shows what a career you're ruining!

Well then, as to all the rest. It seems to me that I am giving you a great deal of pain – some in the most casual way – and therefore I ought to be as plain with you as I can, because half the time I suspect, you're in a fog which I don't see at all. Of course I can't explain what I feel – these are some of the things that strike me. The obvious advantages of marriage stand in my way, I say to myself, anyhow you'll be quite happy with him; and he will give you companionship, children, and a busy life – then I say By God, I will not look upon marriage as a profession. The only people, who know of it, all think it suitable; and that makes me scrutinise my own motives all the more. Then, of course, I feel angry sometimes at the strength of your desire. Possibly, your being a Jew comes in also at this point. You seem so foreign. And then I am fearfully unstable. I pass from hot to cold in an instant, without any reason; except that I believe sheer physical effort and exhaustion influence me. All I can say is that in spite of these feelings which go chasing each other all day long when I am with you, there is some feeling which is permanent, and growing. You want to know of course whether it will ever make me marry you. How can I say? I think it will, because there seems no reason why it shouldn't – But I don't know what the future will bring. I'm half afraid of myself. I sometimes feel that no one ever has or ever can share something – it's the thing that makes you call me like a hill, or a rock. Again, I want everything – love, children, adventure, intimacy, work. (Can you make any sense out of this ramble? I am putting down one thing after another.) So I go from being half in love with you, and wanting you to be with me always, and know everything about me, to the extreme of wildness and aloofness. I sometimes think that if I married you, I could have everything – and then – is it the sexual side of it that comes between us? As I told you brutally the other day, I feel no physical attraction in you. There are moments – when you kissed me the other day was one – when I feel no more than a rock. And yet your caring for me as you do almost overwhelms me. It is so real, and so strange. Why should you? What am I really except a pleasant attractive creature? But it's just because you care so much that I feel I've got to care before I marry you. I feel I must give you everything; and that if I can't, well marriage would only be second-best for you as well as for me. If you still go on, as before, letting me find my own way, as that is what would please me best; and then we must both take the risks. But you have made me very happy too. We both of us want a marriage that is a tremendous living thing, always alive, always hot, not dead and easy in parts as most marriages are. We ask a great deal of life, don't we? Perhaps we shall get it; then, how splendid?

One doesn't get much said in a letter; does one? I haven't touched upon the enormous variety of things that have been happening here – but they can wait.

D'you like this photograph? – rather too noble, I think. Here's another.

Yrs VS.

It is clear from this soul-searching letter that Virginia saw the difficulties that would exist if they married. Equally, it is clear that she regarded Leonard not only as one who was the more successful and superior person, but also as the one person she could really communicate with, the one person who really understood her. We should perhaps bear in mind that at that time she was not the respected author 'Virginia Woolf', but rather a young woman of 30, who knew she had under-achieved and was still struggling to complete her first novel.

Despite Virginia's reservations, she and Leonard were married on 10 August 1912. Because of Leonard's Jewish faith, the ceremony took place in St Pancras Registry Office. Virginia's family and friends were present but Leonard's family were not. The first few nights of the honeymoon were spent at Asheham, near Lewes. From there the Woolfs embarked on a continental holiday, returning in October to Bloomsbury. Briefly to Brunswick Square and then to rented rooms at 13 Clifford's Inn.

The honeymoon had not been a physical success. Virginia, although affectionate, was resistant to having sexual intercourse. Leonard exercised patience for a few days, but then became forceful. His aggressive attempts at penetration simply caused Virginia to panic and he was forced to stop. Certainly Virginia later stated: 'The pleasure of the climax is greatly exaggerated.' Perhaps Leonard's selfishness contributed considerably to the problem. In Ceylon he had a concubine and sometimes used prostitutes, his main concern being his own pleasure.

After a few more half-hearted attempts Leonard finally gave up and accepted the situation. Although they remained physically affectionate through the early years of their marriage, there was no sexual intimacy and, after the honeymoon, they never again slept together.

Despite the physical disaster, the honeymoon could be said to be successful. They developed intense conversations together. They took many long walks together. Their companionship grew quickly to a great strength. They both completed books that they had been working on for some time. Virginia at last drew *The Voyage Out* to a conclusion and Leonard finalised *The Village in the Jungle*, doubtless each helped the other to completion.

Virginia returned from the honeymoon with a lack of appetite and severe headaches. She coped with the move from Brunswick Square to Clifford's Inn but it exhausted her. The winter of 1913 set in and her cyclical depression returned. Nevertheless, she concentrated all her efforts upon the final revisions of *The Voyage Out*. By late spring it was ready for publication. Unable to find a publisher she turned reluctantly to her stepbrother Gerald Duckworth, who owned Duckworth Press. The manuscript was delivered by May of 1913 but was not immediately published. Virginia fretted that it would be badly reviewed and she would become the subject of ridicule. The headaches and poor appetite persisted and now Virginia became indecisive over the smallest matters. Leonard took firm control and began to rule the marriage as he had the natives in Ceylon. On important issues he would tolerate no disagreement or even discussion. Virginia's mind was now in conflict. She resented

190

Leonard's bullying but had to repress her feelings because she was turning ever more to him for support: the more depressed she became, the greater was her dependence on him.

Virginia's condition deteriorated and Leonard consulted Sir George Savage and Dr Michael Craig, telling them that he feared suicide. Sir George again recommended a spell at Miss Thomas's Twickenham nursing home. Virginia was reluctant, but it was finally agreed that she would spend three weeks there, followed by two weeks holiday with Leonard. Virginia left Twickenham on 11 August somewhat improved. Leonard then took her to Asheham. However, Virginia again deteriorated. She would not eat and could not sleep without strong sedation. Leonard, still telling anyone who would listen that he feared Virginia taking her own life, kept her sleeping pills locked away in his private briefcase.

They returned to London. Leonard had lost faith in Doctors Savage and Craig, it seems mainly because they did not concur with his opinion that Virginia was suicidal. He was determined to obtain another opinion and discussed the matter with their mutual friend Roger Fry. He recommended Dr Henry Head, a neurophysiologist. Dr Head saw Virginia and advised immediate admission to a nursing home, rest and a healthy diet. Precisely what Dr Savage had recommended and which had signally failed. They went to tell Vanessa and found her with Mrs Roger Fry. After some discussion, Leonard decided, for some strange reason, that he ought immediately to visit Dr Savage to explain why he had been bypassed. For some equally strange reason he asked Vanessa to accompany him, leaving Virginia with Mrs Fry. Left alone for a few moments, Virginia noticed that Leonard had left his case behind and that it was unlocked. She opened it, took out and swallowed a large quantity of sleeping pills. She soon was fast asleep. Mrs Fry knew of no reason to be concerned. But when Ka Cox arrived, on a chance visit, she was unable to rouse Virginia and they realised something was wrong. Ka Cox immediately phoned Leonard at Dr Savage's consulting rooms; but by the time he arrived, Virginia had fallen into a coma. Rushed to hospital it would be 36 hours before she recovered consciousness.

Leonard had expressed his fears that Virginia might take her own life and he had been watching over her constantly. He was a professional, precise and most careful man. To this day, no one has been able to explain convincingly why Leonard left his unlocked

191

case with Virginia and why he left her with Mrs Fry, who did not know her well. When Virginia recovered she continued to suffer with depression. For many months afterwards she suffered from headaches, insomnia and what, with hindsight, would appear to be the symptoms of the SAD syndrome. Staying on at Clifford's Inn was clearly out of the question and Leonard seriously considered committing Virginia to a mental home. Leonard and Vanessa again consulted with Dr Craig. He said Virginia's mental state was not such that she could be certified and she should not be made to go into a home. George Duckworth came to the rescue by offering the use of his house at Dalingridge. The Woolfs went there with two nurses and stayed for two months, during which Virginia improved enough for her to move to Asheham and, when Leonard was not there, Ka Cox was in attendance. Virginia made further improvement, recommenced reading, and started a diary once more. There she remained until August 1914.

The First World War, which began in August 1914, certainly affected Virginia emotionally. She was a committed pacifist, as was Leonard at that time. Reports of the gradually escalating slaughter of British and French troops did disturb her very greatly. Leonard was by then heavily involved in left-wing socialist politics and, by the outbreak of the war, he was a member of the Fabian Society and a contributor to their publication the *New Statesman*. One of his articles argued that insanity should be grounds for divorce. It is for the reader to make something or nothing of the parallel between Leonard's view on that subject and his view at that time that his wife was mentally unstable.

In August 1914 Virginia was well enough to leave Asheham. Her mind was too active for the serenity of the countryside and her health seemingly could not stand up to the hectic pace of London life. Leonard and Virginia decided to seek a house in Richmond upon Thames. Initially they took lodgings at 17 The Green, and set about finding more permanent residence. In January 1915 they found what they both felt was the ideal house. Hogarth House in Paradise Road was a semi-detached property, with a basement, three upper floors and a 100-foot walled garden. The property was vacant but negotiations for a five-year lease became unusually protracted and, before they could be completed, Virginia's health broke down once more.

Much was happening to disturb and frustrate Virginia at this time. Air raids; harrowing daily reports of the trench warfare, stretching the endurance of everyone's nerves. Also Gerald Duckworth had not yet published her first novel *The Voyage Out*. Leonard suggested they set up their own printing press in the basement of Hogarth House. Virginia was keen, but when they tried to enrol for a course to learn printing operations they were refused because they were not members of the Printers' Union. More frustration. Leonard's novel *The Wise Virgins* had now been published and caused Virginia bitter feelings. Virginia believed he had used her as the model for Camilla, a frigid woman incapable of physical love. Certainly in the book he uses his mother as a caricature of the stereotype Jewish mother: this caused considerable ill-feeling between mother and son, with Virginia caught in the middle. The stress of the anticipated setting up home in the large Hogarth House took its toll. Finally came the usual winter depression. Suddenly, at the end of February 1915, Virginia's fragile nervous system collapsed.

She began with a furious outburst of abuse against Leonard. Next she appeared to be having hallucinations; she thought her mother was in the room and began talking wildly to her. Her emotions became unstable, one moment she was telling Lytton Strachey that she was wonderfully happy with Leonard, but shortly afterwards she was rowing violently with Leonard. All of this happened over the course of a few days, accompanied throughout by severe headaches. Leonard felt he had no choice but to summon nurses and have Virginia taken to the nursing home at Twickenham.

Leonard was convinced that Hogarth House was right for them and he concluded the lease negotiations and moved in on 25 March. He then removed Virginia from the nursing home and she joined him at Hogarth House, in the care of four nurses, on 1 April. At first she was unstable and violent. She would neither feed or clean herself nor allow the nurses to do so. Her anger was pent up and would be released in sudden, savage outbursts, mainly at Leonard. However, the acquisition of Hogarth House was to prove an inspirational move. Leonard still wanted to set up a working printing press in the basement, which he was sure would provide an interest and recreation for Virginia and keep depression at bay. In the last week of April they chanced upon a second-hand printing press for sale, complete with a book of instructions for use. They took immediate delivery. They were to remain at Hogarth House for nine years and establish the Hogarth Press as an important printing house. Virginia threw herself wholeheartedly into the venture. She saw clearly that it was her path to independence, as a writer, from other publishing houses. Her latest breakdown was over. She was not to have another major breakdown until she was nearing the end of her life, 26 years later.

The suggestion is not that the establishment of Hogarth Press prevented Virginia from having further major breakdowns. However, it certainly broke the cycle. It led her away from a dark period dominated by the First World War and into a period when she was able to evaluate her first novel after publication. Only then was she able to work out the future pattern of her novels in what was to become her most prolific writing period.

In the summer of 1915 *The Voyage Out* was at last published. The story of a family embarking on a long and difficult voyage was heavily based upon the lives of Virginia's family and friends. Her mother, father, Vanessa, Lytton Strachey and others all appear in different guises. It was reviewed with admiration and respect in the *Times Literary Supplement* and by E.M. Forster and Lytton Strachey. Generally it was considered an original and promising work, departing as it did from the monotonously familiar Victorian style. Reviews did contain some criticisms; principally that the story-lines were not seamless and the characters were not colourful. Sales were slow, reaching 2,000 copies only after about 15 years, and it made only a very small profit. It did, however, enable Virginia to see the way forward. She had proved herself as an essayist and reviewer, but was aware of her shortcomings as a novelist. Now she would lead the way forward for other women writers: out of the old Victorian structure of novels, into what was to be the forerunner of a completely new style of novel.

From spring 1915 to winter 1916 her time was fully engaged with learning printing processes, assisting Leonard, and writing more than 50 articles printed by various magazines. She simply had no time to miss or yearn for the London social and intellectual scene that Leonard and her (or his!) doctors felt had caused so many of her emotional problems.

By the spring of 1917 Virginia had started her second novel, *Night and Day*. This was her transitional novel. It bridged the gap between her first efforts and the later novels, which were to be a series of different experiments seeking new ways of presenting the relationship between the lives of individuals and the forces of society and history. Although Leonard would only allow work on the novel for about an hour each day, such was the fury of her pace that she had completed 110,000 words before the close of 1917.

Night and Day is in the main a factual novel with no startling material. A good deal of the basic story-lines are plagiarised from Leonard's *The Wise Virgins*. A love story and a social commentary, it moves between the comedy of life and the causes of hostility between people; set against a background of contrasts between the solid houses and streets of Edwardian London and the instability of the ceaseless flowing of the river Thames.

Virginia was unable to maintain her initial furious pace and was diverted into writing several short stories. 'The Mark in the Wall', a fantasy exploring the consciousness of the mind, was completed in the summer of 1917 and, combined with Leonard's 'Three Jews', was the first publication by Hogarth Press under the title *Two Stories*. 'Kew Gardens', 'Solid Objects', 'The Evening Party' and the 'Unwritten Novel' were all work in progress during this period.

By February 1918, Virginia was exhausted and again overtaken by winter depression. This time she needed nothing more than rest, which she took for three weeks. Nevertheless, Virginia was able to complete *Night and Day* by November of 1918. The manuscript went to Gerald Duckworth for publication and this time there was no delay, the volume being launched in July 1919.

The *Times Literary Supplement* gave it a very favourable review. *The Spectator* magazine said: 'A perfection of style which is at once solid and ethereal.' Katherine Mansfield, writer and intimate friend, said in her review: '...it is aloof and unaware of what has been happening, as though the war had never been.' Old friends E.M. Forster and Lytton Strachey were enthusiastic about it and both were later to say it was the best novel she ever wrote. Virginia did not agree, but did derive satisfaction from the sales of the book, which were healthy. Leonard and Virginia now decided that this would be the last book they would ever give to another publishing house.

Leonard was by now exercising very strict physical control over Virginia. He looked upon Virginia as a child needing to be closely watched and protected. At the first sign of any high exuberance, headache, lack of appetite or insomnia he would immediately stop her from all activity and confine her to bed rest and to a strict diet based mainly on milk. Although it is clear that Leonard was a control freak, nevertheless it can be seen that Leonard's actions were beneficial to Virginia. She entered into a period of calmness and prolific writing. However, her involvement with the publishing and printing work of Hogarth Press prevented her from immersing herself totally in writing: and surely this was a good thing; for production of great quantities of writing must inevitably cause the quality to suffer. Virginia began to see benefits attached to these periods of enforced bed rest. It was at these times that she was able to relax and allow her imagination to flow freely without interruption. Almost all the novels and short stories that now followed were originally planned in Virginia's head whilst lying in bed.

The following extract from a letter Virginia later wrote to Ethel Smyth (a long-term mother figure in her life) gives a clear insight into her feelings in 1919.

> I was so tremblingly afraid of my own insanity that I wrote *Night and Day* mainly to prove to my own satisfaction that I could keep entirely off that dangerous ground. I wrote it, lying in bed, allowed to write only for one half hour a day. And I made myself copy from plaster casts, partly to tranquillise, partly to learn anatomy. Bad as the book is, it composed my mind and I think taught me certain elements of composition which I should not have had the patience to learn had I been in the full flush of health always. These little pieces [the short stories] ... were the treats I allowed myself when I had done my exercise in the conventional style. I shall never forget the day I wrote 'The Unwritten Novel'. How I trembled with excitement; and then Leonard came in and I drank my milk and concealed my excitement and wrote I suppose another page of that interminable *Night and Day* ...!

At last the tension and depression caused by the First World War was at an end and now Virginia was exceptionally busy with literary journalism and with her short story 'treats'. The *Times Literary Supplement* asked her to prepare a major obituary to anticipate the death of Thomas Hardy. This meant spending a great deal of time, from 1919 to 1921, rereading Hardy's novels and giving much thought to that popular Victorian writer. At the same time, she wrote or completed several short stories: among others, 'A Haunted House', 'Monday or Tuesday', 'An Unwritten Novel', 'Solid Objects', 'In the Orchard', and 'Lappin and Lappinova'. The two short stories that were outstanding were 'Mrs Dalloway in Bond Street' (from which she was to develop her most famous novel *Mrs Dalloway*), and 'Kew Gardens'.

'Kew Gardens' was to prove a turning point and milestone in the history of Hogarth Press. This short story was an untidy sprawl of long sentences with little connection to the practical world, or to philosophic truths. Virginia had sought to establish her vision that it was the surface of things that mattered, not their names or natures. The quality of this volume was much enhanced with some beautiful woodcut illustrations produced by Vanessa. It was Virginia's first separate publication for Hogarth Press and came out in May 1919. First reviews were mixed. Rupert Brooke thought it 'very poor stuff'. E.M. Forster said there was nothing of neatness about it for it yawned and gaped; yet he admired it. The *National Review* praised its quality of writing and stimulating vocabulary and rated it a highly recommended read. The *Times Literary Supplement* was even more enthusiastic, admiring its fragile impressionism and praising its rhythmic flow. Immediately after publishing 'Kew Gardens', the Woolfs went for a short break to Asheham. When they returned to Richmond they found 150 letters from subscribers, requesting several hundred copies. They quickly arranged with a commercial printer to reprint 'Kew Gardens'. They now had a business and Virginia Woolf had a name. With the publication of *Night and Day* following almost immediately, Virginia now felt a strong sense of security in her career as a writer.

In the autumn of 1919 the lease at Asheham was expiring. The farmer would not renew it because he needed it for his bailiff. Virginia had shared Asheham with Vanessa but following a fierce quarrel with her, mainly about the illustrations for 'Kew Gardens', decided she did not wish to share another country home with her sister. She immediately started looking for another country residence in the East Sussex area and, noticing an agent's advert for a converted windmill, close to Lewes Castle, she bought it sight unseen and without consulting Leonard. As might be expected, when Virginia showed Leonard 'The Round House' he was unenthusiastic and made his reservations clear in no uncertain terms.

On the way back to Asheham, on the Lewes side of the Ouse valley, they saw an auctioneer's board on Monk's House at Rodmell. They knew the house slightly, having walked past it when strolling across the meadows from Asheham. It had an attractive garden and stood in about three acres of land. One could stroll through it and down through the woodland to the river Ouse. Leonard at once said, 'That would have suited us exactly.' In July 1919 they bought it at auction for £700. This was to be a most significant moment in the life and death of Virginia Woolf. It was at Rodmell that she was to spend the last period of her life; and it was from Monk's House that she walked down to the river Ouse to end her life by drowning.

Fortunately Virginia was able to dispose of 'The Round House' a month later with very little loss. Virginia felt immensely reassured by their joint purchase of Monk's House and felt that her relationship with her husband/protector was secure. Combined with her satisfaction at her progress as a writer, and add in her enormous relief at the ending of the war, we can see why she had no further serious mental breakdowns until the approach of the end of her life.

That is not to say that there were no periods of illness and emotional disturbance, both physical and mental; on the contrary, there were many. However, for the next few years, life for Virginia was dominated in equal measure by her writing and by several intimate relationships with female friends. Through the years 1920 to 1923 Leonard's determination to exercise control over Virginia was to some degree assisted by her continuing to suffer from cyclical periods of illness and mild depression. None of this prevented her from continuing to write, constantly exploring different styles. Her main work during this period was a fictional biography, entitled *Jacob's Room*. In this, Virginia sets out to construct a novel more structurally adventurous, more disconnected and less traditional than anything that had gone before it. Nevertheless, the events and experiences are again largely taken from her own life and the anti-hero Jacob is surely her brother Thoby. Also she once more plagiarises, this time from 'The Wind Blows', a story written in 1915 by her intimate friend Katherine Mansfield. Virginia was very pleased with the completed novel and it was immediately printed in 1922 by Hogarth Press. It reviewed well and sales were good.

Virginia had, by 1922, found enough contentment in her work to protect her from any serious mental breakdown. Writers rarely go mad whilst they are writing. However, her physical health continued to be poor. In the winter of 1922 she suffered her normal seasonal depression. By spring it had turned to high temperatures and headaches. Leonard consulted Dr Savage and they agreed that the problem might be with some infection in the roots of Virginia's teeth. Quite astonishingly Dr Savage had a theory that the pulling of teeth might be a cure for insanity. In June 1922 Virginia had three teeth extracted. The only result was an unnecessary disfigurement of one side of her face, particularly noticeable when she smiled. All through the winter and spring of 1923 she suffered with a series of sore throats. Leonard had her examined by Sir Maurice Craig, who found pneumonia germs in her throat and ordered that she be inoculated with 50,000 of them once a week. This had the desired effect; by summer she was again thoroughly depressed.

It is fair to say that her depression at this time was mainly caused by a lack of social life in Richmond. She longed to return to the London social scene. At last she could stand it no longer. In October 1923 she had a long and aggressive argument with Leonard. She felt he was using her frail health as an excuse to live where he wished, in suburbia. She claimed he was doing this because he disliked the social life, which, to her, was so essential. Virginia insisted they must move back to London. Leonard resisted; but eventually he came to recognise that Virginia could not be dissuaded. Matters came to a head later that month. Leonard had gone to Monk's House for a meeting with an author: in his absence Virginia packed a bag and set off to go to London. Leonard caught up with her at Richmond station. Faced with another strong verbal onslaught, he capitulated. Virginia at once began to look for a house in Bloomsbury and her mood instantly changed. Now she felt youthful and vigorous again. Her anticipations rose; so much lay ahead: music, conversation, renewal of friendships. In January 1924 she found a four-storey terraced house with basement at 52 Tavistock Square, with a ten-year lease obtainable. It was not ideal since the ground and first floors were let to a firm of solicitors but Virginia reasoned that they could manage with the two upper floors and the printing press might be fitted into the basement. The Woolfs moved in on 13 March 1924. Leonard did manage to fit the press into the basement and managed to work tolerably well within the confined space. However, as Virginia's mood became more ebullient, Leonard's became more depressed. He complained bitterly that visitors and social life were beginning to take up most of the day and were interfering with his work. It seems Virginia's comments back in Richmond were valid.

The transition of *Mrs Dalloway* from a short story to a full-blown novel and its completion was now Virginia's major project. For light relief she began gathering together her favourite essays, intending to publish them as *The Common Reader*, a guide to how and what to read.

Virginia's social life was now a whirl of parties, music and conversation groups, and with this she was content. This contentment did not flow over into her physical being. She was unfulfilled, she needed a lover. For some time she had been quite open about her preference for the company and physical attractions of women rather than men. Furthermore she was quite certain that Leonard would not countenance an affair with another man. However, he had tolerated her intimate relationship with Katherine Mansfield and he might just accept a discreet affair with a woman. Virginia had someone in mind. She had met Vita Sackville-West in 1922 at a Bloomsbury party given by Clive Bell. It was shortly after the time of Katherine Mansfield's death and Virginia was vulnerable and feeling in need of someone to replace Katherine. She was at once strongly drawn physically to the beautiful, sultry Vita.

Sackville-West came from an aristocratic family dating back 800 years with a home at Knole House, a country mansion in Kent. She was married to Harold Nicholson, who turned out to be a homosexual and a long-term sufferer from venereal disease. Nevertheless, they remained married and very close and understanding friends. Vita had already engaged in lesbian affairs by the time she met Virginia. The longest, and most notorious, was with Violet Trefusis (née Keppel), which lasted from about 1912 until 1917, at which time the two women eloped to France to where they were pursued by the two husbands, who dragged them back home. Between then and late 1922, when she first met Virginia, Vita was engaged in liaisons with several lovers, including an affair with Dorothy Wellesley (then married to the later Duke of Wellington) and a relationship with Geoffrey Scott. In many ways the two 'V's were on much the same wavelength. Their relationships with their husbands were similar, in that they remained soul mates, whilst the husbands tolerated the wives' lesbian affairs. By 1925, when Vita was in love with Virginia, she wrote to her husband:

If you were in love with another woman, or I with another man, we should be finding a natural sexual fulfilment which would inevitably rob our own relationship of something.

Both were writers. Vita was, by 1922, a popular poet and novelist (*The Edwardian* (1930), *Challenge* (1923), 'The Land' (1927)); indeed her novels sold far better than Virginia's. Both were fatalistic. An important difference between them was that Virginia was never interested in being promiscuous.

They saw only a limited amount of each other during 1923, but by 1924 they met constantly; at Knole House (the Sackville family home), at Long Barn, Vita's house, and at the Woolfs' home, Monk's House. Virginia was in love with Vita. An intimate affair was in progress, but the time was not right for it to become full-blown. Virginia was very busy writing, drafting the final revisions to *Mrs Dalloway*, which was to be published that year, and was already deeply engaged in writing her next novel *To the Lighthouse*. In the early part of the year Vita was immersed in a difficult termination of her affair with Geoffrey Scott, and from early summer she too was busy writing.

In the summer of 1925 Hogarth Press published *Mrs Dalloway*. The story takes place on a single day in London in June 1923. It follows Clarissa Dalloway from early morning until late at night as she prepares and gives a large formal party. Her day is greatly disrupted by a visit from her former lover Peter Walsh and by her own visits to Septimus Smith, a young shell-shocked and disabled ex-military serviceman. When news of Septimus's suicide breaks at the party, Virginia gives us an insight into the minds of the social classes of the day. Although the novel begins and ends with a tribute to endurance, survival and happiness, still Virginia's fascination with death intervenes. This was Virginia's fourth novel and by far her most successful. It has survived the years to remain her most read novel. As recently as 2003 it was the subject of an award-winning film *The Hours* (Virginia's original first title for the novel) with Nicole Kidman winning a best actress Oscar, allowing herself to be made up to resemble an unattractive Virginia in her mid forties. Initial reviews were mixed, as was usual with Virginia's novels. The *Times Literary Supplement* showed much foresight in declaring it '... a novel that breaks the mould, brushing aside the unimaginative style restricted by social correctness which has for too long been in vogue. It will in its time become a classic.' The Bloomsbury set and close friends were full of praise. Desmond McCarthy called it '... a fearless and exhilarating examination of today's society.' E.M. Forster said, '... outstanding; a new method that will stand the test of time.' Vita Sackville-West wrote: 'Awe-inspiring. It took my breath away at times.' On the downside, Lytton Strachey said it was 'flawed'. Arnold Bennett declared: 'It was hard work. It beat me; I could not finish it.' Max Beerbohm wrote to Virginia, 'You forget your readers and think only of your theme and method.'

This mixture of reviews continued down the years. *The New Yorker* was to say: 'This book's stream of consciousness is one of the few genuine innovations in the history of the novel.' However, others were not so kind. David Sexton, an important reviewer in the late twentieth, early twenty-first century, found it 'insufferable'; and the Professor of English at Princeton University, Elaine Showalter, noted that the novel revealed Woolf as more limited intellectually than James Joyce and interested only in the moment and certain philosophic theories of time.

Initial sales were good, which was the most important thing so far as Leonard was concerned. Unusually, Virginia was not unduly concerned with the reviews. She had two other very important matters on her mind. Very shortly after the publication of *Mrs Dalloway* she began her next novel *To the Lighthouse*. Fired up, she raced through 10,000 words in two weeks. Inevitably she then fell ill. Mainly exhaustion, headaches and lack of appetite. This was exacerbated by Vita's news in September that her husband had been posted to Tehran and that she would join him in January. For this was the other thing on Virginia's mind; she was in love with Vita. By December Virginia was so low that in desperation Leonard contacted Vita and suggested she might invite Virginia for a weekend at Long Barn before Vita left for Tehran. Vita was more than happy to do so and collected Virginia from Bloomsbury by car, having first dropped off Geoffrey Scott. They spent four days at Long Barn. On 18 December they became lovers. At the age of 43, Virginia lost her virginity.

Vita departed for Tehran in January 1926, with a promise to return to Virginia. They wrote many letters to each other, the content being almost entirely of their passion, each for the other. Vita returned in June 1926 and immediately spent two nights at

202

Monk's House with the Woolfs. On the second night Leonard had to go to London. The lovers took their opportunity to share a bed together. Throughout the summer of 1926 they saw as much of each other as possible. Parties and theatres in London and visits at Long Barn and Monk's House. Vita returned to her husband in Tehran in April 1927, with both swearing to write many passionate letters until Vita's return, which they did. Although Vita's departure depressed Virginia, the impact was lessened by excitement surrounding the completion and publication of Virginia's next novel *To the Lighthouse*. She had written the book at great speed during 1926, between bouts of illness. Perhaps it came easily to her because it is an autobiographical novel, almost an exercise in self-analysis. It centres upon her mother and father and Virginia's childhood in Cornwall. It is a carefully structured novel, but much of it is symbolic. Virginia thought it '... easily my best novel.' Leonard read it prior to publication and told her, 'It is a masterpiece.' Roger Fry said the novel was '... beautifully structured but has a symbolic meaning which escapes me.' Vanessa wrote, '... as far as portrait painting (of mother and father) goes you seem to me to be a supreme artist.' Vita told her, '*To the Lighthouse* makes me afraid of you, afraid of your loveliness and genius.' John Middleton Murray, essayist and reviewer, said that, like most of Woolf's work, it was a failure and no one would read her novels in the foreseeable future. Aldous Huxley said she had lost touch with the real world. Arnold Bennett said it was '... fragmentary, but an improvement on *Mrs Dalloway*.' Most of the literary review magazines treated it favourably. It won the prestigious literary award, The Femina Prize, and, because of its biographical content, Virginia became well known. Sales were very good here and in America and the Woolfs bought their first car, a second-hand Austin, but Virginia steadfastly refused to learn to drive.

Vita was back in June to receive the Hawthornden Literature Prize for her poem 'The Land'. She was at once physically back in Virginia's life. Virginia immediately tried to spend as much time as possible with her. Inevitably she tried to do too much and suffered with severe headaches at several times that summer.

At the end of July, the Woolfs spent a long weekend at Long Barn, with Vita, Harold, Vita's father Lord Sackville and his mistress. Here Vita confessed to Virginia that she had just finished brief affairs with Mary Hutchinson (ex-mistress of Clive Bell), and

Margaret Voight. What Vita did not tell her, but which Virginia soon discovered, was that she was about to embark upon a passionate, foolhardy and utterly disastrous affair with Mary Campbell. Virginia was badly shaken by these revelations and ultimately infuriated. It was to change the pattern of the remainder of their relationship. On top of all this, a scenario of sexual scenes began to unfold all around her. Clive Bell began an affair with Valerie Taylor (the actress); Vanessa Bell and Duncan Grant were not only lovers, but were working and painting together. Two female friends from Bloomsbury, Ethel Sands and Nancy Hudson, were living together as 'man and wife' in Dieppe. Philip Morrell, Bloomsbury roué, paid her an unexpected visit and poured out his emotions, following this up with a barrage of love letters.

All of this left Virginia somewhat bewildered and she felt a distinct sense of sexual difference. She decided to make a statement by changing her appearance. Her hair, which had always been long and beautiful, she now cut short and with a half parting in the centre. She shaved her eyebrows. Her eyeglasses were now changed to a higher strength and more severe frames. To balance all this severity, she enhanced her lip make-up. Clearly this was a statement made at the time to show the major players in her life, Vita, Vanessa and Leonard, that she was now a steady, mature woman, no longer a child to be protected. However, it was a complete change in her appearance, which she was to retain until the end of her life.

Virginia was now full of ideas for her next novel, *Orlando*, which was to be an uninhibited satire on lesbianism, in the form of a fictional biography, opening in the year 1500 and continuing until the present time. The central character was to be a forever young aristocratic man who changes into a female. It was based upon Vita and Virginia dedicated it to her. As she raced through the opening chapters, she wrote to Vita in October 1927: '*Orlando* is about the lusts of your flesh and the lure of your mind.' Virginia wrote this novel at great speed, completing it in about seven months; even after revising the first drafts several times, it was ready for publication by October 1928. Vita said she was enchanted by it.

In the main it was reviewed well and certainly it sold very well, even though some bookshops refused to stock it due to its homosexual content. Virginia had sailed close to the censorship wind with this book at the very time when the Home Secretary was seizing books with what he considered obscene material and prosecuting their publishers. But Virginia had cunningly self-censored a book which, at root, is critical of sexual censorship and of prejudice against homosexuality and lesbianism. By covering her tracks, Virginia escaped the Home Office censor and set herself up to immediately embark upon another exciting book *A Room of One's Own*.

Written at a furious pace (no sickness now), it was ready for publication by autumn 1929. In essence, it was an essay on women writers of fiction and their backgrounds. It also examined and speculated on the lives and adventures of women in London at that time. 'If you are a woman, everything depends upon having money of one's own and a room of your own.' In many ways it was an autobiography of her own financial history. As was usual in her writing about her family, it was heavily disguised in case anyone should think she had a personal axe to grind.

Virginia wrote *A Room of One's Own* from a point in her life where her income from writing alone was rising dramatically. In 1926 her income from books was £356; in 1927 £545; 1928 (*Orlando*), £1,434; and in 1929, with the successful publication of *A Room of One's Own*, £2,750. Multiply by about one hundred times to understand the equivalent value today. Her fame too was increasing in about direct proportion to her income.

Virginia's affair with Vita Sackville-West had come to an end; and with the publication of *A Room of One's Own* there entered into her life Ethel Smyth, with whom she was to form an intimate and strange relationship.

Dame Ethel Smyth was 72 when she first met Virginia, then 48. Ethel was a writer and a well-known music composer. She was also a woman of immense energy and a militant feminist who had been imprisoned for violence in support of Emily Pankhurst. Stubborn, indomitable and highly emotional. Gaunt, and looking older than her years, she was deaf and a little comical in the way she wore an earpiece attached to a boxed battery, which she carried with her everywhere. Each had known of the other for many years, but the first meeting was prompted by Vita, whom Ethel knew well. Ethel had been invited to chair a BBC radio programme *Points of View*, at which *A Room of One's Own* was to be discussed. Vita suggested Ethel invite Virginia on to the show. There was an immediate rapport between the two. Virginia admired Ethel for her artistic ability, her principles and her energy. She came into Virginia's life at a time when Virginia had lost Vita and craved not a sexual affair, but certainly physical affection. This Ethel gave her in abundance. Indeed Ethel fell in love with her and wrote her many long love letters. Virginia found these amusing and generally made fun of Ethel, sometimes in a slightly spiteful way. She wrote to her nephew, Quentin Bell: 'An old woman of 72 has fallen in love with me. It is at once hideous and horrid and melancholy sad. It is like being caught by a giant crab.' Nevertheless, they developed an intimate friendship, which remained very strong for about five years. Ethel was the affectionate mother figure Virginia yearned for and Virginia was the intellectual companion upon whom Ethel could bestow her feelings of love.

For much of the period of her relationship with Ethel Smyth, Virginia was near her peak as a writer. Later, as the friendship cooled, she used Ethel as a character in her novels. She can be recognised as the lesbian theatrical director Miss La Trobe from *Between the Acts* and is unmistakeably Rose Pargiter, the battle-damaged suffragette, in *The Years*. Ethel's support and her interest in Virginia were vital during an emotionally and physically testing period from 1930 to 1934.

Throughout 1930 to 1932, Virginia was writing and redrafting *The Waves*, which was probably her most difficult work to date. In this novel, six characters are interwoven. She attempts to construct a story that connects scenery, thoughts and events in one smooth movement. Her aim, above all, was to create a rhythmic flow of words. Almost certainly, with this novel, Virginia reached her mental and emotional depths for the first time. *The Waves* was not published until the autumn of 1934; again, the reviews were mixed. Leonard had told her, 'It is a masterpiece, the best of your books.' But Ethel criticised it as being 'too extremely delicate'. E.M. Forster praised it highly and Virginia said he was the only one that mattered. The *Times Literary Supplement* called it '... one of the most important novels of our day'. However, Muriel Bradbrook (Mistress of Girton College, Cambridge) called it 'bloodless' and Virginia 'a very bad writer'. Winifred Holtby, who at that time was writing an authorised biography of Virginia, was enthusiastic and said, 'It is a lovely, poetical story'. Goldsworthy Dickinson, shown a final draft, wrote to Virginia expressing his relish for the book, saying, 'It is great poetry'. Virginia's reply to him is interesting in that it defines her reasons for writing and how her fiction is based upon her own life. She wrote:

The six characters were supposed to be one. I'm getting old myself – I shall be fifty next year; and I come to feel more and more how difficult it is to collect oneself into one Virginia; even though the special Virginia in whose body I live for the moment is violently susceptible to all sorts of separate feelings. Therefore I wanted to give the sense of continuity, instead of which most people say, no you've given the sense of flowing and passing away and that nothing matters. Yet I feel things matter quite immensely. What the significance is, heaven knows I can't guess; but there is significance – that I feel overwhelmingly. Perhaps for me, with my limitations, – I mean lack of reasoning power and so on – all I can do is to make an artistic whole; and leave it at that. But then I'm annoyed to be told that I am nothing but a stringer together of words and words and words. I begin to doubt beautiful words. How one longs sometimes to have done something in the world.

Whatever the reviews, the book sold 5,000 copies in the first week and the sales total for the first 12 months of publication was 13,800.

Writing *The Waves* created great emotional stress for Virginia. This was compounded by several other tense events during this period. In the space of nine months in 1932, three close friends were to die. Lytton Strachey died in January. Lytton was not only her best male friend, he had been a lifelong mentor. She had deeply admired him and had great respect for his writing. She was far from alone in her feelings. Dora Carrington was one who adored Lytton and devoted her life to him, without regard to his homosexuality. Dora was 'Old Bloomsbury' and Virginia had known her for more than 25 years. Lytton's death left Virginia and Dora distraught. Virginia visited her on 12 March and found her in very low spirits. She told Virginia she had nothing to live for. The next day, Dora Carrington shot herself dead. Virginia immediately saw her own life as useless and sank into depression. Leonard ordered bed rest and told her, in harsh terms, to pull herself together. This seemed to work, for on 1 June 1932, she wrote in her diary: 'I am glad to be alive and sorry for the dead: I cannot think why Carrington killed herself.' This comment may carry great weight when we come to consider Virginia's suicide. In August, another long time friend, Goldsworthy Dickinson died. The impact of this upon Virginia was magnified by their correspondence only a few weeks earlier about *The Waves*.

She also suffered a difficult summer with Leonard. A committed socialist, he was deeply frustrated by the Labour Party's defeat that summer. Further frustrations followed at work. There were major confrontations between Leonard and the staff at Hogarth Press, mainly caused by Leonard's overbearing attitude, with Virginia caught in the middle. Leonard began to suffer severe nervous tension and this transferred itself to Virginia. In September, she suffered exhaustion and fainting fits. However, by November she was in fine spirits, noting in her diary: 'I don't think we have ever been so happy ... life like this is wholly satisfactory, to me anyhow.' Significantly, she avoided the usual 'winter blues'.

In 1932, whilst still redrafting *The Waves*, she began to write her next book, *The Years*. Virginia's original idea had been for a novel set in the period 1880 to 1930 and using a unique mixture of fiction and factual essays to explain education, literature and sexual behaviour in everyday life. This style caused her many stressful problems and eventually she found it unworkable. She then pushed on with *The Years* as a fictional novel in the form of a family saga. It was to take her three years to complete.

1934 was the year her menopause began with all its usual effects. That summer, George Duckworth and Roger Fry died. Obviously she was distressed by her stepbrother's death, but Fry's sudden demise hit her harder. They had been close friends and correspondents since Bloomsbury days.

We can see that the years 1930–34 were amongst the most traumatic Virginia had suffered since childhood. Yet she did not have a serious breakdown. Throughout 1935 her thoughts appear to have been clear and stable. One good example is her carefully thought out decision to refuse the 'Companion of Honour' status offered to her that summer by the Prime Minister. However, by Christmas 1935, she was under tremendous pressure to complete the final revisions to *The Years*. She had committed herself to having it ready for printing by January 1936; it was a commitment she could not keep. Under increasing strain, she battled on, cutting out all social activity. As we might expect, this caused depression. Headaches forced her to work in short bursts. Finally the work was completed and sent to the printers in April 1936.

Now the grief from the deaths of her friends, the emotional demands of writing and the physical exhaustion from spending much time with Ethel Smyth came together in one wave of stressful pressure.

She collapsed with headaches, lack of appetite and insomnia. The ever fearful Leonard decided this was a serious physical breakdown and took her off to Rodmell, where he instituted his usual prescription of complete bed rest. Apart from a brief visit to London to deal with proofs for *The Years*, Virginia was to remain there for five months. Recovery was slow. Her weight fell dramatically; it seems that a bread and milk diet was not so nourishing as Leonard had thought. In November, Leonard read and approved the final proofs for *The Years*. He did not like the book, but he lied to Virginia, telling her it was '... remarkable, and I have no shadow of doubt that it must be published'. Immediately Virginia's mental state and general health improved and by Christmas she was over the episode.

Leonard, however, was not. Frustrations with staff at the Hogarth Press, mainly of his own creation, were causing him severe tension. This caused him to develop acute muscular pains. Perhaps too, he was worn down by years of caring for Virginia. By February 1937 he was suffering with trembling hands, eczema and handicapped by pain. Although consultations with several physicians confirmed that the cause was psychological, Leonard did not improve. He had for many years been very active in the Labour Party. He had been editor of *Political Quarterly* and was Secretary to the Advisory Committee on International Questions. The defeat of the Labour Party in 1931 had hit him hard emotionally. Now Hitler and Mussolini had taken over in Europe and anti-Semitic feeling was sweeping through the continent. Leonard and Virginia had always shared pacifist views. With his mind in turmoil, Leonard did a U-turn and sought to persuade all his contacts to call for rearmament and preparation for war. Virginia argued violently with Leonard about this, telling him the pen was mightier than the sword and that she would use the pen. This only caused the chasm between them to widen on this fundamental matter. Leonard continued to deteriorate and by December 1937 the question of confining him to a nursing home had to be considered. Virginia strongly resisted this. She would look after Leonard. A complete reversal of their lifestyles had now come about. Vanessa also fell ill at this time, engulfed by grief at the death of her son Julian in the Spanish Civil War. Virginia also took on the responsibility of caring for her sister, visiting her daily at Charleston.

Virginia was also completing *Three Guineas*, in which she describes her pacifist feelings about war. A good deal of this book stems from her extensive reading of Freud. Her central theme here was that latent Fascism was there in the English society of that era. *Three Guineas* was published in 1938. It is not surprising that it received a poor reception from reviewers; the general consensus was that the keynote was repugnant and disturbing.

Virginia and Leonard now encountered a new problem. Demolition and extensive new building work around Tavistock Square was creating noise at a level intolerable to the Woolfs. They also felt they needed larger, more airy rooms. Leonard found suitable premises a short distance away at 37 Mecklenburgh Square, WC1. The rent at £250 per annum was at the upper limit of their budget and this was compounded by their failure to dispose of the lease on 52 Tavistock Square. Nevertheless, they took the property and moved everything, including the Press, starting on 17 August 1939. Virginia found the moving process extremely stressful but everything was successfully completed by 24 August.

At the same time, Virginia was labouring away, trying to draw together the threads of three years' detailed research for a biography of Roger Fry. She began writing it in earnest in April 1938. She regarded the biography as a boring chore, but felt she had an obligation to Roger to write it. She also saw it as an opportunity to defend the Bloomsbury set, in which Roger had been a leading light. What to leave out? His homosexuality; certainly. His penchant for pornography? How could one deny that. The madness of his first wife; his feelings about that must be described, but was he the cause of her disorder and distress? His affair with Vanessa? No, that subject was taboo. So it was that in 1940, when she completed it, much was left unsaid. Paradoxically, the Victorian literary censorship that she had fought throughout her literary career was now re-enacted in this, her wartime writing.

This book completed the final turnaround in Virginia's relationship with Leonard. When she showed the final drafts to Leonard he told her in vehement terms that it was dull, boring, lifeless. Virginia was stunned. She was sure that it was a fine historical essay and that Leonard was wrong. She put it down to his lack of interest in anyone's personality, and for the first time she saw changes in him – he had become petty and dictatorial, with an immature predisposition to condemnation. It is probable that Leonard had developed these characteristics in Ceylon, but Virginia had so much relied upon him in the past that she had not recognised this.

The biography of Roger Fry was published in July 1940, but the critics were slow to review it, seemingly uninterested. However, old friends Desmond McCarthy and E.M. Forster came to the rescue. McCarthy gave it a long and enthusiastic review in The *Sunday Times*; Forster was quoted in several journals saying, 'This is a well-researched book, which makes a noble and convincing defence of civilisation.' Herbert Read, a poet and writer, who had left Hogarth Press to be published by Faber, said Fry, the subject, was a dull, selfish and damnable man. The book was as much about the Bloomsbury Group as about Fry and naturally attracted criticism from those who considered Bloomsbury a depraved set, mainly interested in debauchery. Initial sales were slow, but eventually it paid its way.

It is especially interesting that during this period Virginia had no serious mental or physical breakdowns. It seemed that she had so much on her mind, with caring for Leonard and Vanessa, the Fry book and starting her new novel *Between the Acts*, that she simply had no time for introspection. This relatively calm period could not last and it was the Second World War that was to bring back to her those dark, depressive clouds that she feared so much.

All that summer there was continuous aerial bombardment of England by Germany. Great damage was being done to London. Virginia and Leonard were spending most of their time at Rodmell, but their thoughts were constantly with London and particularly their home and the Press at 37 Mecklenburgh Square. On 14 September 1940, a bomb exploded, destroying the residential parts of No. 37 and causing chaos in the Press offices. Miraculously, the printing machinery suffered little damage. With the greatest difficulty, they moved their personal effects and a myriad books and papers to Rodmell, where they rented some storage rooms. With the help of their manager, John Lehmann, they moved the Hogarth Press, and its staff, to Letchworth in Hertfordshire.

Leonard was at his lowest point, filled with deep gloom. The backwash from Leonard's rapid decline into hypochondria and depression had now reached Virginia. Depression now set in for her, for what was to prove the last time. What had caused it? The war was her second experience of worldwide confrontation; this time the bombing and the Battle of Britain brought it all much closer to her. It moved her deeply and her pacifist ideals were shaken to their foundations. Curiously enough, Virginia now began to worry about money. Throughout the 1930s they had lived fully up to their excellent income. Now, with the war slowing down the sale of books and *Roger Fry* having taken up so much time for so little reward, their income was not matching their expenditure; Virginia was having to face the unpleasant prospect of returning to reviewing other writers' books to earn money. She was struggling with *Between the Acts*, which she felt was not good enough for publication. This time the depression set in so quickly that Leonard failed to recognise the signs. Virginia's mood was dark and she had no appetite for food. The usual headaches were in attendance. Winter came early in 1940 and, by the end of October, her usual winter blues added to the existing problems. Virginia's mental disturbance was now severe, as is evidenced by a number of entries in her diary towards the end of 1940. I give just one example by way of illustration:

29.11.1940
I was thinking about vampires. Leeches. Anyone with £500 per year and education is at once sucked by leeches. Put me and Leonard into Rodmell pool and we are sucked and sucked and sucked. Last night Leonard's lecture attracted suckers.

By the beginning of November, Virginia's reluctance to eat had resulted in a serious weight loss. Leonard began to tell Virginia's family and close contacts that he thought she was 'going mad' and he feared she might attempt suicide. He insisted that there was again a need for a serious consultation with a physician. But with whom? Leonard had called in a dozen different doctors during their marriage, including Herbert Seton, Elinor Rendel, Sir George Savage and Sir Maurice Craig. Virginia would have none of those. Perhaps she remembered that all they ever prescribed were sedatives, bed-rest and control by her husband. They agreed to consult Virginia's cousin, Dr Octavia Wilberforce. She was head physician at the New Sussex Hospital for Women, was manager of a rest home for women and had a general practice. They knew her quite well and liked her as a person. She had the advantage of being near at hand; she was living in Brighton with her lesbian partner Elizabeth Robbins, an actress. Octavia attended Virginia at Rodmell in November and made the obvious diagnoses of anorexia and poor blood circulation. She found no problems of mental disturbance (but we should note that Octavia was not a psychiatrist). The treatment prescribed was fresh air and plenty of exercise. It seems Virginia did not take this advice. She confined herself much to the house, desperately trying to revise and redraft *Between the Acts*. Her health and her mind continued to deteriorate.

Further consultations followed in December 1940. Octavia became strongly attached to Virginia and Virginia responded. By January and February of 1941 she was writing to Vita Sackville-West and Ethel Smyth, telling them she had found a new love and that she would seek to see as much of her as possible. However, deterioration continued and by late February she was having trembling fits and hallucinations. She spoke constantly to Octavia, rehearsing and relating in depth details of her past family life, and moaning about how depressed she was. By mid-March, Octavia was angry enough with her to tell her in the sharpest terms to cease her obsessive thinking about her family past and generally to pull herself together and get on with her writing. Much of Virginia's depression at this time was centred around her writing. She had told Octavia, 'I have lost all power over words, can't do a thing with them.' A good deal of this feeling of failure must be related to her final novel, *Between the Acts*. She intended it to be an examination of English literature from ancient times through the present and into the future. The central theme was to be Peace. The characters range from an embattled middle-class family, through to various unhappy, adulterous and homosexual people. An Elizabethan pageant play is introduced into the story, to a background of news flashes and propaganda. For research she had set herself the massive task of reading all past classic English literature and had set herself a time target of two years.

Virginia had great difficulty in trying to pull together a muddling string of thoughts and ideas. Increasingly she began to feel that the history of literature had little value. She despaired of trying to imagine what the future of literature would be. She realised that, beset by the greatest war the world had ever known, the audience for books was in severe decline. Somehow she staggered on and completed the final draft of the book by the beginning of March. On 14 March 1941, she had a meeting with John Lehmann and Leonard to review the book. She at once began to tell them that it was worthless, could not be published, must be scrapped. Gently, but with great determination, Leonard contradicted her and rebuked her for having such an attitude to a work into which she had put so much time. Lehmann said he would read the final draft and give an unbiased opinion.

Virginia returned home in what appeared to be a more contented frame of mind. On 18 March, Lehmann told her he thought the novel should be published. That same day, Virginia went for a walk and arrived back at Monk's House soaking wet and told Leonard that she had fallen by accident into a water-filled ditch. It is highly significant that Leonard accepted this explanation and had not the slightest thought that Virginia might have attempted suicide. Virginia continued to write her diary until 24 March and there is nothing written there to suggest she was contemplating suicide.

Virginia had spent much time and effort on *Between the Acts* and now felt it was worthless. On 20 March she wrote to John Lehmann that *Between the Acts* was 'no good ... too slight and sketchy'. Lehmann replied that it was too late to stop publication as the book had already been advertised for spring publication. This upset Virginia and she responded on 27 March, telling John not to publish; 'it is too silly and trivial; I will revise it.' This letter she gave to Leonard to forward; Leonard added a note of his own, telling John that Virginia was on the verge of a nervous breakdown and proposing that publication be delayed until the autumn. Lehmann did not receive these letters until after Virginia's death.

Leonard had also told Vanessa that Virginia was mentally ill and Vanessa visited on 20 March. She saw nothing serious and wrote to Virginia the next day, the gist of her letter being that Virginia should pull herself together and not try to exhaust herself physically and mentally with mundane tasks but rather to take more rest. Leonard, himself physically ill and mentally depressed, was not content to let matters rest. He contacted Octavia Wilberforce on 26 March, telling her he was very worried about Virginia and uncertain of whether to get nursing help or send her away to a psychiatric home for a rest cure. One wonders why Leonard wanted Octavia to examine Virginia; he was well aware that Dr Wilberforce had little psychiatric knowledge. Octavia agreed to see Virginia on the afternoon of 27 March at Octavia's surgery in Brighton. Dr Wilberforce found her to be underweight and with poor blood circulation. Virginia insisted it was 'quite unnecessary to have come' and insisted she did not wish to go to a 'home'. Octavia found nothing psychologically wrong with Virginia and advised her to take a break from writing; to rest physically and to force herself to eat more. Leonard was later to tell Dr Wilberforce that Virginia had returned home to Rodmell in a cheerful mood and seemed quite different.

On the morning of 28 March 1941, Virginia went out to the lodge at Rodmell. There she is said to have written a letter to Leonard, which she left for him on the writer's block. The original is housed in the British Library and is here reprinted in full:

Dearest.

I want to tell you that you have given me complete happiness. No one could have done more than you have done. Please believe that. But I know that I shall never get over this and I am wasting your life. It is this madness. Nothing anyone says can persuade me. You can work and you will be much better without me. You see I can't write this even, which shows I am right. All I want to say is that until this disease came on we were perfectly happy. It was all due to you. No one could have been so good as you have been. From the very first day till now.

The letter ends there, but there is an addition in different ink. 'Everyone knows that. V.' On the reverse of the page she writes, 'Will you destroy all my papers.' Leonard went out to her at 11 a.m. They returned to the house together. She told Leonard she would go for a walk and then rest for half an hour before lunch. She was seen by the housekeeper, Louie, going back out to the lodge and then returning to the house. Here she put on her fur coat, took her walking stick and departed on her walk. She walked towards the river Ouse, where she was seen at about 11.35 a.m. by a farm worker. The last person to see her alive was Bert Skinner, a villager, who saw her just before midday, proceeding along the river towards Southease bridge.

At 1 p.m. the housekeeper rang the bell for lunch. Virginia had not returned. Leonard did not go in to lunch. He went instead to the sitting room to listen to the news on the radio. Here he found two letters, one addressed to him and the other to Vanessa. They were similar in content to the one left for Leonard in the lodge.

215

Leonard read his letter, called the housekeeper to tell her he thought something had happened to Virginia, then left the house and rushed down to the river. The housekeeper had sent for the local police constable. PC Collins arrived at the river, about a mile up from Southease bridge. Here he found Leonard fishing Virginia's stick out of the river.

Leonard immediately explained that Virginia had been under tremendous mental stress and may have tried to drown herself. PC Collins dived into the river several times at different points, but with no success. The village blacksmith brought ropes and irons to the river and dragging began. Leonard returned to the house and now found the third letter in the lodge. He firmly believed all three letters were written that same morning. By chance, Vanessa arrived shortly afterwards. Leonard told her he thought Virginia had committed suicide. Vanessa was shocked but also very surprised. She had last seen Virginia on 20 March and had seen nothing unusual and had no suspicion that she was in danger. Leonard drove Vanessa back to Charleston. The only decipherable note in his diary for that day is a record of his car mileage.

Dragging of the river continued the next day but no trace of Virginia could be found. Although the body had not been found, Leonard wrote to *The Times* two days later, telling the editor that Virginia had been drowned. Her obituary duly appeared in *The Times* on 3 April. The BBC radio news announced her death that night. The local Brighton paper picked up the news and interviewed Leonard who said, 'Mrs Woolf is presumed to be dead. She went for a walk on Friday (28 March), leaving a letter behind and it is thought she has been drowned.' It is little wonder that this was the general opinion, since Leonard had also already written exactly this to Vita Sackville-West, Ethel Smyth and others. Virginia's body was recovered on April 18. It was found by children playing at Southease bridge, some way downstream from where Leonard had directed the original search. It was partly obscured by river vegetation, which had trapped the body and prevented it from being swept out to sea. The police removed the body to Newhaven mortuary and immediately called Leonard to identify it. On doing so, Leonard discovered a large stone in the pocket of Virginia's coat, which he showed to the police. It was assumed that she had placed it there to weigh her down and assist drowning. Leonard asked that the inquest be held as soon as possible. It was held the next day at

Newhaven Coroner's Court. Leonard attended alone. He submitted the two suicide letters to Mr Hoare, the coroner. In his statement, he told the coroner that his wife had suffered from acute nervous exhaustion all her life. He also said he had been concerned at the time of the final events on 28 March that she would commit suicide. This latter statement is at odds with his statements to Octavia Wilberforce, Vanessa and others that on the morning of 28 March Virginia seemed calm, was recovered and perfectly normal.

The coroner returned a verdict of 'suicide whilst the balance of mind was disturbed'. Leonard asked for the immediate release of the body and this was granted. He arranged the cremation, which took place two days later at the Downs Crematorium in Brighton. He was the only witness; friends and family had not been informed. The next day Leonard buried the ashes under a huge elm tree in the garden at Monk's House. But this was far from being the end of Virginia Woolf.

John Lehmann, in his own autobiography, tells us that before Virginia's body had even been found Leonard had discussed with him his plans to 'husband' the huge amount of Virginia's unpublished material; to release it at carefully timed intervals over two or three decades. He did this to such good effect that it was not until the mid 1960s that Virginia Woolf became one of the most widely read writers of the twentieth century. This provided Leonard with a good income for the rest of this life and this income was enhanced by his lectures, radio and television interviews about Virginia's life.

Leonard remained at Monk's House for several months before moving back to Mecklenburgh Square, Bloomsbury. Here he found solace among some of the Woolfs' former friends and acquaintances. Among them was artist and lithographer Trekkie Parsons, now married to a painter and living in Victoria Square, Belgravia. In September 1942, Leonard moved to Victoria Square. He formed a very close relationship with Trekkie, which was to last until his death 25 years later. Together they travelled extensively abroad. At times they stayed together at Monk's House. When Leonard died, he left the property to Trekkie.

Certain aspects of Virginia's death remain a mystery. Questions have arisen and there are some who have speculated that her death may not have been suicide.

What of the three suicide letters? Quentin Bell and Leonard Woolf both believe all were written the day of Virginia's death.

The two letters to Leonard were very similar in content. Does this make sense? Why write three letters in the short space of two hours on one morning? In the third letter, found by Leonard after Virginia's death, the handwriting is very shaky and in parts difficult to decipher. We have it from John Lehmann, and Leonard, that her handwriting was shaky in those last months prior to her death. On the other hand, Leonard's own doctors have recorded that he had suffered with trembling hands for some years and this had grown worse since the outbreak of the war. Could the final letter have been forged by Leonard? Many writers who have written about Virginia (led by Nigel Nicholson and Joanne Trautmann), hold the view that the first two letters were suicide notes, written at the time of an attempt on 18 March, when Virginia returned from a walk soaking wet. They say she either failed or abandoned the attempt, which presumably was to drown herself in the river. Why then make the attempt a few days later with exactly the same method? She had other less painful methods to hand, not least now that Leonard no longer kept strict control of her tablets, and indeed there were Leonard's own tablets, prescribed for depression and trembling. Death by drowning in the icy winter waters of an English river must have been painful and horrible. It would not have been quick. Virginia was a very good swimmer – it is inconceivable that she would have panicked and filled her lungs with water.

A single large stone in her pocket would not have carried sufficient weight to have pinned her down under the water. Why was the stone not discovered until Leonard found it in her coat at the mortuary?

PC Collins must have been on the scene and diving repeatedly into the river, at the place to which Leonard directed him, little more than an hour after Virginia's death, yet could find no trace of her. Shortly afterwards the river was thoroughly dragged; again no trace was found. Did Leonard direct the searchers to the correct area? If he did not, was this deliberate? It could not have been in error, for he states that it was the place where he found Virginia's walking stick in the river. Yet why did she need the stick in the river?

Did Leonard play any part in Virginia's death? Leonard says that when he went to look for Virginia he found only her walking stick in the river. Could he have come upon a fainted Virginia, placed a large stone in her coat pocket and pushed her into the river? Could he have found Virginia and been subjected to a torrent of anger, as at Richmond station, sufficient to provoke his fury; could he then have struck Virginia down, perhaps with her stick, and, possibly panicking, bundled body and stick into the river? Is it conceivable that Virginia simply fainted and fell into the river?

No one saw Virginia walk into the river or saw her drown. Therefore anything is possible. The acceptance by the police and the coroner that Virginia committed suicide is based entirely upon Leonard's producing the stick and the letters and upon his statement alone that she was suicidal at the time. The latter statement Leonard made only to the police and the coroner. To others he states completely the reverse, saying that on the evening prior to and the morning of her death, she seemed much recovered and perfectly normal.

If we have doubts, it may be useful to examine Virginia's suicide as it would be by today's legal system and with the advantage of hindsight.

In any inquiry today into the suspicious death of a wife, reported by her husband, the first possible suspect to be considered would be the husband. The prime questions always are: was there motive and opportunity? What motive could Leonard have had? Certainly there was money, including property and future personal wealth from control of publications, broadcasts and lectures about Virginia. Perhaps Leonard had come to the final point where he wanted to end what must have been an unsatisfactory marriage by normal standards. A marriage never properly consummated and without sex. A married life where he had spent most of it nursing a mental and physical invalid to the point where his own health had broken down. It is not unreasonable to suspect that Leonard had come to the stage where he wanted a new life of his own. What do we make of his swiftly forming an intimate long-term relationship with someone he already knew, Trekkie Parsons? All of these matters might be seen as motives.

Leonard was the only one we know of with opportunity and indeed it was the perfect opportunity.

If the events surrounding Virginia's death had taken place today, I believe that, since no one saw Virginia take her own life, and considering Leonard's opportunity and possible motives, a post-mortem examination would have taken place. It may, of course, have found nothing untoward. We shall never know. Leonard's

219

speed in arranging the cremation of the body have ensured that. Why did Leonard alone attend the inquest; surely at least Dr Wilberforce and Vanessa ought to have been asked to give evidence? Why did Leonard alone attend the funeral service and the cremation? It seems none of Virginia's wide circle of friends and relatives were informed.

The coroner's verdict was suicide and this has been almost universally accepted. At this stage we can do no more than accept it and consider why she committed the act.

Was the balance of her mind disturbed? We know her history: by the age of 33 she had suffered three major bouts of mental breakdown. But she did not have another serious breakdown during the remaining 26 years until her death. Was she having a mental breakdown at the time of her death? Her doctor, Octavia Wilberforce, examined her the day before her death and found nothing wrong with her mental health. Leonard told Dr Wilberforce that immediately prior to her death Virginia was perfectly normal. However, we cannot doubt her mental and physical frailty throughout most of her life. Having lived through the First World War in her prime years, she was now having to live through the second international conflict in her declining years; undoubtedly this depressed her greatly. At that time there was a real fear that the Germans would invade Britain. Virginia knew well what would happen to an intellectual Jew and his wife if that happened. Indeed, Leonard and Virginia had made a pact that if invasion occurred they would commit suicide together. Despite her final letters to Leonard, her marriage must have been in many ways unsatisfactory. No sexual relationship, which surely led to so much physical frustration that eventually she had affairs with other women. No children from the marriage, of course. Virginia was extremely unhappy with her last piece of writing, *Between the Acts* and her work prior to that, on Roger Fry, had been unsuccessful. She was struggling to express herself in her writing. Did she feel she no longer had the ability to write? Was she a manic depressive? Or was she, as I believe, one who suffered from a severe form of the cyclical depression, which we now acknowledge as SAD syndrome, perhaps combined with porphyria, which we now know causes excitement, depression and hallucinations? Possibly a combination of all these factors finally crushed her spirit and her will to live. Posthumously, a reputation has been built around Virginia Woolf that she was a brilliant writer, manic depressive and now an icon of feminism. Fierce debate continues today as to whether these attributes are true, with opinions conflicting violently on either side.

The circumstances surrounding her suicide remain an enigma.

Hunter S. Thompson

The Great Gonzo

Hunter Stockton Thompson created 'Gonzo' journalism. He did not invent the word 'gonzo'. The word was first used in 1970 by William Cardoso, editor of the *Boston Globe Sunday Magazine*. Acclaiming 'The Kentucky Derby is Decadent and Depraved', an article written by Thompson for sports magazine *Scanlan's Monthly*, Cardoso said, 'This is it, this is pure Gonzo. If this is a start, keep rolling.' Thompson embraced the word immediately. He told his lifelong friend Ralph Steadman, 'Okay, that's what I do. Gonzo.'

The Gonzo writing style discards impartiality and engages the writer's manic personal views. The distinction between author and

Photo: Getty Images

subject, fiction and non-fiction becomes blurred. In journalism, when reporting an event, the writer is an essential part of the story. The method is stream of consciousness writing.

Thompson's style of Gonzo was fuelled by vast quantities of cocaine, acid, bourbon and cigarettes while the writing unfolded. That he reached the age of 67, and might have lasted much longer if he had not taken his own life, is one of the imponderables of medical history. We can take into account that many of the stories of his gross excesses may have been wildly exaggerated. Thompson himself said, many times, 'Obviously my drug and drink use is exaggerated, or I would be long since dead.' On the other hand, after Thompson was examined by an international team of medical experts, at Indiana University Medical School, in 1991, Dr Bradley Hollingsworth, a leading international liver consultant, declared that Thompson's liver had regenerated itself more than once. Dr Hollingsworth's prognosis: 'He'll outlive us all.'

Hunter Thompson was one of the most important authors and journalists of the twentieth century, a key player in the development of the genre of New Journalism. He has become a cult figure; myths and controversy surround him.

Not least of the controversies concerns his date of birth. It is stated by various authors to be different dates between 1937 and 1939. On the Internet there is an entire web page given over to consideration of Thompson's year of birth. I am satisfied with the birth certificate entered at the Kentucky State Bureau of Vital Statistics. This gives Thompson's date of birth as 18 July 1937. Other information given shows that Hunter was born in the suburb of Norton in Louisville, Kentucky. At birth he weighed 11 pounds; yet another example of a huge weight for a child, later to become an author who commits suicide: see Caesar Pavese and Ernest Hemingway.

Hunter's father, Jack, an engineering insurance salesman, was 42 at the time of Hunter's birth. It was his second marriage; he had one child, Jack, from his first marriage. His mother, Virginia, was 13 years younger and her work was to look after the home and Hunter, with his two younger brothers, Davison and James. Virginia's father was an alcoholic and she soon followed in his footsteps, although she blamed the problem partly upon Hunter, saying that he caused difficulties from the moment of his birth.

Certainly Hunter was troublesome. He quickly grew into a very big child. His physique, together with an aggressive attitude towards authority, soon established him as the leader of his peers. Most of his group were afraid of him due to his bad temper and uncontrollable violence. By the age of ten he had a small rifle and a bullwhip, and he didn't hesitate to use them to shoot or whip at other boys or animals. His mother could not control Hunter, but his father did exercise some control and on occasion did beat him with a heavy, buckled strap.

Hunter began to use his writing talents at a very early age. His first job was as sports writer for *The Southern Star* newspaper at the age of ten.

It seems he could have been a professional sportsman if he had put his mind to it. He starred as a short stop in a baseball team, the Cherokee Colonels, when only twelve. At his junior high school he was on the basketball team. He later was one of the top athletes at Castlewood Athletic Club. He was also a strong swimmer. Several friends from his youth believed that he could have played American pro football. Certainly he had the physique for it. By his late teens he had grown to 6' 4" in height and weighed 198 pounds. He had a strong desire to be a professional athlete, but he simply did not have the requisite concentration and competitive spirit, so it did not happen. He compensated for that, to some degree, particularly in his early years, by using some of his journalistic time to report sports. His articles were weird and wacky, with Hunter's experiences a central theme, rather than a report on the event.

His first main school was Atherton, where he was on the football team. However, he foolishly taunted fellow team players with claims that he intended to leave and join Louisville Male High School because they had a better team. His teammates responded in an appropriate fashion by beating him up. This encouraged him to move on to Male High School. It does seem that frustration born of the knowledge that he would never be a professional athlete was the catalyst for embarking upon a lifetime pattern of outrageous, couldn't-care-less behaviour. A strong contributor to Hunter's behaviour of that time was the death of his father, Jack, in July 1952, from a brain haemorrhage. Hunter had time for his father and it hit him badly.

In 1954 and 1955, Hunter was arrested several times and came before the court on four occasions. The first two occasions were for drunkenness and assault. The third time was for a series of robberies and vandalism at a petrol station on the Bardstown Road in Louisville. During this time, he had also been suspended from Male High School for rape; although he always maintained he was not guilty. It is difficult to believe that charge. Hunter was tall, dark, good-looking, a leader of his peers. Several women, including Lou Ann Murphy and Susan Peabody, have stated that all the girls were crazy about Hunter.

His fourth appearance in court was on 15 June 1955. He was accused of robbing an individual, Joe Monin, at Hogan's Fountain, Louisville on 11 May 1955. Thompson was sentenced to 60 days in the Jefferson County jail. Here he enrolled on a correspondence course in journalism, which he later completed. He was released after 30 days; unfortunately this was too late for him to graduate with the rest of his class.

He now took a job as a truck driver. That soon ended with a crashed truck, courtesy of a bottle of tequila. By now he was 18 and on standby for conscription into the US Army. To beat this he enlisted in the US Air Force. Based at Eglin Air Proving Ground in Florida, he was assigned to duties as sports writer for the base newspaper. Here he produced offbeat but enthusiastic reports. However, being Hunter, he had to flout air force regulations. Whilst serving in the air force, at one point he was also a sports journalist for one Florida newspaper, sports editor for another and press release office for a wrestling promotions company.

Frustrated and enraged at being unable to progress beyond Air Force Man Second Class, he began to bombard the Senate with reasons and requests for him to be allowed to leave the air force on a 'duty completed' basis. Eventually, because he was such a nuisance, he was given a discharge in November 1957. His commanding officer, Colonel W. Evans, wrote, 'In summary, this Airman, although talented, will not be guided by policy. He has little consideration for military bearing or dress and seems to dislike the service and want out as soon as possible. Sometimes his rebel and superior attitude seems to rub off on other airmen staff members.' Hunter said his classification upon release was 'totally unclassifiable'.

Thompson had continued his studies whilst serving and now received his graduation diploma. Next Hunter took advantage of concessions in the GI Bill to enrol at Columbia University's School of General Studies. Here he took a course in short story writing.

In 1958 he worked for *Time* magazine as a copy boy. Whilst

there he typed out the whole of Ernest Hemingway's *A Farewell to Arms*. This he used to study Hemingway's style of writing. This soon led him to reading all of Hemingway's works. He now became greatly influenced by Hemingway. This was to last for the rest of Hunter's life. Hemingway also influenced his lifestyle and became his literary hero. In 1959, after threatening his line manager with gross physical violence, Hunter was fired for 'insubordination'. He then went to work for the *Middleton Daily Record* in New York. Here his favourite pursuit was to kick the office vending machine until it unloaded packets of sweets, which he would then distribute to the other office workers. What really got him sacked was arguing violently with the owner of a local restaurant, who was also a major advertiser in the paper.

At this time Hunter was living in a shabby basement apartment in Greenwich Village. A great deal of his time was spent getting drunk with his male friends and womanising. He was very much the handsome lout about town. This did not stop him working on his first novel, *Prince Jellyfish*. When it was finished, he declared it a masterpiece and set about hawking it around every publishing house in New York. To a man the publishers declared it rubbish. At the time of writing, this book has never been published.

Around this time, Hunter met Sandra Conklin. A Long Island, New York, girl, she was tall, with long blonde hair, a good figure, highlighted by a trim waist. She had many boyfriends. Described by her friends as 'gorgeous. A nice person', it is difficult to tell whether she was the antithesis or the counterpart to Hunter. That they fell for each other immediately is clear. By New Year's Eve 1959, within a few weeks of meeting, they were having a full on relationship, sometimes spending days on end in bed, making uninhibited love together. They were to spend the next 20 years together.

In 1960 Thompson took a job with a tenpin bowling magazine, *El Sportivo*. Based in Beach Shack, in Puerto Rico, he took Sandra Conklin and her ex-boyfriend, Peter Flanders, to live with him. *El Sportivo* soon went out of production, but Thompson kept his Puerto Rican base, from where he travelled widely through South America and the Caribbean, writing articles as a freelance for several USA daily newspapers. The living he made was meagre, but Sandra and he still lived as though they were on honeymoon. Hunter still worked at trying to write a novel and, by the end of 1960, he had

227

completed *The Rum Diary*. Again he could not find a publisher. By now, almost penniless, Thompson decided he had to get back to New York to find work. He found a sailing vessel, which would give himself, Sandra and Peter passage from Puerto Rico to Bermuda as crew. The voyage took seven days. Confinement on board was difficult for Hunter, but an even bigger problem was that there was no alcohol on board. Hunter had been drinking heavily every day for the past year; now withdrawal symptoms set in. They made it to Bermuda and soon found passage to New York.

Unable to find work in New York, or to get a publisher for *The Rum Diary*, Hunter's economic situation was getting desperate. Just as he had decided to move on, he was lucky enough to find himself in drinking company with Michael Murphy, whose grandmother owned an estate in Big Sur, California. Murphy took to Hunter, as most drinking buddies did, with the result that he was invited to visit for a few days. Once there, Hunter ingratiated himself with Virginia, the grandmother. He was given the job of caretaker at the hot springs unit on the estate and, with it, accommodation for himself and Sandra, but no salary. One of his ex-editors, Adam Smith, said Hunter brought several guns with him to Big Sur: 'He would sit in the caretaker's shack, firing away at the homosexuals who climbed the fence.' Hunter would also go out at night, shooting for food. That was an indication of their poverty; indeed if Sandra had not taken temporary work, they would have been in a desperate position. Sandra twice fell pregnant whilst they were in Big Sur. Each time she had an abortion. They simply were not ready for children; they were too poor.

In fairness, one must record that Hunter continued writing articles, which he would send to *Argosy* and *Esquire* magazines, although with little success. One article, which was accepted and published by *Argosy*, was about life in Big Sur and in this he claimed that the hot springs were a meeting place for gays. Homosexuals were generally accepted in California at that time, but not by Hunter who was violently prejudiced against them. The article cost him his job. Virginia simply told him he had to leave.

Hunter and Sandra returned to New York. Sandra found herself a typing job with a nuclear research company and Hunter advertised in the *Editor & Publisher* for work. In May 1962 the *National Observer* agreed to pay him on a per article basis for reports on life and events in South America; subject to him paying his own way there. This he was able to do thanks to a timely small inheritance from his grandmother. The plan was for Hunter to send copy back to Sandra in New York for her to type and send out to the *National Observer* and to travel sections of major newspapers. This worked very well until Sandra discovered Hunter was in Rio de Janeiro, getting drunk by day and consorting with prostitutes by night. She appeared in Rio immediately. Many stories about Hunter let loose in Rio have circulated. In one instance, Hunter was noted walking around Rio with a monkey in his pocket; Hunter was drunk, so was the monkey. Asked to explain this, Hunter said they were both lonely and enjoyed each other's company. When Hunter drank, the monkey drank. Subsequently the monkey committed suicide by jumping off the balcony of Hunter's upper storey hotel room; the theory was that the monkey was suffering from delirium tremens and tried to fly. Although Hunter was even then, at 25, no stranger to drunkenness and debauchery, he now found himself in company with older, more experienced writers from the big daily newspapers of New York and Los Angeles, who were heavyweight reprobates. There is little doubt that they encouraged Hunter to descend into a libertine lifestyle.

Hunter did not stay long in Rio with Sandra. The *Observer* offered him the opportunity to travel through South America, reporting on the domestic issues of the various countries. Sandra was sent back to her mother in the USA. Hunter continued to travel the South American continent for the *Observer* until mid 1964. Much of his time was spent in brothels, bottle of bourbon always to hand. One of Hunter's most interesting articles was his report on Ernest Hemingway's death. Thompson travelled to Ketchum, Idaho, to investigate the reasons for Hemingway's suicide. His article on the drug-fuelled journey was as interesting as his on-site report. Whilst at Hemingway's house he became convinced that he was Hemingway's alter ego. Hemingway was to remain a hero and role model for the rest of Thompson's life. Being Thompson, he could not leave without stealing a souvenir. He chose a pair of elk horns.

Suddenly, in May 1963, Hunter decided to visit his mother in Louisville. It was not because he loved her. He did not. He hated her all of his adult life. He despised her drunkenness; the very alcoholism that he indulged in to gross excess for 50 years. The visit was to see Sandra, who was on a working holiday in Louisville

229

and staying with Virginia. Shortly after arrival, Hunter told Sandra to bundle up her clothes and prepare for a trip (of several hundred miles) to Jacksonville, Indiana. When Sandra asked why they were going there, he told her quite simply, 'We're getting married'. They did get married there on 19 May 1963. The marriage was consummated in the back of Hunter's old, white Rambler car. Their only child, Juan Fitzgerald Thompson, was born ten months later in March 1964. Sandra was to have three miscarriages and lose two full-term babies during the 17 years they were married.

Towards the end of 1964 Thompson decided to write for *The Spider*, a Californian underground newspaper. To facilitate this, he moved temporarily to San Francisco. This caused a falling out and termination of his work with the *National Observer*. Hunter now immersed himself in the drug-fuelled hippie culture of the swinging sixties. Already, at 27, an alcoholic and habitual user of marijuana, mescal (compressed cactus tip juice) and speed, Thompson now found himself inducted into some really heavy drugs. Acid, which he was to use continuously from now on, gave him hallucinations, the horror of which would often terrify him. He called ether 'that rotten stuff' and said that it made that person irresponsible, powerless and depraved; but he continued to take it for the next 40 years. There is little doubt that Hunter's San Francisco experience drove him through drink and drug addiction into a permanent lifestyle of narcotic, alcohol and tobacco abuse. It was around this time that he took to carrying two Magnum 44 guns around with him everywhere and shooting them off at random.

Hunter now discarded journalism in an effort to write a novel based on the cultural revolution of the early sixties era. The novel would not come, writer's block descended and the Thompsons found themselves penniless. Sandra was forced to steal food to prevent them starving. At the same time, Hunter was mail-ordering expensive custom-made shirts; though whether he ever paid for them is doubtful.

Early in 1965, at a point when the Thompsons had reached the position of financial desperation, Carey McWilliams, editor of *The Nation*, offered Hunter $100 to write an article on the motorbike gang, the Hell's Angels. Hunter replied, 'Of course. I'll do anything for $100.' Hunter had no way of knowing this was to be a critical turning point in his career. He spent a week with the Hell's Angels guys, he got on OK with them and the article was written. *The*

Nation published it in May 1965, under the heading 'The Motorcycle Gangs: Losers and Outsiders'. Several editors thought it good material and some suggested Hunter write a book. Bernie Shircliff, editor at Ballantine Books, was the first to make a firm offer. He wrote to Hunter, 'I think there's a paperback book in this; and if you're willing to try it, I'm willing to offer you $6,000.' Was he willing to do it? You bet he was.

Hunter approached Sonny Barger, President of the California Chapter of the Hell's Angels, and asked if he could hang around them and write a book. Barger had liked the article. What's in it for us? he asked. Knowing the guys, Hunter offered a keg of beer on completion. Accepted.

So Hunter spent about a year, summer of 1965 to summer 1966, hanging around with the Hell's Angels. He mostly turned up at weekends. He didn't dress like them; to the Angels he seemed more like someone dressed for a hunting trip than for a motorcycle burn up. He rode with them a little, but his BSA was not well received amongst their Harley Davidsons. However, Hunter got to know their ways well enough and obtained some kudos with them by always carrying a Magnum gun and firing it off indiscriminately. He made notes on their road rallies, their codes of conduct, their sexual adventures and their home lives away from biking. His objective was to describe the gang and their activities whilst highlighting the part the media played in establishing their reputation for brutality. Ballantine set Thompson a deadline of April 1966 and he began to send in material. Bernie Shircliff immediately recognised that this work merited more than a paperback. Ballantine did a deal for Random House to publish it in hardback. Hunter met the deadline. Random House published the book in August 1966 under the title *Hell's Angels: the Strange and Terrible Saga of the Outlaw Motorcycle Gang*, subtitle: *Oh Nerdish Ones*.

The critics received it very well: the *San Francisco Chronicle* said, 'Shattering ... truly rough and stomach turning ... a fascinating view of modern sociology', while the *New York Times* said, 'His language reports of a world most of us would never dare encounter.'

The book sold 500,000 copies during its first year of publication. It became a bestseller and is still in print today and read as classic American literature. Thompson's career is established with his first published book. On 3 September 1966 Hunter meets with the Hell's Angels to show them the book. The gang are not happy. They

231

have not received their keg of beer. Sonny Barger notes the book price at $5. They realise book sales amount to a large sum of money. They ask what is their share. Hunter tells them that it takes a lot of time and much ability to write a book and their share is nothing. It is not surprising that the Hell's Angels then give Hunter a savage kicking, sufficient to confine him to hospital for several days. Undismayed, Hunter used the incident for the new jacket to the paperback, on which he states, 'I met, I rode with and I was almost killed by the Hell's Angels.'

The success of this first book gave Thompson an entrée into the literary and socialite worlds. From 1967 to 1969 he was on a continuous alcoholic binge. He lived mainly on his earnings from *Hell's Angels*, and little work was done. He was engaged as a columnist by *Ramparts*, but does not appear to have written anything of significance. In January 1967 he wrote a six-page article 'Lifestyles: The Cyclist' for *Esquire* magazine. For *Pageant* magazine he wrote 'Why Boys Will be Girls' in August 1967 and 'Presenting: The Richard Nixon Doll' in July 1968. With the latter piece, we discover his loathing of President Richard Nixon, which carried through to his 1972 book *Fear and Loathing on the Campaign Trail '72*.

During this 1967 to 1969 period an element of boredom prevailed. Hunter now developed the habit of not rising from bed until 3 p.m., and this continued for the rest of his life. It was during this period, whilst vacationing at Woody Creek, Aspen, Colorado, that Hunter found a property, which was to remain his home for 38 years until his death. It was basically a large log cabin, with a smaller house adjacent and 130 acres of land. Hunter called it 'my fortified compound'. By the time Hunter had stolen furniture from all around the valley to fit it out, and stocked it with a large number of rifles, handguns, grenades and explosives, then it definitely was that. Sandra named it 'Owl Farm'. There certainly were many owls, but the primary birds were to be a magnificent collection of peacocks, which Hunter built up over his lifetime.

Early in 1970, *Scanlan's Monthly* gave Hunter an assignment to write an article on the appearance at Vermont of triple Olympic gold medallist skier, Jean-Claude Killy. Based in a hotel at Manchester, New Hampshire, Hunter was still finding it difficult to write. He hyped himself up on amphetamines and bourbon and did complete the piece on Killy. The downside was that, having completed, he lost complete control of himself and let out his aggression by smashing up his hotel room. He totally wrecked it and was lucky to escape the arrival of the police. *Scanlan's* were not concerned with the bill for damages, which they didn't have the means to pay anyway. They were happy with the article and next commissioned him to write a piece on the Kentucky Derby.

This point in Hunter's career was highly significant. It was to be his first contact with the artist Ralph Steadman, whom *Scanlan's* had sent to provide the illustration for Thompson's report. The very British and correct Steadman went on to illustrate *Fear and Loathing in Las Vegas*, *Fear and Loathing on the Campaign Trail '72* and *The Curse of Lono* for Thompson. He also went on to become a loyal, lifetime friend and to be thoroughly corrupted by Hunter. 'The Kentucky Derby is Decadent and Depraved' was Hunter's title for the piece. That was almost as far as he got. Try as he did, he could not meet the deadline. In last-minute desperation, Warren Hinkle, *Scanlan's* editor, told him to send simply his notes. Hunter said that he could not; they were crazy gibberish. Hinkle said he must send them anyway, so Hunter tore out the pages from his notebook and despatched them. Hinkle printed them, unedited. Hunter was convinced it was a disaster, but to the astonishment of himself, Steadman, Hinkle and others, it was highly commended by the critics. Bill Cardoso, editor of the *Boston Globe Sunday Magazine*, called it 'pure Gonzo', a phrase he claimed derived from the French Canadian *gonzeaux* and which he meant to indicate a shining new path in journalism. Other critics called it a breakthrough in journalism, a stroke of genius and a new way ahead in combining fact with fiction. So much for critics trying to evaluate what they do not understand! Anyway, the description 'Gonzo' stuck, as we now know. However, this surprising success did not alleviate Thompson's boredom.

His next move was to apply to the Universal Life Church for a doctorate in Divinity. This he achieved by purchase and final interview. For the rest of his life, he insisted on being referred to as Dr Hunter S. Thompson.

In August 1970 he had a flash of inspiration for some major mischief that he could get up to. Election of local officers was due in Aspen. Ned Vare, a local maverick friend of Hunter's was up for election as County Commissioner. Vare was sure to be opposed by the sheriff, Carrol Whitmer, who was himself up for re-election. Hunter decided to run for election as Sheriff of Pitkin County, under the banner 'Freak Power Party'. He would be a kind of stalking horse and draw the attention of Whitmer and his supporters away from Vare. Hunter thought it a rare piece of fun. He set out his programme:

1. Decriminalize the use of drugs. No decriminalization of drug trafficking. Stocks to be set up on the Court House lawn to enable the honest drug-taking public to punish greedy drug dealers as they see fit.
2. Sheriff to have an unspecified number of days off for psychedelic experience.
3. Pedestrianize all streets and lay them to lawn.
4. No building allowed that obscures the view of the mountains.
5. Aspen, Colorado to be renamed 'Fat City'.

Then a problem arose. The ordinary folk of Aspen took to Hunter's crazy programme and his hippie style of presentation. It was no longer a piece of quick mayhem and mischief. It began to look as though Hunter would win. The national press got hold of the story and the campaign was widely reported. The *San Francisco Examiner*'s caption was, 'Aspen may get new Sheriff. Polls show Pitkin County voters set to elect Dr Hunter S. Thompson on Freak Power ticket'. The *New York Times* reported, 'The fact is that Hunter Thompson's bizarre campaign may well make him the next Sheriff of Pitkin County.' The headline in the *Los Angeles Times* said, 'Freak Power Candidate May Be Winner In Aspen Sheriff's Race'. Thompson went to *Rolling Stone* magazine and told the editor, Jan Wenner, that he was about to be elected sheriff and that he wished to submit an article about the campaign. *Rolling Stone* was, at that time, a drug-fuelled music magazine, but Wenner wanted the magazine to expand into events, sports and politics; he therefore commissioned Hunter to write the article. The piece appeared on 1 October 1970 under the title 'The Battle of Aspen' by Dr Hunter S. Thompson (Candidate For Sheriff)'. It was to be the start of a relationship with *Rolling Stone* that would last the rest of Thompson's life and during which they were to publish all his best work.

In the event, the Aspen property developers, estate agents and company owners were so scared of Hunter's programme that they mounted a last-minute surge that just defeated him. The final polls showed the incumbent, Whitmer, pushing Hunter into second place by only 470 votes. Hunter's reaction was, 'If we can't win with Freak Power in Aspen, we can't win anywhere.'

About this time, *Scanlan's Monthly* went bankrupt and Hunter was left with big credit card bills for his 'expenses', including charges for the destruction of his hotel room in Manchester. He also had a large tax bill to pay and was almost penniless. He had taken up the pseudonym of Raoul Duke and his only work now was a few small articles for *Rolling Stone*.

Hunter was in the Polo Lounge at the Beverley Hills Hotel, getting drunk with a friend, lawyer Oscar Acosta, when a life-changing telephone call came through. *Sports Illustrated* offered him $250 plus expenses to write a 250-word caption covering a motorcycle race, the Mint 400. The race was to take place across the Nevada Desert, close to Las Vegas, and Hunter was to depart immediately in order to register as a journalist with access to the riders and the race. Never one to travel alone if a drug-taking, drinking companion was to hand, Hunter invited Acosta along. The first move was to get together sufficient drugs for the journey. Together the pair roar through the Nevada Desert in a hire car at 100 mph stoned out of their minds. They arrive saturated with acid, mescal and ether and subside into grotesque hallucinations. Hunter misses the Mint 400 race, but fills his notebook with gibberish about it. He submits about 2,000 words to *Sports Illustrated*, who reject it aggressively, describing it as rubbish. Without a commission and surrounded by bills, Hunter, already deserted by Acosta, prepares to flee. At the last moment, an assignment comes through from *Rolling Stone* to stay in Las Vegas and cover the National Police Officers' Convention taking place there. Rejoined by Acosta, drug-fuelled mayhem ensues, but little is written about the convention. What is written about is Thompson's search for 'the American Dream' and his antics with Acosta, whom he describes as 'my 300-pound Samoan lawyer Dr Gonzo'. Hunter submits about 10,000 words to Jan Wenner at *Rolling Stone*, partly pages torn from his notebook, plus conversations on audio tape. Wenner liked it and scheduled it for publication. Sarah Lazin, for *Rolling Stone*, transcribed the tape. She says that on the tape two men, one with a Spanish accent and another who continually mumbled, were talking to a waitress in a Las Vegas fast food cafe. The woman couldn't understand Hunter or Acosta and Lazin had trouble understanding any of it. Lazin recalls that whatever it sounded like to her she would type, complete with her own grammar and punctuation. 'Half of it I really felt like I had made up'. However, when it was printed, it was verbatim as Lazin had typed it. Hunter never changed a word.

Encouraged by Wenner and *Rolling Stone*, Hunter withdrew to the basement of his 'fortified compound' at Woody Creek and there completed *Fear and Loathing in Las Vegas*, a short book of about 60,000 words. Little is written of The Mint 400 or the National Police Officers' Convention. Much is written of his drug-crazed antics with Oscar Acosta and the trail of mayhem and bewildered people they left behind them.

Rolling Stone previewed the book in two parts in their magazines of 11 and 25 November 1971 under the pen name Raoul Duke, and with some wonderful illustrations by Ralph Steadman. The book was published early in 1972 by Straight Arrow Books. It quickly became a word-of-mouth publishing sensation, and eventually became a worldwide bestseller. It has since been reprinted 25 times. For the *New York Times*, Chris Lehmann heralded it as 'the best book on the Dope Decade ... mad, corrosive poetry ... it's funny'. For the same broadsheet, Crawford Woods heralded it as 'a desperate and important book, a wired nightmare, the funniest piece of American prose since *Naked Lunch*'. Michael Putney, in the *National Observer*, wrote, 'If you suspend your disbelief and climb out on that precarious psychic limb with Thompson ... then, and only then, *Fear and Loathing* comes off as a mad, manic masterpiece.' Pete Clark, writing later for the *London Evening Standard*, said that Thompson crashed through the barriers of taste and decorum whilst being a fearless seeker of truth. John Raban wrote, for the London magazine *The New Mongrel*, 'No hood or cop could be as unbuttoned, as obscene and sensitive and open as Hunter, motherfucking his way over the typewriter keys like a secretary attentive to his own subconscious.'

His fellow authors were equally enthusiastic. Tom Wolfe called it 'a scorching epochal sensation'. Tom Robbins said, 'It lifts you out of your seat when you're reading it. His prose style reads like he's careening down a mountain highway at 110 miles an hour, steering with his knees.' William Kennedy, writing much later in 1998, called it, 'One of the funniest, most original books of the last three decades.' I share Kennedy's view.

There is little doubt that with *Fear and Loathing in Las Vegas*,

Hunter Thompson peaked as an author at the age of 34. Although he went on to write a further dozen books, none had the impact of *Fear and Loathing in Las Vegas*; albeit *Fear and Loathing on the Campaign Trail '72* was reprinted six times. Hunter also continued to write productively for a variety of magazines for the rest of his life. His main outlet for several years was *Rolling Stone*, for whom he wrote prolifically until 1975, then sporadically as National Affairs Editor until 1984. But it was a slow downhill slide; he never quite reclaimed the brilliance of *Fear and Loathing in Las Vegas*.

A major change in Thompson's character, and in his writing, developed after the phenomenal success of *Fear and Loathing in Las Vegas*. He became even more violent, and now towards his wife, and with disregard for his own actions and little respect for those around him. He was constantly 'wired' and struggled to write coherently and to meet deadlines. Fellow writer and friend of many years, David Felton, said there were two main causes. His new found celebrity had changed his lifestyle. He now began to use cocaine. Felton says the first time he started to use it was around 1973. Robert Altman, the film director, who knew Thompson well, said Hunter despised cocaine in his San Francisco days in the late sixties and never took it until the beginning of the seventies. It did increasingly gain a hold over Hunter, and in his later years, he used it copiously and often continuously throughout a day. There are many authentic reports of his excessive use of cocaine. One of the most frequent statements from journalists and media presenters is that in later years Hunter would not give an interview unless supplied with large quantities of 'Charlie'. He would go to a cloakroom and test the cocaine, and only if it was of the highest quality would he then grant an interview.

In 1972 *Rolling Stone* commissioned Hunter to write a series of articles on the election campaigns, covering Richard Nixon, standing for a second term, and the Democratic nomination contest, which was wide open. Nixon, as incumbent President, did little campaigning and Hunter did not interview him. As an early supporter of Senator George McGovern, Thompson spent nearly the whole year of 1972 travelling with the McGovern camp as they strove to obtain the Democratic nomination for their man. It is fair to say that Thompson's coverage, in which he continuously praised McGovern and ridiculed his main opponents, Ed Muskie and Hubert Humphrey, aided by the rapidly increasing circulation of *Rolling Stone*, did contribute to McGovern winning the nomination. Hunter and George McGovern warmed to each other. When Thompson's articles were published as a 500-page book, *Fear and Loathing on the Campaign Trail '72*, in 1973 McGovern said, 'He was very perceptive. He was pretty good at capturing the spirit of the times. There is no doubt that what he wrote in 1972 was the most valuable book on the campaign.' Conversely, Thompson developed a hatred of the incumbent President, Richard Nixon. Of him, Hunter was to say, 'Nixon will be remembered as a classic case of a smart man shitting in his own nest. But he also shit in our nests. He was a man who could shake your hand and stab you in the back at the same time. His casket should have been launched into one of those open-sewage canals that empty into the ocean south of Los Angeles.'

The book was too long, too detailed about the behind the action in-fighting of American primary elections. Yet the descriptions of Hunter's drug-fuelled antics (his drug of choice at that time being speed) remained hilarious. Some of the duller moments of the book were relieved by Ralph Steadman's brilliantly humorous cartoons – maybe they were drug-induced too. Opinions about the book were mixed. The *New York Times* review said, 'Obscene ... repellent ... urgent, candid, a fascinating, compelling book ... the best campaign book ever published.' But Sunny Kumar (*Daily Herald*) called it 'Lengthy trivia about the American primary elections. Boring and only of interest to addicts of the American political scene. Following *Fear and Loathing in Las Vegas* Thompson's drug anecdotes become almost as predictable as his use of the words "fear and loathing". They wear very thin. Partially rescued by Ralph Steadman's droll cartoons.' Frank Mankiewicz, political director of McGovern's campaign, said it was the most accurate and least factual book about the 1972 campaign that he had read. The book did well commercially and is still in print today. Hunter had established his credentials as a political journalist and had exposed the political journalism of the era as feeble. However, *Fear and Loathing on the Campaign Trail '72* marks the decline in his writing powers from the peak of *Fear and Loathing in Las Vegas*.

Exactly as with the aftermath of the Las Vegas book, his behaviour begins to deteriorate further. His use of cocaine and amphetamines (speed) increases. He becomes more violent, physically and verbally, and particularly towards his wife, Sandra. He starts having affairs

238

with other women; his close friend of that era, Gene McGarr (a TV commercial producer) says that his attitude was that he could get laid as often as he wanted, but his wife was not to be laid by anyone but him.

Hunter's output of writing now slows down, but his outrageous conduct does not. Through 1973 to 1975 he continues to provide articles for *Rolling Stone*, principal among them reports on the Super Bowl tournament of 1973 and 1974 and the Watergate affair. In 1974 *Playboy* magazine commissions him to go to Cozumel, Mexico, to report on an international fishing tournament. Whilst there he runs up such an enormous bill for booze and 'ancillary products' that the hosts, Striker Yachts, bar him. As usual, Hunter found himself a drug-taking friend to accompany him. This time it was Michael Solheim, who later stated that they were on cocaine and acid most of the time. Thompson writes little about the fishing tournament, but does tell his readers that he went fishing one night, stoned on acid, and caught a shark. He gathers together a quantity of his late sixties (pre-Gonzo) and early seventies work and submits it to *Playboy*, who publish it as 'The Great Shark Hunt' in December 1974. Expanded, it is published in book form by Summit Books in 1979 under the title *Gonzo Papers Volume 1: The Great Shark Hunt, Strange Tales From a Strange Time*. It is whilst in Cozumel that Sandra discovers that Hunter has been having a sexual affair for the past two years with a beautiful young Labor Party secretary. The first serious problem in their marriage has arisen and Sandra might well have left Hunter had it not been for their mutual love of their son, Juan.

In the late autumn of 1974, Thompson was engaged for a lecture tour of major American universities. It hardly started before it was over. Arriving at Duke University, drunk on bourbon, he began to throw objects and insults at the audience until security guards removed him. The rest of the tour was cancelled. Hunter's only concern was whether he would be paid. He was not.

Now, having no money and time on his hands, he persuaded *Rolling Stone* to send him to Zaire to cover the Ali–Foreman fight, 'The Rumble in the Jungle'. As ever he was in need of a companion drunk. *Rolling Stone* was coerced to send his illustrator friend Ralph Steadman. Immediately upon arrival Hunter purchased a huge bag of marijuana; he then set up shop in his hotel room and thereafter sold it in screws to all-comers. He never went to the fight and wrote only a minor quantity of rubbish, which *Rolling Stone* never published. Thompson called it 'The biggest fucked up story in the history of journalism.' He did, however, run up a $10,000 (equivalent in 2007 to say $125,000) bill before hastily exiting the country. Before leaving, he purchased two elephant tusks, paying for them with invalid travellers cheques. These were initially impounded at the airport, but Hunter successfully stole them back, loaded them into a newly purchased golf bag and smuggled them back to the USA without paying the customs duty.

Shortly after landing at Woody Creek, with gifts of one tusk each for Sandra and Juan, Hunter departs for London. He is to interview David Frost. He demands that his friend and illustrator Ralph Steadman make all his arrangements, including hotel, drugs and whores. He stays at Brown's hotel in Piccadilly. After creating mayhem there, including overturning his bath, thus bringing down the ceiling of the suite below, he receives a telegram from *Rolling Stone* asking if he is interested in covering the 1976 presidential elections. Hunter departs. Certain bills for 'personal services' are left unpaid.

An advance had been agreed for covering the elections, but the editor, Jan Wenner, cancelled the assignment at the last moment. It may have been because Hunter failed to get an interview with Jimmy Carter or because of Hunter's reaction to this, which was to set fire to the hotel room door of Hammy Jordan (Carter's campaign manager) whilst Jordan was still in the room. Instead, Wenner commissioned Hunter to report on what appeared to be the ending of the war in Vietnam. Without funds, and still awaiting the advance payment ($75,000) for *The Great Shark Hunt* book, Hunter had little option but to accept. Armed with a $2,000 advance for arrival expenses, Thompson departed for Saigon. Just as he was about to leave he heard that Wenner had put *Rolling Stone*'s book division into liquidation. Thompson had lost his $75,000 advance. He immediately wrote a vitriolic letter to Wenner.

Arriving in Saigon, Hunter quickly spent his expense advance on drugs and telegraphed *Rolling Stone* for a further advance. By now Wenner had received Thompson's highly insulting letter about the closure of Straight Arrow Books. Wenner and Hunter had been at loggerheads for some time and for Wenner this seems to have been the final straw. Certainly he flew into a rage and pulled the plug on the Vietnam project. Now Hunter was stranded without financial support, health insurance, a hotel or transportation at a time when the troops were withdrawing and the country was in chaos. Hunter survived and did complete his report on the fall of Saigon, but it would not be published in *Rolling Stone* until ten years later.

From Thompson's viewpoint these three incidents severely strained his relationship with *Rolling Stone* and he would contribute very little to the publication in his remaining years.

Indeed Thompson would do very little writing for the next five years. He relies now upon his reputation and this is so powerful that he has entry to most social, sporting, political and media arenas. He lives the social life to excess, his drug-taking escalates and his violence towards his wife increases.

About this time, commencing in 1975, Garry Trudeau, an American cartoonist, started producing a comic strip for Universal Press entitled 'Doonesbury'. The main character is modelled on Hunter Thompson, appearing as Uncle Duke (readers will recall Raoul Duke was a pseudonym used by Thompson). This cartoon strip ran very successfully up to and beyond Thompson's death. It was much resented by Hunter, who sent several abusive letters to Trudeau and threatened various retributions, including setting Trudeau on fire.

Late in 1977 Hunter's Las Vegas companion Oscar Acosta, disappears in mysterious circumstances, never revealed; Hunter writes an article about Oscar for *Rolling Stone* under the headline 'Banshee Screams for Buffalo Meat: Fear and Loathing in the Graveyard of the Weird'. This leads to Universal Studios paying $100,000 for the rights to a film, *Where the Buffalo Roam*, about Hunter's lifestyle and his relationship with Oscar. The scriptwriter is John Kaye, the director Art Linson. Bill Murray stars as Hunter and Peter Boyle as Oscar. Hunter spends much time on the film set, bonding and boozing with Bill Murray. John Kaye recalls that Thompson was high on cocaine most of the time and constantly interfered with the script. To Murray's credit he tried hard to understand the character he was playing, even spending some time at Owl Farm with Hunter, probably to the detriment of his own health and sanity. Despite Murray's best efforts, aided by a fine performance by Peter Boyle, the film received a poor response from the critics. *Los Angeles* magazine (Merrill Schindler) called it 'at best Gonzo dreck'; Sunny Kumar (*The Herald*) said,

241

'Unintelligible. Who cares about the antics of a drug-addicted, out of control journalist?' Robert Altman (blockbuster film director) later said it was the worst film Bill Murray ever made. The film bombed at the box office, losing Universal and Art Linson several million dollars.

Publication of *The Great Shark Hunt* is in the autumn of 1979. In essence it is a personal anthology of Hunter's journalistic work from 1956 to the 1970s. David Felton (author and long-term friend) said there was no order to the book and that it was self-indulgent, mainly pre-Gonzo stuff that was flat and uninspired. Unsurprisingly, most critics commented on Thompson rather than the book. The *Chicago Tribune* (Nelson Agren) wrote, 'No other reporter reveals how much we have to fear and loathe, within and without, yet does it so hilariously.' Norman Mailer said Thompson was unarguably an enormously significant sociological wonder. Laurence Devine, for the *Boston Globe*, wrote, 'Thompson the writer and the man is wildly undisciplined, immature, self-indulgent, self-destructive and distractedly discursive. He is also one of the best writers around.' For *Le Figaro Magazine*, Harry Middleton stated, 'Any chronicle of the sixties will have to include some of Thompson's frenzied, atomised history of those years, even though now, a decade later, his hopped-up, rampaging prose is already losing its pizzazz, and races along as directionless as a tailless kite.' On 1979 TV show *Bookaholic*, Ricky Sebak said, 'He knows how to make his observations and opinions as important as the events he's covering.'

The book was not a great success but I report the reviews here in some detail because they give us a sense of what Gonzo journalism was and where Thompson was at by 1980.

It is from this point that we can observe the inexorable decline in Thompson's writing powers, his inability to control drugs, alcohol and his character. His treatment of women becomes a particular matter of concern.

His wife Sandra is in fear of his violent behaviour. She has taken several beatings from Hunter and in 1980 she takes one too many. She obtains a divorce. Hunter is perplexed and angry. The fact that he beats his wife, uses whores, is drunk most of the time and drives his wife into alcoholism; why should these things cause Sandra to want a divorce? Hunter's attitude is: that's me, that's who I am. As author Nick von Hoffman said, 'For Hunter to wreck that marriage took a lot of work.' There is no doubt that Hunter was devastated by Sandra's rejection and that it accelerated his downward path. He now becomes paranoid and believes he is being followed and/or bugged by the police. He obtains a police scanner and spends much time listening in to police conversations.

In December 1980, *Running* magazine commissions him to cover the Honolulu marathon from Hawaii. He demands that Ralph Steadman comes with him as illustrator and also takes with him his regular girlfriend, Laila. Once again, little was written about the event and much about Hunter. However, *Running* magazine did publish the piece in April 1981 under the title 'Charge of the Weird Brigade'. An enormous bill had of course been run up.

Hunter decided to stay on in Hawaii to try to write a novel. Laila stayed with him. Steadman was called back from London to collaborate with him on the book, which was to become *The Curse of Lono*. The book is a mixture of reporting on events in Hawaii, mythologies of the island, previously published work, factual and fictional tales of Hunter's long, eventful journey there and his usual antics. Its manic, incongruous images led some critics to hail it as a return to his 'Las Vegas' style of writing. The *Louisville Times* (Archie Scott) wrote, 'Thompson, with characteristic paranoia, finds paradise rife with racial tensions and violence that reduces the melting pot to a myth.' *The Independent* (UK) said, 'The book races along like the runners the author was supposed to be covering – but instead we find him drinking margaritas, ingesting hillocks of cocaine and mescaline, lighting fire crackers and nearly drowning: ... and it's the druggy sixties anarchy that gives his writing a manic glee.' Rod Felder (editor at *Playboy*) was surprised by the degeneration in Hunter's work and said, 'The best story had already been published, the rest ... was mostly a series of false starts and half-baked ideas.'

In fact, Thompson had found it a difficult struggle to write new material for a book. There were the usual diversions of drink and drugs. In his hallucinatory phases he imagined himself as the local god Lono, famed for bringing curses upon those who displeased him. The only curse Hunter actually suffered was writer's block. A new diversion, learning to skipper a fishing ship, did not help. He also diverted a lot of time and energy copulating alfresco with Hawaiian girls who were actually sent to him by the locals. Thompson did not finish the book until the autumn of 1983. It was published by Bantam, with excerpts published by *Playboy*.

The book just about washed its face and even this was mainly due to some brilliant illustrations by Steadman. The book disappeared from sight for more than 20 years, until publishers Taschen printed a limited edition with additional illustrations by Steadman.

Hunter continues to try to create new work, particularly a novel. The more this eludes him, the more frustrated he becomes.

Playboy offers him a project to write a magazine story about feminist pornography. Jaded and plagued by writer's block, Thompson accepts and immediately departs Hawaii for San Francisco. Laila was left behind. In San Francisco, he establishes himself at the O'Farrell Theatre, a nightclub featuring nude showgirls and lesbian sex acts. He now negotiates a deal with a publisher to expand his articles for *Playboy* into a book with the title *The Night Manager*. Hunter had already found a new live-in girlfriend, Maria Kahn, a young, very pretty girl with a kind temperament, who adored him and followed him around, writing down everything he said in her notebooks. Hunter loved that kind of flattery. But it did not stop him falling in love with the O'Farrell Theatre's queen of porn, the gorgeous blonde, Debbi Sundahl. Sundahl encouraged some attention from him, since she had just commenced producing a women's erotica magazine, *On Our Backs*, and she obviously felt he might be an entrée into the publishing world. However, Sundahl did not reciprocate Hunter's love. This drove Hunter further into depression and, according to his contemporaries, he was taking cocaine and acid continuously during his waking hours. *The Night Manager* was never finished and thus never published. This leaves Thompson without money again.

It may well be that Hunter was saved further deterioration by his old friend Warren Hinkle. In the summer of 1985, Hinkle becomes editor of the *San Francisco Examiner*. He offers Thompson a weekly column as media critic. Thompson asks for $5,000 a column; he is offered $1,200 on a take it or leave it basis; wisely he accepts. The column continues until 1990. Little of significance is written. 'The American Dream' (May 1987), in which he denounces Senator Gary Hart as a sex fiend, and 'Remembering Oscar' (December 1987), reminiscences of his old fellow addict Oscar Acosta, perhaps being exceptions. Most of the reports are faxed through at the very last moment from his home in Aspen.

This enables Hunter to spend long spells holed up in his fortified compound at Woody Creek, surrounded by his personal arsenal of weapons, ammunition and dynamite.

244

There were occasional sorties out into the normal world but, of course, Hunter's antics were anything but normal. Since Hunter constantly drank and took drugs, it follows that he habitually drove whilst under the influence. Many times he was stopped but released by local police in Aspen and Buena Vista, but in the summer of 1985, and again in 1998, he is arrested in San Francisco, heavily fined and ordered to pay damages.

In February 1990 his aggressive antics with women backfired on him. Gail Palmer-Slater, a gorgeous, seductive brunette, a former *Playboy* 'Girl of the Month' and producer of pornographic films, asked for a meeting with Hunter. Her purpose seems to have been straightforward. With her husband, she had bought land in Aspen and intended to build; she wanted some advice on local conditions. She was now a fledgling writer and wanted to talk to Hunter about his books and have his advice on publishing. Hunter had seen her film, *The Erotic Adventures of Candy*, and enthusiastically invited her to visit him at Owl Farm. When Gail arrived, she found that Hunter's current girlfriend, Terri Chafee (Maria Kahn had been despatched some time earlier) was away at college. Her sister Cathy was there 'looking after' Hunter in Terri's place. Gail was comfortable with this and at first the visit went very well. Gail had drinks, talked about Hunter's books and, in Gail's words, 'I was having a really great time.' Hunter gave her a tour of the house, ending up in the Jacuzzi room. Gail's version of the events that followed was that Hunter asked her to get into the hot tub with him, but she refused. Hunter then asked Cathy to persuade her; Gail again refused and when Cathy reported this back to Hunter he flew into a wild rage and attacked Cathy; Gail tried to intervene and Hunter assaulted her, in particular grabbing her tits. She then left the house and returned to her husband. Hunter's version is that Gail got drunk and came on to him, demanding sex; he found her unattractive and wanted to get rid of her and may have pushed her as a consequence of this. Gail did not wish to pursue the matter, but her husband insisted the local police be informed. The police did wish to pursue the matter.

There is little doubt that the police saw it as a prime opportunity to search Owl Farm. Search it they did, spending about 12 hours ransacking Hunter's house. Thompson was duly charged with possession of illegal drugs, illegal possession of a machine-gun, a 12-gauge shotgun, dynamite and other explosive materials. He was also charged with sexual assault and possession of child pornography. This all amounted to five felonies and three misdemeanours, which, if proven, would carry a maximum prison sentence of 50 years. In fact the police found relatively small amounts of drugs: marijuana and cocaine, about 40 LSD tablets, and some amphetamines. Gail Palmer-Slater was later to state that Hunter had been warned that he was about to be raided. She has never named the person who warned Hunter; there has been speculation that it was Gail herself.

At the pre-trial, in Aspen District Court, Mrs Palmer-Slater was an unco-operative prosecution witness and said clearly that she did not wish to press any charges. Hunter's lawyer said the drugs were not his and that the machine-gun was an antique souvenir. The matter was sent down for trial on 30 May 1990, but on the day, the prosecution dropped all charges, stating that they could not be sustained beyond some doubt. Hunter drove off from court at tremendous speed, shooting off a blank-firing pistol indiscriminately and screaming, 'We beat them like stupid rats. We beat them like dogs' (*Sunday Times*, June 1990).

In 1991 the stunningly beautiful writer E. Jean Carroll was invited to Owl Farm, ostensibly to discuss writing a biography of Hunter. The true reason was probably that Hunter lusted after her. Carroll remained for several weeks, which is greatly to her credit, in view of the debauchery, drug-taking and drinking to which she was made party. Eventually Hunter threw her out at 3.30 a.m. on the day they were supposed to get married. Interestingly enough, despite some depraved experiences at Hunter's hands, Carroll describes him as a splendid, generous man and the most important living author in America. The result was Carroll's hilarious and revealing biography, *Hunter: The Strange and Savage Life of Hunter S. Thompson*.

In 1992 the *Observer* gave Hunter a commission to write, in his Gonzo style, about the royal family. Suggested events were the Highland Games, or the Queen's family holiday at Balmoral. Expenses for a five-day stay in the UK would be paid. Hunter arrived at Gatwick in style, with ten cases, most of which were trollied through customs by his latest girlfriend, Nicole Bradley, a petite 25-year-old blonde. The luggage contained guns and drugs, without which Hunter would not travel. Had he known the ease with which they would pass through customs, he would have brought much more. Hunter had expressed a wish to stay at Brown's Hotel,

246

but they recalled him well and would not have him. A luxurious suite was booked for him at The Metropole, which is a five-star hotel ideally located at Marble Arch. It was not to Hunter's liking. He described the suite as a dog pound, locked himself in the room for two days and then departed for the USA without informing his hosts. The suite was described by the hotel management as being in comprehensive disarray. Nothing had been written on the project beyond a few notes, which the *Observer* somehow embellished into an article.

Now begins Hunter's long, slow descent towards death. Cocaine and acid have failed to make much impact upon him, but alcohol is beginning to take a toll on his well-being. He still has strong sexual desires and with his legendary charisma and fame, he is still able to attract beautiful young women. However, he now finds great difficulty in obtaining an erection. The pneumatic model and soft porn actress Anna Nicole Smith recalled him as charming, sensitive, a powerful communicator with an aura about him. She fell for Hunter instantly. However, when they went to bed together, she experienced what she described as disappointment and humiliation. Similar comments were attributed to an unnamed blonde movie star, possibly Goldie Hawn, by E. Jean Carroll in her book *Hunter*. In simple terms, Hunter could not get it up. I suspect his impotence was due mainly to alcoholism. Hunter had long been noted for his short temper, fiery outbursts and foul language; these now became chronic. Ronnie Rosenbaum, writing in the *New York Times*, said of him that he was stewing in his own bitterness in Woody Creek.

Hunter now found himself unable to create any new writing in book form, and many of his former fans complained that he was just rehashing old material. *Songs of the Doomed: More Notes on the Death of the American Dream* was published in late 1990, the third in an anthology of his previous newspaper and magazine articles with a smattering of new work (the previous two were *The Great Shark Hunt* and *Generation of Swine*). The fourth and final part of these Gonzo papers was *Better Than Sex: Confessions of a Political Junkie*, published in 1994. This included his account of Clinton's 1992 election campaign (viewed on television from his armchair at Owl Farm) and his visceral but vicious obituary of Richard Nixon: 'He has poisoned our water forever. By disgracing and degrading the Presidency of the United States, by fleeing the

White House like a diseased cur, Richard Nixon broke the heart of the American Dream.'

Hunter had long been obsessed by the 'American Dream', which, in his view, was to find truth of thought, word and action in the American people and their politicians. In his early years, Thompson had searched for it long and hard but, by the end of the mid-1990s, he had lost all hope of finding it and this was a major factor in the deep disillusionment that he was to suffer during the next ten years as his life drew to a close.

Hunter did continue to write as a journalist, but output was spasmodic and little was noteworthy. His work as media critic for the *San Francisco Examiner* had ended. He was now writing occasional magazine articles, mainly for *Esquire*. Harry Hayes and Terry McDonnell at *Esquire* gave him an opportunity to write a regular page for the magazine, but he began by submitting 12,000 plus words of rambling rubbish and they quickly lost patience with him. He still continued to write from time to time for *Rolling Stone*, but little was notable. An exception was 'Fear and Loathing in Elko', a fictional rallying cry against Judge Clarence Thomas. Since Thomas was accused of sexual harassment, this was somewhat tongue-in-cheek by Hunter, who had certainly done his share of committing the same offence. This seems strange, since Hunter was considered by critics to be a writer who reported as he saw it with no punches pulled. What seems even stranger is that both fans and critics not only received it well, but considered it a return to Hunter's earlier rampaging style.

Thompson had been contemplating suicide for some long time. In 1978, with Ralph Steadman's help, he drew up plans for his own funeral, including an impressive monument. These plans were shown on a BBC programme at the time, *Fear and Loathing in Gonzovision*. There are several people to whom he had confided in the eighties and nineties that he was happy in the knowledge that he could commit suicide at any moment, but if there ever came a time when he did not feel certain of that, then this would be when he would commit the act. The earliest time to which I can trace that remark is 1980, when he stated it to Steadman. After Hunter's death, Steadman said that his suicide was inevitable. By the mid-1990s, Thompson seemed ready to take his own life. This would appear to be confirmed by his suicide note, which we shall consider later. That he did not do so was due, I believe, to fate twice offering him a new lease of life.

His son Juan had married in August 1994 and by 1995 Hunter was in anticipation of having a grandchild. It meant a great deal to Hunter to know that his lineage would continue, and he determined to see it established through his grandson William's early years.

In 1997 Universal Studios decided to turn *Fear and Loathing in Las Vegas* into a film. It was 25 years since the book's publication and Hunter had long since sold the film rights. It came as a surprise to Hunter and it certainly revitalised him. After much infighting at Universal (which delighted Hunter), Terry Gilliam was hired to direct, Johnny Depp starred as Hunter and Benicio Del Toro as Oscar ('Dr Gonzo'). Depp moved into Owl Farm for several weeks to study Hunter and the pair went hunting and drinking together and got on terribly well. Thompson asked for, and was given, a cameo role in the film as one of the customers at the Matrix Club. Involvement in the film kept Hunter busy until its release in late 1998. Hunter declared it 'a masterpiece; an eerie trumpet call over a lost battlefield'. Hunter's use of the words 'a lost battlefield' seem to indicate his resignation about his failure to find the American Dream. Critics did not receive it well. Nigel Kneale (author of *The Quatermass Experiment* and screenwriter) said the film script failed to translate the two great characters from the novel. The film did not do well at the box office. Yet, like the book, it slowly gained an adoring cult following, and it can still be obtained today on DVD. It also revived interest in the novel, which went into several reprints. Also awakened was renewed interest in Thompson's earlier works. His long-lost novel, *The Rum Diary*, was rushed into publication, yet although the book sold well, it was not critically acclaimed, it being generally thought the product of an immature Thompson. Hunter had always wanted the book to be made into a film, but this was not to happen in his lifetime.

Thompson was now approaching the end of his writing career. *Kingdom of Fear* was published in 2003. A collection of his early work, newspaper cuttings and a small amount of new work, critics saw it as a fierce but funny attack on the passing of the American twentieth century. His last continuous work, through 2004, was a sports column on the Internet for ESPN; in 2005 a selection of these articles was published in book form, entitled *Hey Rube: Blood Sport, the Bush Doctrine and the Downward Spiral of Dumbness*. He remained on the *Rolling Stone* masthead with the title Chief of National Affairs. Occasionally he would contribute articles: his last was to be 'Fear and Loathing, Campaign 2004', his views on the Bush/Kerry presidential campaign. He hated George W. Bush almost as much as he had reviled Nixon. In 2000 he had written that Bush's victory over Al Gore in the Florida fiasco was 'the most brutal seizure of power since Hitler burned the German Reichstag in 1933 and declared himself the new Boss of Germany'. In 2004 he used his Internet column for another blast against the Bush administration: 'Who does vote for these dishonest shitheads? They are the racists and hatemongers among us; they are the Ku Klux Klan. I piss down the throats of these Nazis.' It was to be his swansong statement against an Establishment that he had rebelled in defiance of all his life. He was now coming to the end of his journey along life's path.

Thompson was now beset by a number of physical ailments, which were causing him pain and restricting his movements. He had clinical arthritis affecting his arms and hands. A hip replacement plus spinal stenosis combined to cause pain and numbness to his legs. This was exacerbated by his breaking his left leg in 2003 and again in 2004. He now needed frequent physiotherapy. Whiskey and painkillers eased the pain, but the vast quantities he was now consuming were affecting his liver; causing oedema (fluid in the abdomen), loss of appetite, lethargy and confusion. An enlarged prostate was a constant and incontinent nuisance. Chain-smoking had damaged his lungs, causing breathlessness.

A new lease of life, albeit short, came to him on 24 April 2003. He had finally persuaded his long-time (and long-suffering) assistant, Anita Bejmuk, to marry him. Young, slim, fit, sweet-natured and laid-back in a style sometimes reminiscent of the sixties Californian hippies, she was very much the close friend that Hunter needed around him at that time.

He did have many famous friends, who came to visit him at Woody Creek in those, his last days. Johnny Depp, Keith Richards, George McGovern, Bill Murray, Sean Penn, Jimmy Carter are but a few among them. However, his famous billionaire Aspen neighbours – Michael Douglas and Catherine Zeta Jones, Rupert Murdoch, Jack Nicholson, Donald Trump, Barbra Streisand – carefully avoided him on their occasional visits.

Within himself, Hunter felt a terrible loneliness. He spent many hours in front of the television, obsessively watching American football. He could no longer write, he was impotent, cocaine and acid no longer made the adrenalin flow. The selection of Bush for a second term had broken his spirit; he now felt that his 'American Dream' was vanquished for ever. He was paranoid that his friends and acquaintances were using him to get money. Hallucinations were taking over; he was seeing golf balls inside his head and little green men in yellow raincoats outside his fortified compound. It was time to depart. He knew how he would do it. He would follow in the footsteps of his hero, Hemingway. But he could only do it when his mood was right and he would know when the right moment was at hand. Ideally he would like to have his family around him in his last moments. On 16 February 2005 he delivered the following suicide note to his wife, Anita:

No more games. No more bombs. No more walking. No more fun. No more swimming. 67. That is 17 years past 50. 17 more than I needed or wanted. Boring. I am always bitchy. No fun – for anybody. 67. You are getting greedy. Act your old age. Relax – this won't hurt.

At 5.40 p.m. on 20 February 2005 he is alone in his kitchen/ workplace, seated at the bar, typewriter before him with a sheet of paper in place bearing the single word 'counsellor'. In the lounge are his son Juan, with wife Jennifer, and Hunter's grandson, Will. His family are around him. Hunter lifts the phone and rings his wife Anita, who is at the gym. His last words are for her alone. As she listens, he places the barrel of a .44 Magnum gun against the side of his head and fires. The bullet passes through his brain, causing instant death; it passes on, terminating by thudding into the cooker ventilation hood. In the next room his family were unaware, hearing only a noise, which they associated with Hunter knocking or throwing down a book. His body was eventually found by Juan, who had gone to the kitchen for a glass of water.

The funeral was not celebrated until 20 August 2005. This was due to the elaborate arrangements set out in plans drawn up in 1978. Hunter's ashes were fired from a cannon sited on top of a 150-foot tower, designed as a double-thumbed fist. Simultaneously, green, red, white and blue fireworks were exploded. The ceremony was played out to the tune of 'Mr Tambourine Man' by Bob Dylan. Some 300 people attended, mainly celebrities whom it would be superfluous to mention individually. Johnny Depp paid for the ceremony.

During his life, Thompson wrote an estimated 20,000 letters; he always kept copies. Posthumously, many of these have been published in a series of books entitled *The Fear and Loathing Letters*, edited by Thompson's official biographer, Douglas Brinkley. The last of these appeared in 2007.

So Hunter S. Thompson has gone. His first person style was humorous and eccentric. His aim was to personalise and exaggerate events to make them more entertaining. His achievement was to bring a new movement to journalism in the sixties and seventies, which enabled it to break free of the unbiased and detached style of that era. He leaves behind a void, which may never be filled.

Why did he decide, more than 25 years before his death, that he would choose his own time and place and end his own life? Was he strongly influenced by that day in 1964 when he visited the site of the suicide of his hero Hemingway? Being Hunter Thompson, one thing is certain, he would not let anyone else take his life for him and that includes God. But what made him choose the time to commit the final act?

How much weight should we give to the serious disruption of Hunter's youth by the early death of his father and his mother's alcoholism?

For most of his life Hunter had been a charming, entertaining, kind and generous human being; eccentric and aggressive perhaps, but much loved by many. What broke his spirit? Was it really the collapse of his American Dream and his deep hatred of the major politicians of his time, Nixon and George W. Bush? Was it his own physical deterioration? From his mid-teens until his mid-thirties, he had been a very handsome, well-built and strong man. It must have hurt him badly to see himself later on; bald, his face and body ravaged with alcohol, huge spectacles, limping along, a shell of his former self. There had been many women in his life and an abundance of sex; but, now he was impotent, it wasn't much fun any more. Depression played its part, as it does with many writers when they cannot write. Drink and drugs played their part. It is unlikely that drugs had much influence on Hunter's mood. The mind and body often become immune to cocaine and acid if they are used habitually. The vast amount of alcohol that Hunter consumed would certainly have been a cause of most of his physical ailments and it seems likely, from his letters, that he was suffering from occasional bouts of delirium tremens.

What did the 'Fear and Loathing' that Hunter referred to throughout his writing career mean to him? The fear was of what drugs, particularly ether and acid, could do to him. The loathing was for the loss of the American Dream and for the politicians who destroyed it.

I believe the reader will not find it difficult to understand why this exceptional writer, who loved guns, came to choose one to destroy himself when he came to hate life.

Anne Sexton

The Promiscuous Poet

Anne Sexton was sexually abused as a child, poorly educated and in regular psychiatric therapy from 15 years old. By the age of 28 she had made two suicide attempts, was psychotic, had a permanent psychiatrist and had not written any poetry. Yet within the remaining 20 years of her life she was to become one of the most revered and famous American female poets of all time. Pulitzer Prize-winner, wife, mother, bisexual lover of many, hers is a remarkable story of love, lust, mental disorder, alcoholism and artistic creativity.

Anne Sexton did not write any poetry until she was 28. Should we be interested in her years before then? Almost certainly yes.

Photo: Time and Life Pictures/Getty Images

255

My research into internationally acclaimed writers who have committed suicide has convinced me that many of the demons that led to their ends originated in their early years. So let us look briefly at Anne's beginnings.

Anne Gray Harvey was born in Newton, Massachusetts on 9 November 1928. She was the third of three daughters: her sisters were Jane (born 1923) and Blanche (1925). Until the age of five Anne spent most of her time locked in her room.

Her father, Ralph, was a tall man, always immaculately groomed, who, at the time of Anne's birth, had just started his own company, selling processed wool. By the beginning of Anne's teenage years, the business had become successful and, with more leisure time available, Ralph Harvey began to drink heavily and soon became an alcoholic. Anne's relationship with him was in the main difficult. Anne described during psychotherapy, and in several of her poems ('Briar Rose' from the collection *Transformations* is a good example), how in her pre-teens her father would enter her bed, kiss her and fondle her private parts. Anne also suffered verbal and physical aggression during her father's drunkenness.

Anne's mother, Mary Gray Staples, was born at Lewiston, Maine, into an influential family. Her father was publisher of the *Lewiston Evening Journal* and her uncle had been a US congressman. An only child, born late in the marriage, she was given excessive attention and treated as though she were a princess. It probably was this background that caused her to be cold and undemonstrative towards Anne. Later Anne competed with mother for attention and this led Mary Gray to belittle her daughter's early achievements. Subsequently Mary Gray became, secretly, a heavy drinker.

In the early years of their marriage, Ralph and Mary Gray were a very close couple. This resulted in Anne and her sisters being often excluded so that the Harveys could socialise or enjoy their own company privately.

The other important emotional influence on Anne's early life was her great aunt, Anna Ladd Dingley, always referred to as 'Nana'. A spinster, Nana had lived in Europe for three years and, returning home to Maine, she had become an editor and shareholder in the *Lewiston Evening Journal*. Left homeless by the death of her brother-in-law, she was given rooms in the Harvey home at Weston. Anne was Nana's favourite and Nana treated her like a granddaughter. Nana was very tactile with Anne, giving her back

256

rubs and cuddling her intimately in bed. Indeed the impression Anne gave to some of her closest friends was that the cuddling amounted to sexual abuse. It would almost certainly be seen to be so today.

There is no doubt that throughout her life, whenever Anne turned to anyone for comfort, reassurance and physical cuddling, she thought of that person as being Nana. Anne felt comfortable and safe with Nana and when Nana had a nervous breakdown through 1943 and 1944, Anne was devastated.

Anne attended Brown's School in Wellesley and Junior High School in Weston. She was not a good pupil. Excitable, inattentive and sometimes absent, by age 12 she had not passed beyond fifth grade. However, over the next three years she matured at a pace almost certainly too fast for her. She grew tall (she was 5' 8" at 16) and slim, with long, dark hair and, although her complexion was marred with acne, she was considered very attractive. She began to smoke, a habit that would develop into chain-smoking for the rest of her life. At 13 she had her first romance; significantly they were to remain in each other's memories for the rest of their lives. He was Michael Bearpark, an English boy sent to relatives in Weston to shelter from the Second World War. With Michael, Anne was to have her first kiss. More than 20 years later, she wrote to him in England, telling him that it was an experience in her life that sent her 'along quite a long trail'. It certainly did; Anne was to have many affairs, many lovers.

Michael Bearpark soon had a rival and a serious one, who was to see him displaced. Jack McCarthy was young, always well dressed, a student from Boston. From the age of 14 until 18, Jack was Anne's steady boyfriend. They believed they were in love and they became engaged to marry. This did not stop Anne flirting outrageously with many other boys. Jack and Anne shared a surprisingly sophisticated lifestyle for young teenagers. They went to cocktail bars and cosmopolitan dance halls and were regularly at the Boston Playhouse. They visited New York with Anne's parents, staying at the Waldorf and visiting 21 Club, Jack Dempsey's restaurant and The El Morocco nightclub.

Anne's parents now noted that she was boy crazy and, in 1945, to counter this, they sent her to a girls' boarding school, Rogers Hall, in Lowell, Massachusetts. The plan did not work. Anne simply began dating several different boys from the nearby Phillips Academy and exchanging secret love letters with some of them. Jack McCarthy and Anne also exchanged letters frequently, but for Jack, absence did not make the heart grow fonder and, in 1946, he broke off the engagement and they quickly lost contact. Anne was by now used to the adoration of young men and this rejection hit her hard.

Anne was now more interested in finding a young man suitable for marriage than in studying. As a consequence, she obtained only modest grades at Rogers Hall. From there she was sent to Garland Junior College in Boston, regarded at that time as a 'finishing' school. Anne was still focused on getting married, although, in fairness to her, readers should be aware that in the late 1940s through the early 1950s, marriage was the target of most young American girls. Anne did get engaged to Bruce Howard, a young student from Boston whom she had known for about four months and whose father was a wealthy industrialist. A grand wedding was planned but Anne was still writing flirtatious letters to other boys, some of whom she had not met. One such was Alfred 'Kayo' Sexton, a 20-year-old medical student at Colgate University, Hamilton, New York State. Kayo invited Anne to a dance at Longwood Cricket Club, Chesnut Hill, in the first week of July. It seems to have been love at first sight and, before the month was out, they became passionate lovers. Anne was later to write that, having lost her virginity to Kayo, she began to have intercourse with Bruce, since Anne felt it was his due as her fiancé. Early in August of 1948, Anne found that her period was much overdue. She consulted with her mother, who advised her to elope. Anne did elope with Kayo, in classic style. Kayo fixed the ladder and Anne climbed out of the second-storey window of her parents' house at 3 a.m.

They could not marry in Massachusetts, where the age of consent was 21. Anne took one of the family cars and they drove to North Carolina, where the age for marriage was 18. In fact, Anne's period started before they crossed the State line; but there is no doubt that they were in love and the marriage proceeded as planned. They were married at Sunbury, North Carolina, on 16 August 1948. The honeymoon was at a five-star hotel on Virginia Beach.

Afterwards, Kayo returned to Colgate and the couple lived in rented accommodation on a farm near the university. Married life was rather a shock for Anne, who had never before cooked or washed up or laundered. By the end of the year, Kayo, fed up with financial dependence on their parents, left university and took

258

a job selling wool. The couple spent most of 1949 living with their parents, but at the end of that year they moved into a flat of their own in Cochituate, Middlesex County, Massachusetts. Anne took a job selling lingerie and enrolled in a modelling class; later she modelled for the Hart Agency in Boston. There were some indications that Anne would have been content to make modelling her career. However, upon her own admission, the acne scars from her teenage years kept her out of the front rank of models; and already Anne's mindset was that she would only do something if she thought she could be the best.

The Sextons now began to socialise freely. Their best friends were the Bensons. Johnny was a young surgeon, just completing his qualifications at Harvard, and his wife had been a university peer of Kayo's. Johnny and Anne soon began a passionate relationship and they went to Anne's mother to tell her they were thinking of living together.

Mary Gray demanded that Anne stop seeing Johnny immediately. Anne's reaction was to take an overdose of phenobarbitone. Fortunately Mary Gray and Johnny heard Anne fall to the floor in her bedroom and they were able to arouse her in time and force her to sick up most of the tablets.

It was then that Mary Gray insisted that Anne start psychotherapy. She was sent to Dr Martha Brunner-Orne, who had previously treated Ralph Harvey and his sister, Frances, for alcoholism. It took several weeks of treatment until Anne changed her mind about leaving Kayo, but Johnny Benson never left her heart, despite many love affairs that were to follow.

After her decision to stay with Kayo, it seems Anne felt that what was missing was children. However, this desire was to be temporarily thwarted. The USA declared war on North Korea in 1950; Kayo signed on for the naval reserve in November and by May of 1951 he was on active service in the Far East.

Denied the attentions of Kayo and of her mother, Anne now became bored and restless. She began dating and having affairs with other men. Mary Gray picked up on this and, in the autumn of 1952, she persuaded Anne to go to San Francisco to join Kayo, whose ship was in dock for overhaul. Anne and Kayo immediately resumed their strong, physical relationship. By the end of the year Anne was pregnant.

Linda Sexton was born on 21 July 1953 and Joyce Sexton on 4

August 1955. Anne's family was now complete; but Anne was very far from being content.

Linda's babyhood had brought new physical and psychological strains upon Anne. Before she was able to cope with these demands, Anne was hit by the terrible blow of the death of her beloved 'Nana' in August 1954. Anne was devastated emotionally and her psyche never recovered during her lifetime. Nana's death was quickly followed by pregnancy and, following the birth of Joyce, Anne suffered severe post natal depression. At that time she had little support from Kayo, who had accepted a job as a travelling salesman for his father-in-law's company, and was rarely at home.

By November 1955 Anne was having serious mental health problems. There was a degree of manic depression, her moods swinging between low spirits and excitability. The mood swings sometimes showed split personalities indicative of Multiple Personality Disorder. She was experiencing dream-like trances. Uncontrollable rages would overcome her and she would physically attack Linda. She developed an unwholesome phobia of being left alone with the children. Severe stomach pains proved to be psychological rather than physical. All of this culminated in another suicide attempt in July 1956. Anne took up her bottle of sleeping pills and a picture of Nana and sat quietly on her porch preparing herself to join Nana. Kayo found her just in time, before she had taken the pills, but the situation was considered serious enough to send her back to Dr Brunner-Orne, her psychiatrist. The children were sent away, Linda to her Aunt Blanche and Joy to her grandmother, Billie.

Dr Brunner-Orne committed her to Westwood Lodge institution ('the mental hospital', Anne called it), where she was to stay for three weeks. Dr Brunner-Orne's decision was to prove probably the most important ever made in Anne's life.

Throughout the rest of her life, Anne was to return time and again to Westwood Lodge. She came to regard it as a safe haven away from stress and responsibility; indeed she wrote some of her best poetry whilst hospitalised there. More significantly, during the 1956 visit, her diagnostic tests were carried out by Dr Martin Orne, Dr Brunner-Orne's son. Martin Orne was to become a major influence in Anne Sexton's life. Released in the first week of August, Anne found Dr Brunner-Orne was on vacation and she turned to Dr Martin Orne for psychiatric treatment. He would remain her psychiatrist for the next eight years. During that time Anne, prompted by Martin Orne, would begin writing the poetry that would catapult her to world fame. They would have an intense relationship, which some have suspected was partly sexual. Ultimately Dr Orne would astound his fellow psychiatrists by releasing tape recordings of their treatment sessions. Many medical and psychiatric doctors denounced him for unprofessional conduct likely to adversely affect trust in the profession.

Dr Martin Orne quickly established the root of Anne's mental problems. He correctly determined that Anne's depression was caused by an overwhelming lack of self-esteem. He also found that Anne had a poor memory; this had contributed to her poor academic achievement, which in turn led to her believing that she was unable to accomplish anything that was expected of her. The other contributing factor to her lack of confidence was the failure of her parents to give her that special attention that every child needs in their formative years. Dr Orne diagnosed Anne as an hysteric. It appears that in doing so he was deliberately trying to avoid any empathy on the depressive side of Anne's psyche. It would seem, on the evidence, that a diagnosis of manic depression would have been more appropriate. With hindsight we can understand Martin Orne's approach to the problem. He concentrated on channelling Anne's thoughts into considering what things she could do well. Anne's immediate reaction was that her only ability was to please men and help them to feel sexually potent. She believed that her only talent might be to be a good prostitute. This was subsequently proven not true since Anne became a great poet and entertainer.

Martin Orne rightly dismissed this and, returning to the subject, he suggested Anne try writing, particularly about her feelings connected with her breakdown. This sparked a flame somewhere within Anne's subconscious and she began to bring poetry to her psychiatric sessions: she was able to discuss them critically with Martin Orne and he encouraged her strongly to continue. From these sessions Anne was able to look at her self-esteem with a critical sensitivity. This gave her the impetus to move forward. Poetry became part of her therapy and, by the summer of 1957, she had gathered enough strength to enrol in a poetry workshop held in the evenings at the Boston Center for Adult Education, taught by Professor John Holmes. She remained enrolled for two years. During that period she also took a week-long course tutored by William Snodgrass, and enrolled in a Boston University course taught by Robert Lowell. She met many other emerging poets who were to go on to international fame and who were to remain close to her for much of the remainder of her life. Amongst them were Sylvia Plath, who became her short-term companion in mischief and life-long correspondent, and Maxine Kumin, with whom she collaborated on several children's books and who was her closest friend until the very end of Anne's life. Another was George Starbuck, a young poet and editor at Houghton Mifflin, who was revealed in Plath's diaries as one of Anne's lovers. By the end of those two highly formative years she had made unusually rapid progress, mastering formal techniques that were to gain her widespread attention.

She was now Anne Sexton, poet. Her poetry became the most important thing in her life. Her style was 'confessional' and many of her female readers were able to identify with her fears and angst about menstruation and abortion, which they had suffered themselves. She began to be much compared to Sylvia Plath. A major difference between these two poets was already obvious. Sexton was able to struggle with, confront and write about the issues that evaded Plath in therapy.

At the time Sexton attended the short W.D. Snodgrass course in the summer of 1958, only half a dozen of her poems had been published. *The Christian Science Monitor* had published 'The Reading' and 'The Balance Wheel'. The *Antioch Review* had scheduled 'For Johnny Pole on the Forgotten Beach' for publication. *Harper's Magazine* and *The New Yorker* had accepted poems. The *Fiddlehead Review* had published 'Eden Revisited'. The impact of Snodgrass can readily be assessed by the fact that some 40 of Sexton's poems were accepted for publication in the 12 months following the course. It is clear from the comments made later by both parties that Sexton sought to seduce Snodgrass and that he resisted, albeit with difficulty. What is beyond doubt is that this one-week course made a substantial contribution to Anne's stability during this period.

By the middle of 1958, Anne was able to take Joyce back from grandmother Billie. She was able to cope with a visit from her mother, who had been diagnosed with breast cancer and whose demands for constant attention had grown worse than ever. She was also able to cope with the shock of her father's hospitalisation following a stroke. Throughout the autumn months of 1958 her poetry flowed. Several of her poems were published. Perhaps the most important is 'The Farmer's Wife', published by *Harper's* in October. In this poem, Anne's dissatisfaction with her marriage to Kayo becomes apparent. 'The Double Image', one of the most significant poems she was ever to write, was being worked on throughout this time. A lengthy poem of seven stanzas, it is addressed to her daughter, Joyce. The double image is the pair of portraits her mother had commissioned when taking Anne on a recuperation trip after her hospitalisation in the summer of 1955; in essence, it interprets the emotional forces in play between Anne and Mary Gray. The intellectual resemblance between Anne and her mother is analysed. Anne makes it clear that between herself and Joyce, Anne sees herself as the entitled daughter, not a mother. In the following extract from 'The Double Image', Anne returns to the question of why she would rather die than love her daughter.

And you came each weekend. But I lie.
You seldom came. I just pretended
you, small piglet, butterfly
girl with jelly bean cheeks,
disobedient three, my splendid
stranger. And I had to learn
why I would rather
die than love, how your innocence
would hurt and how I gather
guilt like a young intern
his symptoms, his certain evidence.

However, by mid-November, the stress of everything had caught up with Anne; she was hearing witch-like voices in her head and admitted herself to Westwood Lodge for a few days therapy. There, in an atmosphere of calm, she was able to complete 'The Double Image'. The poem was accepted by New York literary journal *The Hudson Review* and published in February 1959. The journal's editor, Frederick Morgan, said the poem was essentially strong and authentic, and he told Anne her work showed power allied to control. Ted Hughes, then in Boston with his wife Sylvia Plath, said, 'Technically excellent. The unexpected rhythms of her verse reveal the authentic poet.'

Anne Sexton's work had now been recognised. Encouraged by her tutor, Robert Lowell, she worked furiously through 1958 to mid-1959 on writing poems and collating them for a first book. One would have thought she had little time for nervous breakdowns and she maintained a façade of stability. Nevertheless, when the breakdown in November 1958 was followed by news that her father had suffered a stroke and that her mother was terminally ill with cancer, Anne, unable to cope, went back to Westwood Lodge for a few days. Once again she found peace there and was able to write a new poem, 'Ringing the Bells'. Almost certainly Anne's ability to recognise the warning signs of her mental instability at that time saved her from being committed to an institution for a much longer period of time.

We should understand that, whilst Robert Lowell's course matured Anne as a poet, it probably had an adverse effect on her mental state. Lowell himself was a manic-depressive. A well-built man, tall, at 6' 3", dark and handsome, Lowell habitually had affairs with his students. Surprisingly, Anne, who was promiscuous, did not have an affair with him; possibly, she preferred those without psychiatric problems. Several poets who attended the course had psychiatric problems. Sylvia Plath went on to commit suicide, so did John Berryman, who, as a guest reader, chose to read from Lowell's Pulitzer Prize-winning book *Lord Weary's Castle*.

1959 opened with surprising events for Anne. First, the death of her mother from breast cancer. Her father, whose relationship with Anne had always been distant, suddenly began to visit her frequently. The cause lay in his loneliness and depression following the death of his wife. Now he began to date a local widow and suddenly announced that he would marry her. This being just a few weeks after Mary Gray's death had caused great consternation within the family. Anne, together with her sisters Jane and Blanche, and others, managed to sabotage the wedding. However, the strain of this, coupled with the stress of trying to keep another love affair secret from Kayo, broke Anne down. It was back to Westwood Lodge for a few days. Released from there on 2 June, she had to face, the next day, the news that her father had died from a stroke. Settlement of his estate brought further shocks. Ralph Harvey had sold the shares in his company to pay for his lavish, drunken lifestyle. Kayo would not inherit the company and it seemed he would remain forever a travelling salesman. Anne was so infuriated that she took her father's picture, smashed it to the floor and ground her heel into it.

Through the remainder of 1959 and 1960 there was enough going on in Anne Sexton's life to prevent her from dwelling upon the state of her mental health.

Physically, she had several causes for concern. In September 1959 she caught pneumonia. During treatment, an ovarian cyst was discovered and in October this was surgically removed. It proved to be non-malignant, but the threat of cancer prompted recurring memories of her mother's death. She was constantly wracked with headaches.

The death of her father-in-law, George Sexton, in March 1960, in an automobile accident, was as sudden and unexpected as had been her father's. Anne had been close to George and he had been paying one half of all her psychiatric bills and had once been the responsible adult who was required to stay with her at the psychiatric hospital. He had also played a large part in looking after Joyce and Linda, which task Anne had delegated to her in-laws in the wake of her poor mental and physical health. Anne was deeply depressed by these three family deaths within the space of one year.

The next trauma for Anne was to discover that she was pregnant. Kayo wanted another child, but Anne was not sure it was his; it may have been from George Starbuck, with whom she had been having a love affair. In May she resolved the problem by having an illegal abortion. This did nothing to resolve her problems with Kayo.

Anne was fortified through this period with long daily telephone calls with Maxine Kumin and daily romantic correspondence with James Wright, an established poet whom she had met at Robert Lowell's class in the summer of 1959. Wright had come from a poor, working-class family but, through the diligence of his studies, had won a Fulbright scholarship to the university of Vienna. Although married, he quickly fell for the beauty of Anne's presence, her physical beauty and the beauty of her poetry. In turn, Anne was captivated by the maturity of Wright's fusion of American and European experience and by his tall, dark and reasonably handsome looks. Their letters soon carried plenty of sexual references and by July of 1960 they were lovers, using the Long Island home of fellow poet Hy Sobiloff to rendezvous.

To combat all of this, Anne fought back by writing a series of poems. The final drafts of the poems for a first book, *To Bedlam and Part Way Back*, were completed and the book put to press. 'Old Dwarf Heart', 'Ghosts', 'With Mercy for the Greedy', 'In the Deep Museum', 'The Abortion', 'For God While Sleeping' and 'The Starry Night' were all completed during this period and appear in her second book, *All My Pretty Ones*. Anne also wrote a play, *Ladybug, Fly Away Home*, at this time. It is an intriguing, short work in which the leading character is a young student whose psychiatrist persuades her to have an abortion. Could it have been that this advice came from Dr Orne? Might he have assessed that Anne's failure to cope with her existing children, together with the state of her mental health, made it unsafe for her to have another child, particularly as she was uncertain of the fatherhood?

To Bedlam and Part Way Back was published by Houghton Mifflin at the end of April 1960. It received extensive attention; unusual for a first book of poems. Allen Grossman, a professor at Brandeis University said, 'The jacket shows a woman in great pain. The poems seem to me incredibly distinguished and compassionate. They reach me, hold me and give me pleasure. Her poetry reflects the recuperation of self in the aftermath of madness and then of medical treatment.' The *New York Times* said, '... the theme has a natural built-in interest: a mental breakdown pictured with a pitiless eye and a clairvoyant sharpness'. In England, the *Observer* (A. Alvarez) called it a major work from a new, female poet destined to become a star on the American scene. Ted Hughes declared, 'The first book of confessional poet Anne Sexton, *To Bedlam and Part Way Back*, is painfully applicable to every reader. Her control of rhythm marks her out as a serious poet of importance.' James Dickey, writing in *Poetry Magazine*, did not agree with Hughes. Dickey felt Sexton was still an apprentice and her work no better than that expected of a final year student.

With hindsight, we can say that sales of *To Bedlam and Part Way Back* prove Dickey wrong. Over the 30-odd years since Anne's death, the collection has achieved worldwide distribution and, as part of various anthologies, has been reprinted many times.

It is for the reader to decide which poems from the collection they feel are the most interesting. My own selection of those of special significance is: 'Music Swims Back to Me', 'Ringing the Bells', 'The Farmer's Wife', 'The Double Image', 'Her Kind'. The following short extracts are offered to give the reader a flavour of Anne's early work.

Music Swims Back to Me

Wait Mister. Which way is home?
They turned the light out
and the dark is moving in the corner.
La la la, Oh music swims back to me
and I can feel the tune they played
the night they left me
in this private institution on a hill.

. . .

They lock me in this chair at eight a.m.
Oh, la la la,
this music swims back to me.
The night I came I danced a circle
and was not afraid.
Mister?

Ringing the Bells

And this is the way they ring the bells
in Bedlam
and this is the bell-lady
who comes each Tuesday morning
to give us a music lesson

. . .

and this is always my bell responding
to my hand that responds to the lady
who points at me, E flat;
and although we are not better for it,
they tell you to go. And you do.

The Farmer's Wife

. . .

they name just
ten years now
that she has been his habit;

267

as again tonight he'll say
honey bunch let's go
and she will not say how there
must be more to living
than this brief bright bridge
of the raucous bed or even
the slow braille touch of him
like a heavy god grown light,
that old pantomime of love
that she wants although
it leaves her still alone...

and then how she watches him,
still strong in the blowzy bag
of his usual sleep while
her young years bungle past
their same marriage bed
and she wishes him cripple, or poet,
or even lonely, or sometimes,
better, my lover, dead.

Her Kind

I have gone out, a possessed witch,
haunting the black air, braver at night;
dreaming evil, I have done my hitch
over the plain houses, light by light
lonely thing, twelve-fingered, out of mind.
A woman like that is not a woman, quite.
I have been her kind.

. . .

I have ridden in your cart, driver,
waved my nude arms at villages going by,
learning the last bright routes, survivor
where your flames still bite my thigh
and my ribs crack where your wheels wind.
A woman like that is not ashamed to die.
I have been her kind.

To Bedlam and Part Way Back deals, in personal terms, with Anne's efforts to retain her sanity at only 30 years of age. As such it struck a chord with many young readers right across the United States, Australia and Great Britain. So began the fame of Anne Sexton with all its adverse trappings and its final, fateful conclusion. She receives numerous requests for public appearances and readings. This widens her circle of contacts and upgrades her social life. The money is also useful!

Spring of 1961 is hectic. She is still attending John Holmes' group classes. Being with a group creates adrenalin and inspires her to keep revising her work. Persistent revision, always seeking perfection, is the greatest strength of Anne's work. Now she is invited on to a poets panel at Boston College: other members are William Snodgrass and John Holmes. Here she again meets up with her ex-lover, Jack McCarthy, who is a tutor in the English department. At Cornell University she gives readings, together with her erstwhile lover George Starbuck and her rumoured lover Maxine Kumin. Sexton is now chain-smoking and, together with Kumin, is drinking heavily. In New York she meets up with James Wright once more and she also meets a new friend with whom she is to have a relationship. He is Tony Hecht, a *Hudson Review* poet, separated from his wife. Tony and Anne are on the same intellectual wavelength. He tells Anne he is in love with her, but when she pushes for sex he refuses. Interestingly enough, the same thing happens that spring with James Wright and George Starbuck, who both refuse to enter into further sexual adventures with her. In fairness to Anne, we should take into account that Kayo was frequently away as a travelling salesman and part of Anne's illness was her uncontrollable need for demonstrations of love for her. She told Dr Orne that she does not want to go to bed with these men, but she does so because she wants to be sure that they love her. She says that when she does have sex, the men are only substitutes for those who are unavailable.

Her relationship with Kayo remains disturbed. Anne continues to take barbiturates and sleeping pills, although Kayo is strongly opposed. Anne is not the housewife type and constantly treats Kayo as though he were her father or Nana. They have quarrels and these lead to serious physical attacks on Anne by Kayo. Anne issues an ultimatum, either Kayo enters therapy or they divorce. Kayo does enter therapy, gains some self-control and the beatings stop. Later Anne told Dr Orne that she then found that she did not want them to stop.

In the autumn of 1961, Harvard University introduce The Radcliffe Institute, a new programme for women whose intellectual careers had been interrupted. Twenty Fellowship grants, each of $2,000, would be given. At least 200 women applied for grants. Anne Sexton was accepted. She spent the $2,000 on a porch extension, which she used as a study, and a swimming pool. At last Anne felt equal to all her university-educated friends and contacts. Certainly being a 'Radcliffe Institute' student increased her standing in the literary world. *Newsweek* and *The New Yorker* began to feature her. Her speaking fees were raised to $250, at a time when the average was below $100. Only a very few poets could now command higher fees than Anne, and those that could had been published for many years and had undertaken publicity tours. Of her many readings in 1961, 'In the Deep Museum' was particularly controversial. This poem discusses the healing power of art, but accepts the inevitability of death. What was particularly interesting was that Anne chose to recite it using a voice intended to be Christ in the tomb.

Through all this action in 1961, Anne is trying hard to work on poems for a second book, *All My Pretty Ones*. She is handicapped by her bad memory and by her habit of falling into trance-like states, which often last several hours. She is helped by constant support from Maxine Kumin. Anne creates a poem for her, 'My Friend, My Friend' and, after much revision, it appears in the book as 'With Mercy for the Greedy'. Maxine responds with 'For Anne at Passover', which appears in Kumin's collection *Halfway*. Anne's strongest quality, persistence, sees her through; *All My Pretty Ones* is completed by the end of the year and is published in 1962.

The title for the book comes from a speech by Macduff in Shakespeare's *Macbeth*. The book contains 31 poems. In the title poem, 'All My Pretty Ones', and in 'The House', Anne communicates her feelings of loss, her mixed emotions towards her parents and her reactions to their deaths. Other outstanding poems are 'The Abortion', 'The Fortress', in principle dedicated to Dr Orne, and 'Doors, Doors, Doors'. In part three of 'Doors – Young Girl', we can understand why Anne is labelled both a confessional poet and one with special powers of observation.

Doors, Doors, Doors – Young Girl

Dear love, as simple as some distant evil
we walk a little drunk up these three flights
where you tacked a Dufy print above your army cot.

The thin apartment doors on the way up will
not tell us. We are saying, we have our rights
and let them see the sandwiches and wine we bought

for we do not explain my husband's insane abuse
and we do not say why your wild-haired wife has fled
or that my father opened like a walnut and then was dead.
Your palms fold over me like knees. Love is the only use.

Both a little drunk in the middle afternoon
with the forgotten smart of August on our skin
we hold hands as if we were still children who trudge

up the wooden tower, on up past that close platoon
of doors, past the dear old man who always asks us in
and the one who sews like a wasp and will not budge.

Climbing the dark halls, I ignore their papers and pails,
the twelve coats of rubbish of someone else's dim life.
Tell them need is an excuse for love. Tell them need prevails.
Tell them I remake and smooth your bed and am your wife.

Part two of *All My Pretty Ones* includes Anne's 'With Mercy for
the Greedy', her dedication to Maxine. It contains Anne's
uncompromising view of poetry:

My friend, my friend, I was born
doing reference work in sin, and born
confessing it. This is what poems are:
with mercy
for the greedy,
they are the tongue's wrangle,
the world's pottage, the rat's star.

With the odd exception, *All My Pretty Ones* was very well received. Charles Simmons, writing in *The Saturday Review*, felt that the poems were touching, human and frighteningly intense, '... qualities one might think guaranteed good writing'. Sylvia Plath wrote to Anne, 'I was absolutely stunned and delighted with the new book.' Philip Larkin said, 'A really exciting book. Examines the mind and body of the inner woman. It is full of wild, uninhibited feelings.' James Dickey slated it, as he had done with *Bedlam*. Writing in the *New York Times* Book Review he said, 'It would be hard to find a writer who dwells more insistently on the pathetic and disgusting aspects of bodily experience.' Sales of the book were excellent; 5,000 in the first year, 20,000 by the time of her death and about 50,000 to date. Anne now really was the self-made star poet.

It was to be six years before Anne would make another serious suicide attempt. However, she remained mentally unstable, her mind emotional rather than objective, subject to trances and vivid, horrific dreams. During this period admittances to Westwood Lodge continued. Her psychiatric treatment with Dr Orne continued until the summer of 1964. It remained a difficult relationship for both parties. A major problem is indicated in a note by Anne to Martin Orne in the spring of 1962:

> I would like to lie down beside you and go to sleep, and you will never leave me because I am a good girl. But I can't have sex with you because I can't have sex with Nana.

Anne, always determined to have her own way, now began to go into deep sleep trances in many of her sessions with Dr Orne. Clearly he had great difficulty in progressing his treatment of her.

Throughout this period Anne found her services for readings in high demand. She was already working her way towards a third book of poetry, greatly helped by constant liaison with Maxine Kumin and she was collaborating with Maxine on the production of two children's books, *Eggs of Things* and *More Eggs of Things*.

1962 brought further drama into Anne's life. In May 1962 her first mentor, John Holmes, was diagnosed with cancer. By June he was dead. Anne was traumatised by his sudden decline and she poured all her feelings in to a long elegy for him, 'Somewhere in Africa'.

(Verses 6 to 8)

Let there be this God who is a woman who will place you
upon her shallow boat, who is a woman naked to the waist
Moist with palm oil and sweat, a woman of some virtue
and wild breasts, her limbs excellent, unbruised and chaste

Let her take you. She will put twelve strong men at the oars
for you are stronger than mahogany and your bones fill
the boat high with fruit and bark from the interior
She will have you now, you whom the funeral cannot kill

John Holmes, cut from a single tree, lie heavy in her hold
and go down that river with the ivory, the copra and the gold.

This tragedy for Anne was swiftly followed by the suicide of her
close friend, the poet Sylvia Plath. Again Anne was heavily depressed
but again she was rescued by her poetry, penning 'Sylvia's Death'.
Some critics have said that in that poem there is the suggestion
that Sexton and Plath were lovers. I cannot see the reference and
I cannot think that it was true in life. Anne may have had female
lovers, but Sylvia's taste was very much for men.

Throughout 1962 Anne had lengthy and intense correspondence
with a Roman Catholic monk, who has always wished to remain
anonymous. The correspondence had begun suddenly, with a
complimentary letter to Anne upon her poetry, and it was ended
just as suddenly by the monk in 1963, when he moved on to a
life outside the monastery. The correspondence is significant in that
it gives Anne her first insights into religion and from then onwards
religious themes enter frequently into her poetry.

In October 1962 *Poetry Magazine* awarded her the prestigious
Levinson Prize for seven poems, which they had published as an
extract from *All My Pretty Ones*. Spring 1963 brought further
awards. The Ford Foundation granted her $5,000 for work in the
theatre; she had already begun drafting a play. In May The American
Academy of Arts and Letters awarded Anne a travelling fellowship
of $6,500 costs for spending a year abroad. The AAA award caused
Anne as much distress as delight. Agoraphobic by nature, Anne
could not contemplate being so far away from home for a month,
certainly not a year. At the same time, she was aware of the

273

derision she would be met with if she refused such an honour. She resolved the conundrum by persuading friend and neighbour Sandra Robart to accompany her. Anne would give half the award to Sandra, who could take the opportunity to visit schools and clinics for retarded children.

Anne was now awarded a second term at Radcliffe. It is of interest to note that most of the scholars at Radcliffe at that time had been or were going through psychiatric treatment. Anne's close friends during this term were Maxine Kumin, the artist Barbara Swann, and Tillie Olsen. Swann drew portraits of Anne and later said that Anne had come into her life like a whirlwind and had taken possession of her; it would seem that briefly they were lovers.

In August Anne and Sandra sailed from New York to Southampton on the first leg of their European adventure. From Southampton to London and then to Paris and from there Belgium, where their battered Volkswagen was broken into and all their luggage stolen. Re-equipped with second-hand clothes, they travelled onward to Amsterdam. As they moved on to Venice, Anne found herself more and more relying upon Sandy Robart; yet Sandy's support enabled Anne to take the many shocks and surprises of virgin European travel in her stride, something she could never have done before. In Venice Anne was captivated by the beauty of the city and, in a highly charged emotional state, she wrote many love letters to Kayo. By October the rains began to sweep into eastern Italy and they moved on to Florence. Sated with culture, they drove to Rome. Unaware of the undisciplined traffic in Rome, they crashed and wrote off their car soon after arrival.

On their first trip to the beach, Anne met a dashing young hairdresser, Louis. They discussed Cesare Pavese, the author, with whom Louis had been imprisoned during the Second World War. They flirted, visited cafes, listened to romantic music, drank, danced and inevitably made love together. Anne was consumed with guilt and soon became distraught with fear that she might be pregnant. She departed with Sandra for Naples and on to Capri. Louis, clearly infatuated, followed, and they soon became entwined again. Now Anne became schizoid. One part of her desired Louis physically, the other part wanted to escape from him. In desperation she made a marathon long-distance telephone call to Boston to Martin Orne. Immediately afterwards she met with Louis; they went to the beach and were again intimate. However, Dr Orne's advice had made the

274

necessary impact and, within a few days, she wrote to tell Kayo that she would be returning to Boston on 27 October.

Within a few days of returning home, Anne's mind became so disorientated that she became suicidal. She turned to Dr Orne, who admitted her to Westwood Lodge. Here she was again in the care of Dr Brunner-Orne. She was denied alcohol and sleeping pills. This exacerbated her condition. Kayo went to see her after three days and was so distressed with her condition that he talked to her at length, finally persuading her to discharge herself the next day.

As soon as Kayo had brought Anne back home he resumed work, travelling around the States, absent several days at a time. Anne always needed physical contact and at these times she turned to her daughter Linda. At night Anne would get into Linda's bed and cling on to her. At the time Linda did not realise that whilst doing this, Anne was masturbating herself. Anne knew, and all her old guilt feelings returned.

To try to break the circle of guilt, Anne threw herself into frenetic attempts to write poems for a new collection. The new volume was to be entitled *Live or Die*.

At the beginning of 1964, Dr Martin Orne informed Anne that he would be moving to Philadelphia in September to take up a new teaching and research appointment. Their eight-year journey together would end. He would help Anne to find another therapist. Anne was stunned, but her first reaction was that she would find her own therapist.

In the summer of 1963, Tillie Olsen had introduced Anne to a friend, Anne Wilder, a psychiatrist. Wilder was seven years older than Sexton, more sophisticated, had a warm personality and a good sense of humour. She was full of the joy of life and was particularly interested in writers. The two Annes immediately hit it off together. In fact, only a short time elapsed before Anne Sexton declared herself in love with Anne Wilder. Now Anne hoped Wilder would become her therapist. Wilder, however, had contracted lupus (a chronic degenerative skin disease) and was running down her practice and giving over the time to writing novels. She therefore would not accept Anne as a patient. Nevertheless, they did enter into lengthy and intimate correspondence and telephone calls. Indeed, Anne poured her heart out to Anne Wilder, making her privy to comprehensive details about Sexton's life and therapy. Anne Wilder became heavily attracted to Sexton. In May of 1965 Wilder accompanied Anne on a two-week speaking tour from Rochester through to Ann Arbor. It was during this journey that they first became lovers. They remained friends for the remainder of Anne's life.

This did not solve Anne's problem of finding a therapist to replace Martin Orne. When she did find a new psychiatrist, she was to remain with him for five years, during which Anne's suicidal thoughts abated considerably. Frederick Duhl was from Boston, a young married doctor with children. Anne quickly fell for him, seduced him and they became and remained lovers throughout her treatment years. The affair and the therapy only ended when the good doctor tired of it and ensured that his wife found out their adultery in order to provide him with an excuse to terminate everything.

Anne was now drinking very heavily. This did not prevent her from accepting the many speaking engagements, which her popularity as a poet had gained her. Sometimes she was half drunk when she appeared, but this did not diminish the demand for her readings. Nor did it slow down her relentless production and revision of poems for her next book. 'Consorting With Angels', 'Love Song', 'Man And Wife', 'Wanting to Die' and 'Wedding Night' were all completed during this period. She was also hard at work on a play, which she had started and put to one side. Now that she had the Ford grant to fund development and production costs and the Charles Theatre in Boston as a venue, she was inspired to work towards a completed script.

July of 1964 saw another brief breakdown, with voices in her head and spells of incoherence. A confinement of two weeks in Massachusetts General Hospital was needed. During this time it was decided that her future medication should be Thioridazine, an antipsychotic drug, prescribed at that time mainly for schizophrenics. Whilst this treatment had been successful in damping down the over-stimulation of the brain, it did have side-effects, principally restlessness, abnormal facial movements and impairment of eyesight. Anne Sexton might be regarded as an excellent reference case in that she gained the benefits of the drug, but suffered the side-effects. The drug does have a sedative effect and alcohol should be avoided, which Anne did not – big time! Anne's mental problems towards the end of her life can, in part, be attributed to her long-term use of this drug and the effects of coming off it.

276

Upon release, all of Anne's thoughts were taken up with Dr Martin Orne's departure. When he did leave in September, Anne immediately started on her workshop at the Charles Theatre, working on her play, which was to be called *Tell Me Your Answer True*. She worked closely with the theatre's producer, Ben Shaktman, but she could not get the theme of the main character, Daisy, right and when Shaktman left, in March 1965, to take up other productions, she returned to her attempts to write a novel, based on sex in the suburbs. These attempts were not successful; the project was just too large for Anne's concentration span.

Late in June 1966 she was invited by the Kohl Foundation to a conference in Long Island to discuss new thinking to induce collaboration between writers and teachers with the objective of invigorating the teaching of English in secondary schools. She was accompanied by Robert Clawson, a young, married teacher from Weston High School. They only knew each other slightly but they were to spend seven days together at the conference. They straightaway became lovers and remained so throughout the week. Although they remained friends, and exchanged passionate letters for some time afterwards, the physical intimacy did not last beyond that week. Anne immediately returned to Frederick Duhl, her psychiatrist lover.

In August Anne took Kayo on a three-week safari to Africa. Kayo loved hunting, but Anne hated the heat and dust and was reviled by having to eat the flesh of the animals they had hunted. It was her last gift to Kayo; a final, desperate attempt to save her feelings for him and her marriage. It was destined to fail.

In September 1966, *Live or Die* was published by Houghton Mifflin. The volume consisted of 34 poems. The thrust of these poems is to explore the connection between madness and sexuality. As always, Sexton is confessional and her breakdowns and suicide attempts are examined. Anne Sexton's style was changing and her mastery of technique was such that she could by choice ignore the control of metre. Perhaps the best of the poems in this book, certainly the most quoted and remembered were 'Flee on Your Donkey', 'Sylvia's Death', 'For the Year of the Insane', 'Menstruation at Forty' and 'Suicide Note'. I include 'Menstruation at Forty' so that the reader may compare Anne's style and thinking with her poems in *To Bedlam and Part Way Back* and *All My Pretty Ones*.

Menstruation at Forty

I was thinking of a son.
The womb is not a clock
nor a bell tolling,
but in the eleventh month of its life
I feel the November
of the body as well as of the calendar.
In two days it will be my birthday
and as always the earth is done with its harvest.
This time I hunt for death,
the night I lean toward,
the night I want.
Well then—
speak of it!
It was in the womb all along.

I was thinking of a son...
You! The never acquired,
the never seeded or unfastened,
you of the genitals I feared,
the stalk and the puppy's breath.
Will I give you my eyes or his?
Will you be the David or the Susan?
(Those two names I picked and listened for.)
Can you be the man your fathers are—
the leg muscles from Michelangelo,
hands from Yugoslavia
somewhere the peasant, Slavic and determined,
somewhere the survivor bulging with life—
and could it still be possible,
all this with Susan's eyes?

All this without you—
two days gone in blood.
I myself will die without baptism,
a third daughter they didn't bother.
My death will come on my name day.
What's wrong with the name day?
It's only an angel of the sun.

Woman,
weaving a web over your own,
a thin and tangled poison.
Scorpio,
bad spider—
die!

My death from the wrists,
two name tags,
blood worn like a corsage
to bloom
one on the left and one on the right—
It's a warm room,
the place of the blood.
Leave the door open on its hinges!

Two days for your death
and two days until mine.

Love! That red disease—
year after year, David, you would make me wild!
David! Susan! David! David!
full and disheveled, hissing into the night,
never growing old,
waiting always for you on the porch...
year after year,
my carrot, my cabbage,
I would have possessed you before all women,
calling your name,
calling you mine.

I also recommend for the reader's consideration 'Flee on Your Donkey': At 263 lines it is too long to repeat here, suffice it to say that it describes in depth Anne's experiences and feelings in her favourite mental hospital.

Reviews for *Live or Die* were generally, although not wholly, very favourable. The *Saturday Review* (Joseph Slater) praised 'the sure, dramatic movement of whole poems'. *Harper's* said, 'Her previous books were interesting, but now mere self-dramatisation has become a habit.' Other reviewers did not accept Sexton's work

279

as poetry, deriding it as just a record of modern psychiatric treatment. When Oxford University Press published the volume in London in 1967, it attracted numerous poor reviews, many of which compared her work unfavourably with that of Sylvia Plath. Significantly, Ted Hughes said that with *Live or Die* Sexton was approaching her peak. He described her stanzaic patterns and her control of traditional form as models other, less talented, poets ought to aspire to. He told her not to worry about the bad English reviews, telling her that good reviews are bad for poets. I think he meant that they create conceit, whereas a poet should always aspire to continuously improve. In the *London Magazine* Alan Ross wrote, 'Anyone experiencing the process of breakdown knows the impossibility of describing it. Yet for all their burden, these poems rarely sink, for they carry the weight of their own conviction without poetic strain. The rewards of these poems are many, for they are the products of a tough original mind, of an engaging poetic personality.'

It seems the good reviews had much more impact than the bad. In the USA and in Britain the first printings quickly sold out. In the spring of 1967 the book was awarded the Shelley Memorial Prize, followed by the Pulitzer Prize. With hindsight, most critics now agree that *Live or Die* was Anne's finest work.

Anne never quite recovered from receiving the Pulitzer Prize. From that time on she thought it meant that everyone should notice her. If they did not, she would become wild with anger. This represented something of a turning point in her personality; certainly she was no longer agoraphobic.

Celebrating her birthday at home in November 1966, Anne suffered a tumble down the stairs, which resulted in a broken hip. She was hospitalised for ten days and finally the fracture had to be held together with screws. Anne was to be severely restricted for the next six months, being bedridden or using either wheelchair or stick to get around. Her hectic lifestyle was curtailed with a suddenness that shocked her. There is some cause for belief that this ordinary accident was the beginning of the final stage of Anne Sexton's drift into suicide. The hip never fully mended and Anne walked with a limp for the rest of her life. As a result of this immobility Anne put on almost three stones in weight in a very short period of time. Limping, fat, her face twitching and with blurred eyesight (Thioridazine), Anne's physical beauty was no longer captivating most men, and some women, at first sight. This had a big impact on Anne because she always had a deep need to be loved and to have that love physically demonstrated.

In July 1967 Ted Hughes, on behalf of the Arts Council of Great Britain, invited her to read at the five-day Poetry International Festival in London. Still in difficulty with walking, she wanted to take her own wheelchair and she would need a companion. She settled on Lois Ames. Amazingly Sexton was short of funds and had to grub around to raise sponsorship for her expenses. Departing for London on 11 July, Anne complained to Lois that on such a short visit and, handicapped by her hip, 'I will have to look sharp to get any action on this trip.' Her desire met with mixed results. Anne gave a 13-minute reading from *Live or Die* to 2,000 people at the Queen Elizabeth Hall on the first night of the festival. She finished with a flourish, throwing her arms open wide, as if to embrace the audience, and blowing them an exaggerated kiss to invoke their love. She did not get it; she was greeted with a silence that approached disgust. Love she did get, and from a not entirely unexpected source. She had met George Macbeth, a prolifically published poet and a programmer for the BBC, whilst he was touring the USA in early 1966 and later at his Richmond, Surrey, home when she was on holiday with Kayo. This time she recorded a BBC radio interview for Macbeth. Afterwards they spent the day together and ended up in the room Anne shared with Lois at the 69 Hotel. There they made passionate love together, busted hip not withstanding. Unlike Lois, I could not have slept through such a performance.

Returning to Weston, Anne took up a workshop teaching post at Wayland High School in collaboration with her ex-lover, Bob Clawson. This was successful and was extended into 1968 by the school. It was there that one of her students, Steve Rizzo, came up with the idea of setting Anne's poetry to music. This was eventually to lead to Anne Sexton's own chamber rock group.

Anne was now working on her next volume of poetry, which she was to call *Love Poems*. She had resumed the love affair with her married psychiatrist. When he left Boston with his family for an 18-day vacation in December 1967, Anne created a daily series of poems, covering each of the 18 days. Appropriately entitled 'Eighteen Days Without You', they were destined to appear as the final poems in the *Love Poems* book.

1968 saw an important new progression in Anne's career. Bob Clawson developed Steve Rizzo's original idea into a rock band playing back-up rhythms to a selection of Anne's poems. The band would be led by Rizzo on acoustic guitar and would have keyboard, drums, flute, saxophone and, later, bass guitar. Anne would front the band and deliver the words in rhythm with the music. The group would be called Anne Sexton and Her Kind. Readers will recall that the title was taken from a poem in Anne's first book *To Bedlam and Part Way Back*. Rehearsals were continuous throughout spring and early summer. The first performance was in July 1968 in Boston at a benefit night to open a presidential rally for Eugene McCarthy. From then on the band, with Anne, was to tour continuously until 1971.

By 1969 Anne was an established celebrity. This was reflected in her hectic lifestyle. She was teaching, working on her new book of poetry, touring with the band, having psychiatric treatment, drinking very heavily. This frantic pace meant that she was constantly under pressure. It would not be long before this provoked another breakdown.

For now, Anne's mind was focused on the publication of her new book. 'Sexton' was now a brand name and *Love Poems* seemed assured of success. Her style had gradually evolved and there were now trademarks with which she could be identified. Her frequent use of similes, metaphors and repetitions are prime examples, well illustrated in 'The Touch', her own favourite from *Love Poems*.

The Touch

For months my hand was sealed off
in a tin box. Nothing was there but the subway railings.
Perhaps it is bruised, I thought,
and that is why they have locked it up.
You could tell time by this, I thought,
like a clock, by its five knuckles
and the thin underground veins.
It lay there like an unconscious woman
fed by tubes she knew not of.

The hand had collapsed,
a small wood pigeon
that had gone into seclusion.

282

I turned it over and the palm was old,
its lines traced like fine needlepoint
and stitched up into fingers.
It was fat and soft and blind in places.
Nothing but vulnerable.

And all this is metaphor.
An ordinary hand – just lonely
for something to touch
that touches back.
The dog won't do it.
Her tail wags in the swamp for a frog.
I'm no better than a case of dog food.
She owns her own hunger.
My sisters won't do it.
They live in school except for buttons
and tears running down like lemonade.
My father won't do it.
He comes in the house and even at night
he lives in a machine made by my mother
and well oiled by his job, his job.

The trouble is
that I'd let my gestures freeze.
The trouble was not
in the kitchen or the tulips
but only in my head, my head.

Then all this became history.
Your hand found mine.
Life rushed to my fingers like a blood clot.
Oh, my carpenter,
the fingers are rebuilt.
They dance with yours.
They dance in the attic and in Vienna.
My hand is alive all over America.
Not even death will stop it,
death shedding her blood.
Nothing will stop it, for this is the kingdom
and the kingdom come.

Reviews of *Love Poems* in America were good. Anthony Hect (*The Hudson Review*) thoroughly approved the work and perceived a new narrative structure within the volume. Hayden Carruth liked the confessional style, although he said her work again raised the question of where you draw the line in poetry between art and documentary. Linda Wagner-Martin says that Anne's reputation as a poet peaked with the publication of this volume. The book sold 4,000 copies in the first month of publication, 14,000 in the first year and circa 25,000 by the time of her death. Readers will doubtless be aware that represents prodigious sales for a book of poetry.

Love Poems was published in England later in 1969. It was not generally well reviewed and took two years to sell the first 1,000 copies; it was not reprinted. Her publishers, Oxford University Press, told her, 'You do not always convince us that the cause of celebration justifies the fireworks.' Alfred Alvarez (the *Observer*) wrote, 'Her undoubted talent risks being eroded by constant self-flagellation.' Author and reviewer Ian Hamilton said (in *Poetry Magazine*), '*Love Poems* is a dead end for Anne Sexton.' Christopher Driver's view, for the *Guardian*, was that 'Sexton has her own tone of voice which injects whole phrases and stanzas into the memory without one noticing it. That is how poetry secures an audience in its own time, and perhaps for posterity too.'

Anne's other major project in 1969 was the redrafting of her play *45 Mercy Street*. The final draft centres around incest, the defilement of the young female body and sensual relationships between a young woman and one much older. The main characters are Daisy, Aunt Amy and Ace; clearly they represent Anne, Nana and Ralph Harvey. The play opened at the American Place Theatre on 3 October 1969 and ran until 21 November. Marian Seldes starred as Daisy, with Mel Dowd as Aunt Amy. William Prince played Ace. It had lukewarm but favourable reviews and good audiences, who received it well. It could have run for longer if the theatre had not already been committed to other productions. Typical of the reviews was the *New York Times* (Clive Barnes), 'Miss Sexton has written a play to be considered rather than dismissed.' John Osborne, speaking on BBC Radio in London, praised the actors and the ritual and imagery and said the play had poetic strength.

Throughout the rehearsals and performances of the play, Anne was enthusiastic and happy. Yet, early on in the performances, despite favourable audiences and reviews, Anne's feelings about the play turned bitter. She was convinced that she would never be a good playwright. This abrupt turnaround in Anne's attitude to her play and her ability as a playwright is a clear example to support my claim that she was suffering from Multiple Personality Disorder.

It was during this period that an incident occurred that was to have a significant impact on Anne's life and that of her daughter, Linda. For some years Anne had been in the habit of getting into Linda's bed and snuggling up to her. On this occasion, Anne asked her to come to her bed. Linda fell asleep. When she woke in the middle of the night, she found her mother lying upon her, rubbing against her and kissing her on the mouth. Linda jumped up, ran to the bathroom and was sick. She was disgusted and frightened by this attempt at sexual intimacy. It heralded the start of Linda's own psychiatric treatment. From then on, Linda gradually withdrew from the unhealthily close relationship with her mother, which had previously existed. This affected Anne more than it did Linda. Anne always had to have constant demonstrations of adoration by everyone around her.

1969 was a hectic year, with a new book, a first play, a circuit of readings and on the road with *Her Kind*. This resulted in her producing no new poetry in 1969. Anne had been taking amphetamines and alcohol to stimulate her, Thioridazine to tranquillize her and a hypnotic drug for sleeping. Nervous exhaustion from her frenetic lifestyle and the effect of drugs had brought Anne to the edge of another breakdown by the end of 1969.

There was to be no let-up in 1970. Amazingly, Sexton produces almost her last burst of creative energy. She begins two new volumes, *The Book of Folly* and *The Death Notebooks*. Sandwiched between these she produces, in just eight months, a book of 17 lengthy poems, based on Grimm's fairy tales, which she entitles *Transformations*. The title is most apt. The volume represents a substantial change in Sexton's style. It is her most feminist work and steps outside the confessional style tied to her own persona. She does call on her perceived relationships with her mother, father and Nana; but the main themes running through are fear and a mocking of society.

Sexton retells these well-known fairy tales, with black humour, from the perspective of 'a middle-aged witch, me' (her words). She supplies some surprising conclusions, which are not part of the original stories. The following extracts from two poems, 'Briar Rose (*Sleeping Beauty*)' and 'Cinderella' are good examples of the work:

Briar Rose (*Sleeping Beauty*)

. . .

Briar Rose
was an insomniac . . .
She could not nap
or lie in sleep
without the court chemist
mixing her some knock out drops
and never in the prince's presence.
If it is to come, she said
sleep must take me unawares
while I am laughing or dancing
so that I do not know that brutal place
where I lie down with cattle prods,
the hole in my cheek open.
Further, I must not dream
for when I do I see the table set
and a faltering crone at my place,
her eyes burnt by cigarettes
as she eats betrayal like a slice of meat.

. . .

I must not sleep
for while I'm asleep I'm ninety
and think I'm dying.
Death rattles in my throat
like a marble.
I wear tubes like earrings.
I lie as still as a bar of iron.
You can stick a needle
through my kneecap and I won't flinch
I'm all shot up with Novocain.
This trance girl

is yours to do with.
You could lay her in a grave,
an awful package,
and shovel dirt on her face
and she'd never call back: Hello there!
But if you kissed her on the mouth
her eyes would spring open
and she'd call out: Daddy! Daddy!
Presto!
She's out of prison.

. . .

There was a theft.
That much I am told.
I was abandoned.
That much I know.
I was forced backward.
I was forced forward.
I was passed hand to hand
like a bowl of fruit.
Each night I am nailed into place
and forget who I am.
Daddy?
That's another kind of prison
It's not the prince at all,
but my father
drunkenly bent over my bed,
circling the abyss like a shark,
my father thick upon me
like some sleeping jellyfish.
What voyage this, little girl?
This coming out of prison?
God help—
this life after death?

Cinderella

You always read about it:
the plumber with twelve children

287

who wins the Irish Sweepstakes.
From toilets to riches.
That story.

. . .

The prince was getting tired.
He began to feel like a shoe salesman.
But he gave it one last try.
This time Cinderella fits into the shoe
like a love letter into its envelope.

At the wedding ceremony
the two sisters came to curry favour
and the white dove pecked their eyes out.
Two hollow spots were left
like soup spoons.

Cinderella and the prince
lived, they say, happily ever after,
like two dolls in a museum case
never bothered by diapers or dust,
never arguing over the timing of an egg,
never telling the same story twice,
never getting a middle-aged spread,
their darling smiles pasted on for eternity.
Regular Bobbsey Twins.
That story.

In 1970 Anne is also teaching at Boston University. The pace took its toll on Anne by August. She became disorientated and was hallucinating. She had a session with her new psychiatrist, whom she calls Frau Doktor and Mama Brundig. The doctor saw no cause for alarm and advised Anne to go home and rest. In fact Anne went to the house of her friend and neighbour and made wild and uncontrolled telephone calls to Dr Brundig and Maxine Kumin. She then went home and took a large overdose of barbiturates. She then made a further incoherent phone call to Maxine. Alerted, Maxine sent Billie Sexton to stay with Anne. When Kayo arrived, she was in a coma. He drove her to Massachusetts General Hospital, where she was admitted to the psychiatric ward. Presumably this was another suicide attempt. It certainly triggered off a series of health problems for Anne. On this occasion she recovered quickly.

Soon after Anne returned from hospital she was hit with another great shock. She was visited by Azel Mack, an old family friend and godfather to Anne's daughters. He came to reveal a mind-blowing secret. He told Anne that her mother and he had been having an affair from 1927 continuously until Mary Harvey's death. That, in fact, he was Anne's father. Mack produced several proofs to support his story and maintained that he was only now releasing the secret, after 40 years, because he was dying. Eventually Anne came to believe that Azel Mack was her true father. We can imagine the impact this had on a mentally disturbed woman, who believed that she had been physically abused by her 'father' and mentally cowed by her mother.

Despite some misgivings by Anne's publishers, Houghton Mifflin, *Transformations* was published in October 1971. Their fears were unfounded. It was an extremely popular book, earning Anne about $10,000 in its first year of publication. It is still in publication today. The American critics were generally impressed. Christopher Lehmann-Haupt, *New York Times*, called it 'A funny, mad, witty, frightening, charming, haunting book. Delightfully accessible.' However, when it was published in the UK, her publishers also had doubts and this time reviewers were not so kind. The *Times Literary Supplement*, July 1972, said, 'The poems might be expected to appeal to a fairly sophisticated, but undemanding American adolescent, but it is unlikely to find an adult audience here.'

Despite her previous experiences of exhaustion, Anne continued her frenetic pace through 1972. Colgate University appointed her Professor in Literature for the spring semester with a salary of $13,000. Despite being ill-educated, Anne was a fine teacher. At Boston University she was given a five-year contract to lecture part-time with a salary of $10,000 per semester and the rank of professor. In the early part of the year she completed the final drafts of her sixth book, *The Book of Folly*, and throughout the year she was working on her seventh book, *The Death Notebooks*. She continued her well-paid recital tour.

Despite Anne's high earnings, financial worries began to depress her. Kayo had been made redundant and Anne had financed him to start his own company. It was not achieving any early success. It also seems that Anne was spending large amounts of money on alcohol and travelling expenses. Nevertheless, Anne had some areas of contentment. The children were in their late teens, Kayo travelled frequently and Anne felt free from many of the stresses of family life. As is often the case when one has a degree of contentment, Anne was putting on more weight. She admitted to size 18, but probably was a size 20; her size 8 to 10 days of her youth were gone temporarily.

Anne was now very much a feminist. One of the earliest female writers to use the title 'Ms', she frequently called herself 'Ms Dog'. She had intended *The Death Notebooks* for posthumous publication and clearly had been thinking she was near to the time of taking her own life. In the summer of 1972 she decided that *The Death Notebooks* would be published to follow *The Book of Folly* and she wished to be around to observe the reactions of the critics.

Anne called *The Book of Folly* a book of very surreal unconscious poems and some fiction stories. In fact the book returns to the confessional mode with the opening poems 'The Ambition Bird' and two collections of poems, *Angels of the Love Affairs* and *The Death of the Fathers*. Another sequence of nine poems, entitled *The Jesus Papers*, prepares us for the religious theme that looms over Sexton's final collections. From *The Jesus Papers*, I like these extracts from 'Jesus Raises Up The Harlot':

The harlot squatted
with her hands over her red hair
She was not looking for customers
She was in a deep fear.
A delicate body clothed in red,
as red as a smashed fist
and she was bloody as well
for the townspeople were trying
to stone her to death

. . .

Jesus knew that a terrible sickness
dwelt in the harlot and He could lance it
with His two small thumbs

. . .

He lanced her twice. On the spot
He lanced her twice on each breast

290

pushing His thumbs in until the milk ran out,
those two boils of whoredom
The harlot followed Jesus around like a puppy
for He had raised her up
Now she forsook her fornications
and became His pet.
His raising her up made her feel
like a little girl again when she had a father
who brushed the dirt from her eye.
Indeed she took hold of herself,
knowing she owed Jesus a life,
as sure-fire as a trump card.

The Book of Folly was published at the end of 1972 in the USA. In Britain her publishers, Oxford University Press, were again uncertain with the direction Sexton was taking and Anne decided abruptly to cut herself off from them. She signed a contract with Chatto & Windus, but by the time they published it in the UK in 1974, Anne was only months away from suicide.

Reviews of *The Book of Folly* were lukewarm in America and the UK. Critics were pretty much agreed that the confessional style was sourced from Sylvia Plath's work. I feel that Plath was concerned to tell people every little thing about herself and her problems and to vent her rage, whilst Sexton wanted to confess her sins of mind and body in the starkest detail. Gloomy self-preoccupation versus liberating candour.

Sexton's demons were now pursuing her with force, pushing her into a final frenzy of writing. Already she was heavily engaged in the final drafting and preparation for publication of her next book *The Death Notebooks*. Yet in the single month of January 1973 she wrote 40 poems; 39 of these were later collected into one volume *The Awful Rowing Toward God*. It is difficult to estimate in what way this January output was influenced by three days hospitalisation at Westwood Lodge halfway through the month.

She was telephoning Maxine Kumin every day and Maxine was later to say, 'She was writing like a fugitive one length ahead of the posse.' 1973 was also the year Kumin won the Pulitzer Prize for *Up Country*; Anne Sexton was one of the three judges. Anne voted for Maxine, even though she knew that the award of the prize would mean more work and travelling for Kumin with the inevitable result that they would see much less of each other.

In the early days of her marriage Anne had been much dependent upon Kayo and his physical presence. By 1973 they had grown distant from each other. Anne's fame was by now at its peak and provided her with a network of friends, peers and colleagues. Kayo had become jealous and was no longer tolerant of Anne's drunkenness and erratic behaviour. At times he would also occasionally become verbally and physically violent towards the children. By the end of January Anne had decided she wanted freedom from Kayo. She told him to get out of the house and asked for a divorce. Anne maintained that the breakdown of the marriage had been caused by a gradual, and now irreversible, weakening of their sexual relationship. We know that sex was always very important to Anne. She said that the decision had been delayed for some years by her dependence upon Thioridazine. She was now off this drug and, whilst she admitted she still had manic spells, the upside was a new feeling of independence and a desire to make other beneficial choices about her life. Her psychiatrist told Anne that she had made 'significant progress' and agreed that it was a time in her life to 'move on'. This appears to have been a poor diagnosis. Anne had not made significant progress with her mental demons. She was to have further breakdowns, culminating in suicide by 1974. Anne had not improved her alcoholism; she was drinking more heavily than ever.

In the interval between parting with Kayo and the final divorce hearing, Anne fell into serious depression. She added chain-smoking to her constant drinking and carried with her at all times several pillboxes of tranquillisers and antidepressants. Throughout this period Anne was heavily supported by her friends Lois Ames and Louise Conant. Without their support, it is likely that Anne would not have survived this critical period. Anne also received a great boost from Conrad Sousa, the composer and conductor. Sousa devised a light opera based on *Transformations*. The piece previewed in Minneapolis and, at the end of the performance, Sousa invited Anne on to stage to take a bow, which she did at great length and continued by hugging each and every one of the players. One part of Anne really did love the limelight of the stage.

The divorce was finalised in November 1973. One might have

thought that Anne would have a sense of relief and, perhaps, return to the vibrancy of her late thirties. In fact she began to deteriorate further mentally and physically. Through that period she suffered extreme pain from an abscess surrounding some of her teeth and extending into her sinus; this, understandably, caused sleeplessness, even though she was taking maximum doses of sleeping pills. The drug Quinidine, which she was taking to control irregular heart rhythms, together with the latent effects of Thioridazine, was affecting her eyesight; spectacles were now a necessity. She continued to fall into trance-like states and now she was having hallucinations; ceilings, walls and floors seemed to oscillate and would create panic attacks within her.

In August Sexton was admitted to the McLean Hospital in Belmont, where she spent five days undergoing extensive examinations. Measurement of the electrical activity of her brain revealed normal brain functioning and she was released.

Anne's deterioration had not obstructed her from having an intense love affair with Philip Legler, an old flame from her reading tour in 1966. Legler was married with children and now teaching at Northern Michigan University. As soon as he heard of Anne's impending divorce, he immediately sought to renew their relationship. Anne was lonely and very willing. For two months, through July and August, the affair was torrid. Love letters were prolific. In one such, Anne told Philip that he had given her the most intense sexual experience she had ever known and with it he had given her back her body. In several of Anne's letters she asked Philip to end his marriage and marry her.

Early in September Legler wrote a final letter, telling Anne he had decided to remain in his marriage and end their affair. He would return to psychiatric treatment. Anne reacted by getting drunk and taking an overdose of sleeping pills. She had to be admitted to the accident and emergency department at Newton-Wellesley Hospital for treatment but was released late the following day. The next day Anne repeated her antics, adding a large dose of Quinidine. She collapsed and was taken to Westwood Lodge Institution. After three days at Westwood it was decided that Anne should be transferred to the Human Research Institute at Boston for further analysis and treatment. This was much against Anne's will. She believed that the treatment, mainly group therapy, benefited young people mainly in the early stages of mental breakdowns and was inappropriate for persons of her maturity with long-term, deeply rooted psychological problems. Anne was right. She was deeply miserable for most of the four weeks she spent there.

Released at the end of October, Anne found herself with another problem to face. Her writing gift had deserted her. She tried to convince herself that she could still make her typewriter fly along with a stream of words; but the facts denied her. Anne Sexton was to write no more new, publishable poetry.

In December her psychiatrist, 'Doktor Brundig', despaired of Anne's way of life and her lies, and gave up treating her. From now on Anne would receive therapy from Barbara Schwartz. Schwartz was not a psychiatrist. She was a social worker specialising in clients with psychiatric problems. Such was the warmth of her personality and her imperturbability that she soon became one of Anne's close friends.

Of course, *The Death Notebooks* was now at the publishing stage and Anne was, to some small degree, able to focus upon that. The volume consists of 44 poems. Within them Anne acts out her search for spiritual meaning as a way of fighting depression. Publication was at the end of February 1974. Critics generally agreed that the sequences 'O Ye Tongues' and 'The Furies' were rated amongst the finest Anne had ever written. This extract is from 'O Ye Tongues Tenth Psalm':

For as the baby springs out like a starfish into her million light years Anne sees that she must climb her own mountain.

For as she eats wisdom like the halves of a pear she puts one foot in front of the other. She climbs the dark wing.

For as her child grows Anne grows and there is salt and cantaloupe and molasses for all.

For as Anne walks, the music walks and the family lies down in milk.

For I am not locked up.

For I am placing fist over fist on rock and plunging into the altitude of words. The silence of words.

For the husband sells his rain to God and God is well pleased with His family.

For they fling together against hardness and somewhere, in another form, a light is clicked on by gentle fingers.

For death comes to friends, to parents, to sisters. Death comes with its bagful of pain yet they do not curse the key they were given to hold.

For they open each door and it gives them a new day at the yellow window.

For the child grows to a woman, her breasts coming up like the moon while Anne rubs the peace stone.

For the child starts up her own mountain (not being locked in) and reaches the coastline of grapes.

For Anne and her daughter master the mountain and again and again. Then the child finds a man who opens like the sea.

For that daughter must build her own city and fill it with her own oranges, her own words.

For Anne walked up and up and finally over the years until she was old as the moon with its naggy voice.

For Anne had climbed over eight mountains and saw the children washing the tiny statues in the square.

For Anne sat down with the blood of the hammer and built a tombstone for herself and Christopher sat beside her and was well pleased with their red shadow.

For they hung up a picture of a rat and the rat smiled and held out his hand.

For the rat was blessed on that mountain. He was given a white bath.

For the milk in the skies sank down upon them and tucked them in.

For God did not forsake them but put the blood angel to look after them until such time as they would enter their star.

For the sky dogs jumped out and shovelled snow upon us and we lay in our quiet blood.

For God was as large as a sunlamp and laughed his heat at us and therefore we did not cringe at the death hole.

From 'The Furies' I have chosen 'The Fury of Cocks'.

There they are
drooping over the breakfast plates,
angel-like,
folding in their sad wing,
animal sad,
and only the night before
there they were
playing the banjo.
Once more the day's light comes
with its immense sun,
its mother trucks,
its engines of amputation.
Whereas last night
the cock knew its way home,
as stiff as a hammer,
battering in with all
its awful power.
That theatre.
Today it is tender,
a small bird,
as soft as a baby's hand.
She is the house.
He is the steeple.
When they fuck they are God.
When they break away they are God.
When they snore they are God.

In the morning they butter the toast.
They don't say much.
They are still God.
All the cocks of the world are God,
blooming, blooming, blooming,
into the sweet blood of woman.

In Boston and New York the critics, Charles Simmons and James Slater among many, reviewed it favourably. Even former detractors, such as James Dickey, gave positive reviews. It was not published in England until after Anne's death: the leading reviewers in London, A. Alvarez and Ted Hughes, found it stunning in its sensibility.

In March Anne gave a reading of *The Death Notebooks* at the Sanders Theatre in Boston. The event was widely publicised and a packed theatre included many of Anne's friends and lovers. It was one of Sexton's finest performances and the audience rose to applaud a triumph.

It was, however, to be Anne's swansong. There were to be very few public appearances before her end. She did continue teaching at Boston University. However, she was going downhill at speed, both mentally and physically. Alone and lonely in the first week of February, she had deliberately taken an overdose of sleeping pills mixed with Thioridazine pills. She lay comatose for several hours until discovered by a neighbour and rushed by ambulance to Massachusetts General Hospital. This was probably more a cry for help than a genuine suicide attempt. She had already told Eric Edwards, a student in her Boston University class, exactly how she intended to commit the deadly act; as we shall see it was not by an overdose of drugs.

In April, Anne went to Barbara Schwartz's office late one night, sat outside, and took a medley of pills. Just as she was collapsing, a passer-by saw her and took her to Mount Auburn Emergency Hospital. Anne has become very shaky and has lost weight rapidly. She is now, at 5' 9", only 105 lbs and size 6.

Summer came and passed, with Anne becoming increasingly paranoid about being alone. Her friend and neighbour Jan Smith was hired as nurse companion; but Anne continued to deteriorate. As summer moves in to autumn, Anne's end is near. She continues to drink heavily and chain-smoke, with marijuana supplementing cigarettes. She is now addicted to a daily cocktail of pills: Diazepam, antidepressants and hypnotic-type sleeping pills. She has manic spells when teaching or giving readings yet she also has moments of great poise and confidence, never better illustrated than in her sittings for photographer Arthur Furst, who created an interesting portfolio of portraits of her in that last summer of 1974.

Since the time of her voluminous correspondence with a Carmelite monk in 1962/63, Anne had been continuously investigating religion. Now, in her last months, Anne entered into periodic religious instruction from Patricia Handloss, a young student at the Episcopal Divinity College in Boston. There is little doubt that she was seeking spiritual comfort. However, she was not inclined to join a church and, in her usual flippant way, she maintained, 'St Mattress is just as appropriate a place to find the unknown, however doubtful, ever possible, joyous "God" as any religious gathering.'

On the morning of 4 October 1974 Anne Sexton made a deliberate decision to end her life. She was calm and relaxed about her decision. She had a morning meeting with her therapist, Barbara Schwartz. On departing, she left behind her constant companions, cigarettes and lighter; she had no further use for them. From there she went to meet Maxine Kumin for lunch. They discussed the proofs of Anne's next book *The Awful Rowing Toward God* and a children's book, which they were co-authoring, *The Wizard's Tears*. Maxine says they had a light-hearted and rather silly lunch together and that Anne seemed relaxed. Their farewells that day were emotional. Maxine thought this was due to Maxine being about to depart on a long trip to Europe, Iran and Israel. She knew Anne had been dreading having a long period without Maxine's support. But Anne knew that the emotion she felt at leaving Maxine that day was because she would never see her again.

The first thing Anne did when she arrived home was to telephone her date for the evening and change the time of their meeting. She then removed all of her jewellery, put on a fur coat, poured a glass of vodka and went out to her garage. Here she closed the doors, got into her car, switched on the ignition and slowly and peacefully passed away. She left no suicide note.

The funeral of Anne Sexton was arranged by Patricia Handloss and held at the Episcopal Church in Dedham. Anne was cremated, but such was the family grief that it was August of 1976 before her ashes were buried at Forest Hill Cemetery in Boston. In the meantime, *The Awful Rowing Toward God* and *The Wizard's Tears* were published posthumously in 1975.

The Awful Rowing Toward God contains 39 poems, which, taken overall, show us how strenuously Anne strived to understand religion and the spiritual world at the time of her death. The final poem in the collection is 'The Rowing Endeth', in which Anne plays poker with God and loses to a wild card. You may recognise the story from a famous Leonard Cohen song in which the Devil and God are the players.

In 1977 *45 Mercy Street* was published, followed by *Words for Dr Y* in 1978. These were substantially edited by Linda Sexton.

We should pause to reflect that when Anne Sexton committed suicide, she was 47 years old and had been a writer for only 18 years. She died surrounded by unpublished work. Why so young?

During the last few months of her life, Anne's mind had been unsettled about suicide. She had hallucinated about it; in the spring she had told Eric Edwards exactly how she would commit the act, but in the summer she wrote to Erica Jong saying, 'All our lives we'll keep in touch.' In the autumn she coolly committed suicide.

Some reviewers have said that the cause of Anne's early death was an ill-informed diagnosis of her mental condition. It is fair to say that Anne was wrongly diagnosed, by her psychiatrists and herself, as an hysteric. Reviewing her life today we can clearly see that she was manic-depressive and an abuse victim. With the right diagnosis and treatment, Anne would probably have found the strength to survive longer. However, we can hardly attach blame to her psychiatrists, for even today students of Anne's life and work are confounded by the question: what really was Anne Sexton's problem?

There is little doubt that Anne was physically and mentally abused as a child. Later she became a victim of her own substance abuse; this gradually wore her down physically. I believe that she was also mentally exhausted by her prodigious output of writing over a comparatively short period of time. It is interesting to note how Anne Sexton's final furious burst of writing, followed by suicide, mirrors that of Sylvia Plath and Cesare Pavese. Anne probably was also worn down by an addiction to sex. Yet it was another addiction that was to bring about her end. An addiction to suicide.

Conclusion

Suicidal thoughts are as addictive as drugs. This much the reader may deduce by comparing the biographies of eight internationally acclaimed writers produced in this book.

Some of us may have suicidal thoughts, but, if we are lucky, something or someone persuades us to live. For writers it does seem that the higher the creative quality of the writer, the more likely it is that the suicide, which is in the mind, will be translated into lethal practice.

As we consider these eight great writers, we come to see how interwoven their backgrounds, experiences, characteristics and weaknesses are. The following table may assist readers in their consideration of the subject writers.

Fig. 1 Comparison Matrix for Featured Writers

Writer	History of family mental illness	Subject to childhood abuse	Heavy drinker	Drug abuse	Sexually unconventional	Manic and/or depressive	Obsessed with suicide	Determined to commit suicide	Suicide follows period of intensive writing	Age at death
Beddoes			✓	✓	✓	✓		✓		45
Hemingway	✓	✓	✓	✓	✓	✓		✓		62
Kane			✓	✓		✓		✓	✓	28
Pavese		✓	✓			✓	✓		✓	41
Plath	✓	✓		✓		✓			✓	30
Sexton		✓	✓	✓	✓	✓	✓	✓	✓	45
Thompson			✓	✓	✓	✓		✓		67
Woolf	✓	✓			✓	✓				59

This table is by no means comprehensive and readers should add headings, which they deem appropriate for comparison purposes.

We ought also to look at the way in which these writers relate to each other. Thompson, Pavese, Plath and Sexton have deep admiration for Hemingway. For Kane, Sexton was a clear influence. Sexton seems to follow Plath's style, admires Thompson, relates strongly to Woolf and is very interested in Pavese's work. Woolf's later style is in some ways reminiscent of Hemingway – both writers' later work is more about observation than storytelling and their endings leave much unsaid – and she appreciated Beddoes' work. Plath's heroines are Woolf and Sexton. The way in which these writers connect to each other becomes interesting when we focus upon the fact that they all commit suicide.

Is there one common factor that leads to so many important writers committing suicide? That is the question for the reader to ponder.

Many of the people I have spoken to about suicide have said, 'What a horrible thought.' So it is; probably that is why few of us contemplate it and even fewer commit the act. Yet it may be that it is the unique creativity of the great writer's mind that enables them to give thought to the subject. The thought is father to the deed.

Bibliography

Introduction

Books

Jamison, K. R., *Mood Disorders and Patterns of Creativity in British Writers and Artists*. Simon & Schuster, 1989.

Ludwig, Professor Arnold, *The Price of Greatness*. Guilford Press, 1995.

Nettle, Daniel, *Strong Imagination: Madness, Creativity and Human Nature*. Oxford: OUP, 2003.

Articles

Andreasen, N.C., Creativity and Mental Illness: Prevalent Rates in Writers, *American Psychiatric Publishing*, 1987.

Richards, Ruth, Relationship Between Creativity and Psycho-pathology, *American Psychological Association*, 1981.

Internet

To Be or Not to Be: an Investigation of Artists and Suicide. www.rnw.nl/culture/suicide/heroes, 3 July, 2002.

Sylvia Plath

Books

Alexander, Paul, *Rough Magic*. Da Capo Press Inc., 1999.

Appignanesi, Richard, *What do Existentialists Believe?* Granta Books, 2006.

Connors, K. and Bayley, S. (eds), *Eye Rhymes: Sylvia Plath's Art of the Visual*. OUP, 2007.

Hayman, Ronald, *The Death and Life of Sylvia Plath*. W. Heinemann, 1991.

Hughes, Ted, *Birthday Letters*. Faber & Faber, 1998.

Koren, Y. and Neger, E., *A Lover of Unreason: The Life and Tragic Death of Assia Wevill*. Robson Books, 2006.

Kukil, Karen V., *The Journals of Sylvia Plath*. Faber & Faber, 2000.

Northouse, Cameron, *Sylvia Plath and Anne Sexton*. Boston: G.K. Hall & Co., 1974.

Plath, Aurelia Schober, *Letters Home*. Faber & Faber, 1976.

Plath, Sylvia, *The Bell Jar*. W. Heinemann, 1963.

Plath, Sylvia, *Johnny Panic and the Bible of Dreams*. Faber & Faber, 1977.

Plath, Sylvia, *Collected Poems*, Faber & Faber, 2002.

Wagner-Martin, L. and Stevenson, A., Two Views on Sylvia Plath's Life and Career, in Ian Hamilton (ed.). *The Oxford Companion to Twentieth Century Poetry in English*. OUP, 1994.

Articles/essays

The Sylvia Plath Cult, *Vogue Magazine*, October, 1971.

Sylvia Plath: The Road to Suicide, *The Observer*, 14 November, 1971.

Internet

Moses, Kate, *The Real Sylvia Plath*. www.salon.com, 2002.

Museums/libraries/public records

BBC, Written Archives Centre, London WC2.

The Berg Collection, New York Public Library, New York, USA.

The Lilly Library, Indiana University, Indiana, USA.

Public Record Office, Kew, Surrey.

Cesare Pavese

Books

Biasin, Gian-Paolo, *Smile of the Gods: A Thematic Study of Cesare Pavese*. Cornell University Press, 1968.

Heiney, Donald, *Three Italian Novelists*. New Directions, 1968.

Lajolo, Davide, *An Absurd Vice: A Biography of Cesare Pavese*. Milan: Il Saggiatore, 1960.

Pavese, Cesare, *Work Wearies*. Einaudi, 1936.

Pavese, Cesare, *The Harvesters*. Einaudi, 1941.

Pavese, Cesare, *August Holiday*. Einaudi, 1945.

Pavese, Cesare, *Before the Cock Crows*. Einaudi, 1948.

Pavese, Cesare, *The Beautiful Summer*. Einaudi, 1949.

Pavese, Cesare, *The Moon and the Bonfires*. Einaudi, 1950.

Pavese, Cesare, *This Business of Living*. Peter Owen Ltd, 1961.

Articles/essays

Hawkins, Ernest J., Notes on Cesare Pavese, Unpublished, 1952.

Pavese, Cesare, Return to Man, *L'Unita*, May 1945.

Pavese, Cesare, Dialogues with a Comrade, *L'Unita*, May 1946.

Thomas Lovell Beddoes

Books

Donner, H.W., *The Browning Box*. Oxford: OUP, 1935.

Gardner, Helen, *The New Oxford Book of English Verse*. Oxford: OUP, 1972.

Higgens, J. and Bradshaw, M., *Thomas Lovell Beddoes: Selected Poetry*. Carcanet Press, 1999.

Snow, R.H., *Thomas Lovell Beddoes*. New York: Covici, Friede Inc., 1928.

Strachey, Lytton, *Books and Characters*. New York: Harcourt, Brace, 1922.

Thompson, J.R., *Thomas Lovell Beddoes*. Boston: Twayne Publishers, 1985.

Articles/essays

Beddoes: Last of the Alchemists, *The Spectator*, February, 1929.

Blunden, Edmund, The English Vision, *Times Literary Supplement*, November, 1933.

Ernest Hemingway

Books

Hemingway, Ernest, *The Old Man and the Sea*. Scribner, 1953.

Hemingway, Ernest, *The First Forty Nine Stories*. Arrow Books, 1993.

Hemingway, Ernest, *Men Without Women*. Arrow Books, 1994.

Hemingway, Ernest, *Death in the Afternoon*. Vintage Books, 2000.
Hotchner, A.E., *Papa Hemingway*. Simon & Schuster, 1999.
Lynn, Kenneth S., *Hemingway*. Simon & Schuster, 1987.
Myers, Jeffrey, *Hemingway: A Biography*. Macmillan, 1986.
Wagner-Martin, Linda, *A Historical Guide to Ernest Hemingway*. Oxford: OUP, 2000.

Articles/essays
New York Times, 3 July, 1961.

Internet
www.allhemingway.com
BBC Education, *Ernest Hemingway*. July, 2002.

Museums/libraries/public records
John F. Kennedy Library, Boston, USA.

Sarah Kane

Books
Kane, Sarah, *Complete Plays*. Methuen Publishing, 2001.
Saunders, Graham, *Love Me or Kill Me: Sarah Kane and the Theatre of Extremes*. Manchester: Manchester University Press, 2002.
Sierz, Aleks, *In-Yer-Face Theatre*. Faber & Faber, 2001.

Articles/essays
Alberge, Dalya, Drama's Enfant Terrible Takes Her Own Life at 27, *The Times*, 23 February, 1999.
Benedict, David, Disgusting Violence? Actually It's Quite a Peaceful Play, *Independent on Sunday*, 22 January, 1995.
Benedict, David, What Sarah Did Next, *The Independent*, 15 May, 1995.
Billington, Michael, How Do You Judge a 75-minute Suicide Note?, *The Guardian*, 30 June, 2000.
Clapp, Susannah, Blessed Are the Bleak, *The Observer*, 2 July, 2000.
Graham, Polly, Rape Play Girl in Hiding, *Daily Express*, 20 January, 1995.

Greig, David, Obituary, Sarah Kane, *The Herald*, 27 February, 1999.

McGlone, Jackie, Obituary, Sarah Kane, *The Scotsman*, 27 February, 1999.

McKinley, Jesse, A Second Life, *The New York Times*, 24 October, 2004.

O'Connell, Vincent, Short Letters, *The Guardian*, 25 February, 1999.

Ravenhill, Mark, Obituary, Sarah Kane, *The Independent*, 23 February, 1999.

Sierz, Aleks, Love in the Most Violent of Climates, *The Times*, 18 April, 2003.

Sierz, Aleks, The Filth, the Fury and the Shocking Truth, *The Times*, 24 October, 2005.

Wardle, Irving, Theatre. *Independent on Sunday*, 22 January, 1995.

Internet

Bardell, Paula, *The Paradox of Sarah Kane*. www.articlecity.com, November, 2003.

Virginia Woolf

Books

Bell, Quentin, *Bloomsbury*. Weidenfeld & Nicolson, 1968.

Bell, Quentin, *Virginia Woolf: A Biography*. Harcourt Brace Jovanovich, 1972.

Dick, Susan (ed.), *The Collected Shorter Fiction of Virginia Woolf*. Hogarth Press, 1985.

Dunn, Jane, *A Very Close Conspiracy: Vanessa Bell & Virginia Woolf*. Little, Brown, 1990.

Hall, Sarah M., *The Bedside, Bathtub and Armchair Companion to Virginia Woolf*. Continuum Publishing, 2007.

Kemp, Sandra (ed.), *Virginia Woolf: Selected Short Stories*. Penguin Books, 1993.

Lee, Hermione, *Virginia Woolf*. Chatto & Windus, 1996.

Lehmann, John, *Virginia Woolf*. Thames & Hudson, 1975.

Nicolson, Nigel, *Virginia Woolf*. Weidenfeld & Nicolson, 2000.

Stape, J. H., *Virginia Woolf: Interviews and Recollections*. Macmillan, 1995.

Taylor, A.J.P., *English History 1914–45*. Pelican Books, 1965.
Woolf, Virginia, *Night and Day*. Duckworth & Co., 1919.
Woolf, Virginia, *Mrs Dalloway*. Hogarth Press, 1925.
Woolf, Virginia, *Orlando*. Hogarth Press, 1928.
Woolf, Virginia, *A Room of One's Own*. Hogarth Press, 1929.
Woolf, Virginia, *Moments of Being*. Sussex University Press, 1976.

Articles/essays
Hunt, Tristam, Brave Hearts, *Time Magazine*, 11 November, 2004.
Sexton, David, Who's a Fan of Virginia Woolf?, *Evening Standard*, 13 January, 2003.

Internet
Merriman, C.D., *Biography*. www.virginiawoolf.com, 2007.
Our World. www.compuserve.com, 3 July, 2002.

Museums, libraries, public records
The Berg Collection, New York Public Library, Fifth Avenue, New York, USA.
The British Library, London NW1 and WC2.
The Lilly Library, Indiana University, Indiana, USA.

Hunter S. Thompson

Books
Carroll, E. Jean, *Hunter: The Strange and Savage Life of Hunter S. Thompson*. Simon & Schuster, 1993.
Mckeen, William, *Hunter S. Thompson*. Boston: G.K. Hall & Co., 1991.
Steadman, Ralph, *The Joke's Over*. W. Heinemann, 2006.
Thompson, Hunter S., *Hell's Angels*. Random House, 1966.
Thompson, Hunter S., *Fear and Loathing in Las Vegas*. Random House, 1972.
Thompson, Hunter S., *Fear and Loathing on the Campaign Trail '72*. Straight Arrow Books, 1973.
Thompson, Hunter S., *The Great Shark Hunt*. Summit Books, 1979.
Thompson, Hunter S., *The Curse of Lomo*. Bantam Books, 1983.
Thompson, Hunter S., *Songs of the Doomed*. Summit Books, 1990.
Thompson, Hunter S., *Screwjack* (self-published), 1991.

Thompson, Hunter S., *The Rum Diary*. Simon & Schuster, 1998.

Articles/essays
Anson, Robert S., Hunter Thompson Meets Fear & Loathing Face to Face, *Rolling Stone*, 10 December, 1976.
Ashforth, David, Tribute to a Decadent and Depraved Race Goer, *Racing Post*, 26 February, 2005.
Clark, Pete, How Hunter Cast His Spell on My Generation, *Evening Standard*, 22 February, 2005.
Dolan, John, A Hero of Our Time – Hunter S. Thompson 1937–2005, *The Exile*, Moscow, 25 February, 2005
Morgan, Piers, Hunter's Sad End – But What a Way to Go!, *Evening Standard*, 22 February, 2005.
Rolsen, Jeff, Writer Hunter S. Thompson Commits Suicide, *Air Force Times*, 21 February, 2005.
Thompson, Hunter S., The Lost Story, *The Independent*, 23 February, 2005.
Don't Glorify Gonzo Hunter, *Daily Express*, 1 March, 2005.

Anne Sexton

Books
Furst, Arthur, *The Last Summer*. New York: St Martin's Press, 2000.
Hall, Caroline K.B., *Anne Sexton*. Boston: Twayne Publishers, 1989.
Northouse, Cameron, *Sylvia Plath and Anne Sexton*. Boston: G.K. Hall & Co., 1974.
Sexton, Anne, *The Complete Poems*. New York: Houghton Mifflin, 1981.
Wagner-Martin, Linda, *Critical Essays on Anne Sexton*. Boston: G.K. Hall & Co., 1989.
Wood Middlebrook, Diane, *Anne Sexton*. New York: Random House Inc., 1991.